The Pathos of the Real

RETHINKING THEORY
Stephen G. Nichols and Victor E. Taylor, *Series Editors*

The Pathos of the Real

On the Aesthetics of Violence in the Twentieth Century

ROBERT BUCH

The Johns Hopkins University Press

Baltimore

© 2010 The Johns Hopkins University Press
All rights reserved. Published 2010
Printed in the United States of America on acid-free paper
9 8 7 6 5 4 3 2 1

The Johns Hopkins University Press
2715 North Charles Street
Baltimore, Maryland 21218-4363
www.press.jhu.edu

Library of Congress Cataloging-in-Publication Data
Buch, Robert.
    The pathos of the real : on the aesthetics of violence in the twentieth century / Robert Buch.
        p. cm. — (Rethinking theory)
    Includes bibliographical references (p.   ) and index.
    ISBN-13: 978-0-8018-9756-6 (hardcover : alk. paper)
    ISBN-10: 0-8018-9756-4 (hardcover : alk. paper)
    1. Aesthetics, Modern—20th century.   2. Violence—History—20th century.   3. Pathos
—History—20th century.   4. Reality—History—20th century.   I. Title.
    BH301.C88B83 2011
    190.9'04—dc22   2010007499

A catalog record for this book is available from the British Library.

*Special discounts are available for bulk purchases of this book. For more information, please
contact Special Sales at 410-516-6936 or specialsales@press.jhu.edu.*

The Johns Hopkins University Press uses environmentally friendly book materials, including recycled text paper that is composed of at least 30 percent post-consumer waste, whenever possible. All of our book papers are acid-free, and our jackets and covers are printed
on paper with recycled content.

CONTENTS

ACKNOWLEDGMENTS

This book has been in the making for many years. During that time I have benefited from the help and advice of numerous colleagues and friends. First and foremost I want to thank Hans Ulrich Gumbrecht, my dissertation adviser at Stanford University, whose enthusiasm, intellectual range, and extraordinary vitality have motivated and inspired me over many years. In its early conceptual phases the project profited from meticulous readings by my two other mentors in the Bay Area, Russell Berman and Hinrich Seeba. Later on, two further interlocutors, Agata Bielik (Warsaw) and Eric Santner (Chicago), provided crucial impulses that allowed me to finally pull things together and bring it to a close. I am immensely grateful to both of them for their comments, their encouragement, and their friendship. It is a great pleasure, as well, to thank my other friends at Chicago, David Levin, Susanne Lüdemann, David Wellbery, and Christopher Wild, for their collegiality and support. In addition, special thanks are due to Thomas Pavel for his generous comments and suggestions after reading an early draft of the manuscript and to Julia Hell, at Michigan, who has provided me with various opportunities to present and discuss my work. Though it is not always made explicit on the pages that follow, the present book is indebted to the work of Karl Heinz Bohrer, whose encouragement and interest in my project throughout the long process of its development have been very important to me. I am also indebted to the Franke Institute of the Humanities, where parts of this book were written, and the Center of Interdisciplinary Research on German Literature and Culture at the University of Chicago for funding the acquisition of rights for the cover image. Finally, I want to thank a number of colleagues and friends, at Stanford, Chicago, Berlin, and elsewhere, for their comments, criticism, and support over the years: Ewa Atanassow, Frauke Berndt, Dominik Finkelde, Christiane Frey, Julia Kindt, Florian Klinger, Oliver Lubrich, Justin Steinberg, Chenxi Tang, Ralph Ubl, and Jobst Welge.

The Pathos of the Real

Introduction

"La passion du réel"

In a provocative book that attempts nothing less than to sum up what was decisive about the twentieth century, Alain Badiou has placed the years from 1914 to 1989 under the sign of a passion. According to the philosopher's *Le siècle*, translated into English as *The Century*, the "short" twentieth century is not to be conceived of in terms of its "grand narratives," of the great ideas and ideologies that attended its course, but rather as deeply and passionately invested in what he calls the real. The two main areas in which Badiou sees this "passion of the real" at work are the arts and politics, the century's artistic and literary avant-gardes, its great revolutionary struggles, but also the two world wars. The goal of the book, based on a series of lectures given in 1999 and early 2000 at the Collège Internationale de Philosophie, is to understand and recuperate the century's most vital concerns. Its methodological premise is to do so by looking at some of the epoch's accounts of itself, especially as they are articulated in the poetry of the times. The philosopher's *parcours* through the previous age is thus guided by some of the best-known modernist poets, from Mandelstam to Pessoa and Brecht, from Mallarmé to Saint-John Perse and Paul Celan. Other figures who flesh out his proposal to conceive of the century under the sign of the "passion of the real" include Nietzsche, André Breton, Pirandello, Malévitch, Lenin, and Mao.

The guiding motif of the passion of the real is as suggestive as it is vague, combining, it seems, affect and fact, the subjective and objective, evoking at the same time a sense of complexity and reduction. It is indeed both things, a reductive and polemical term, rather than a descriptive category, and a fairly complex notion that seeks to recuperate a lost legacy. The formula's conflicting connotations obviously make up part of its appeal: *passion*, as in the commitment or devotion to a cause, is connected to a term, the *real*, that couldn't be more remote from anything constituting a cause or value about which, at least on the face of it, one could imagine being passionate. There is also some ambiguity in the concept of the real itself. Vacillating between abstraction and concreteness, it could be perceived as an abstract ontological notion or its opposite, as the epitome of facticity (the real as opposed to the semblances of, say, ideology and discourse). But, as quickly becomes apparent, it is a notion that is not quite as simple as it may seem, in spite of its polemical thrust. It is, on the contrary, a rather intricate category that Badiou adapts from Lacanian psychoanalysis, albeit with important modifications.

If we associate the real with horror and disgust, as, say, in the sight of wounds, of bare flesh, of bodies in agony, the kinds of things with which it is frequently linked in Lacan, then Badiou's depiction of the past age is, in some respects, not that different from other accounts of the century that have singled out the unheard-of scale of violence and destruction as its defining characteristic. But as much as the passion of the real may bear responsibility for the century's darkest moments, Badiou tends to recall this passion as the mobilizing force behind the century's most audacious aspirations, refusing, by the same token, to dwell on its tragic aspects. The real is, in fact, very much mobilized against a contemporary historiography that views the century in terms of its aberrations and pathologies, and against a present that has lost touch with the resolve that is the prerequisite of radical change. Against this tendency the recapitulation proposed by Badiou seeks to recover a largely forgotten or misrecognized force.

The ambition to sum up the century in a simple formula is bound to elicit skepticism. There is something provocative, and even preposterous, not only in the formulaic character of the definition but also in the very terms the formula conjoins. I want to introduce the project of this book by way of sounding out some of the connotations of these two terms, the *passion* and the *real*, and their conjunction. Two implications of this formula impose themselves immediately. Placing the twentieth century under the "passion of the real" is to set it against a present that supposedly partakes of no such passions anymore. Passion, as in the passionate commitment to a cause, is what is lacking in the current age, "after" the twentieth century. But passion also implies a lack itself, a desire for something that is missing, something one does not have. Calling this something the real, in turn, suggests that the given, and possibly even reality itself, is somehow not real. In other words, the symbolic order, which constitutes our world and which the real calls into question, is in some way unreal, afflicted with a lack of being, so to speak. For Badiou the real is a political, and indeed an ethical, category, but what it indicates, above all, is a lack in and of reality, a kind of ontological shortcoming. The twentieth century felt this lack acutely, and its defining passion was to counter it.

As we will see shortly, *The Century* elaborates on the notion of the real quite a bit. By contrast, the other term of the book's formula, *passion*, remains largely underdeveloped. It is taken in its colloquial meaning, but this is not to say that Badiou is not aware of its semantic scope. On the contrary, the duplicity of passion and pain, of passionate engagement for a cause, on the one hand, and the torments of desire, on the other, might very well be on his mind. What gives the book its edge, though, is precisely its apparent disregard for this latter dimension, for the suffering implicit in the term *passion*. There is indeed at times an unmistakable nonchalance with which the hardships and horrors of the century are subordinated to its passionate commitments and struggles, even if a closer look reveals that the passion of the real is closely tied to these very hardships and horrors. The provocation of Badiou's definition consists in the fact that he takes passion in a more or less positive, one-sided sense.

One may justifiably wonder whether Badiou's formula, precisely in its suggestiveness, obfuscates and mystifies the realities of the twentieth century rather than casting light on its moving principle. How could the confluence of political, social, economic, cultural, and historical factors that together made the century what it was possibly be subsumed under a single heading? True, what Badiou dubs the passion of the real may intersect with some of these areas and may reflect some characteristics of the age, but why accord it so much significance, especially given its obvious vagueness? Arguably, objections like these miss the thrust of the book. Badiou's *mise au point* of the century does not aim at a comprehensive account in the first place but takes the "age of extremes," as Eric Hobsbawm has called it, at its most extreme.[1] The formula seeks to get at and make sense of the experience of this extremity.

The present book differs in scope and ambition from Badiou's probe into the twentieth century, but it is very much about the appeal of the extreme that *The Century* seeks to recall and, in some sense, to recover. In different ways the engagement with such extremes, with a kind of excess that is beyond our grasp—intellectually, affectively, and, today, if we are to believe Badiou, even historically—is the subject of the works at the center of this study. In some respects the notion of the passion of the real captures what is at stake in their confrontations with this extreme experience, with the experience of violence and excess, quite well. At the same time, the engagement with the real staged by these works often evinces a much greater ambiguity than Badiou allows for, even though it is implied in his formula, at least to some extent and largely *malgré lui*. The instances of violent excess around which the works studied in this book revolve thus corroborate the notion of the passion of the real, yet they also recast it. In preparation for the readings that form the core of this book, the first two sections of this introduction provide a rather detailed account of the notion of the real, both in Badiou's "passion of the real" and in Lacanian psychoanalysis, which is where the term first originated. The remainder of the introduction turns to the concept of pathos and outlines the themes of this book.

Alain Badiou's *The Century*

In Badiou the "passion of the real" is opposed, first and foremost, to any project purporting to derive its legitimacy from the future: "The nineteenth century announced, dreamed, and promised; the twentieth century declared it would make man, here and now. This is what I propose to call the *passion of the real*. I'm convinced it provides the key to understanding the century. There is a conviction, laden with pathos, that we are being summoned to the real of a beginning."[2] A bit later he writes that the twentieth century "is not the century of promise, but that of realization. It is the century of the act, of the effective, of the absolute present, and not the century of portent, of the future" (58). This emphatic sense of presentness that is thus associated with the real can be conceived in two ways: as culmination and finalization of what came before or as discontinuity and rupture. In Badiou it is for the most part the latter conception that prevails.

The Century presents the real alternately as the means to a cause, as the index of that cause, or even as the cause itself, though its features remain vague. Ultimately, the orientation toward the real aims at a radical realignment of the given order. In this it must not be thought of as some inner kernel, an identity or an essence, accessible only by way of stripping the outer layers, as in the century's fantasies of "purification." It is, rather, a realignment that requires a different kind of move, though one that, in many respects, is no less violent than its counterpart. Badiou calls it "subtraction."[3] This subtraction is a form of negation, but unlike ordinary "destruction," which remains beholden to what it destroys, it is a negation that removes itself from that which it seeks to undo. The operation of "subtraction" is thus a kind of removal from and displacement of the order of the given. The passion of the real asserts itself not simply in the direct assault on this order but rather in the rejection of the given terms, of what constitutes reality, including the terms of its termination and transformation. In a sense this is why the real has to remain strangely undefined. It is what is lodged in the difference, in the gap opened up by subtraction, rather than in some kind of depth or beyond. The task is "to purify reality, not in order to annihilate it at its surface, but to subtract it from its apparent unity so as to detect within it the minuscule difference, the vanishing term that constitutes it" (65). Echoing one of Lacan's paradoxical pronouncements, Badiou's "real" is what is impossible. And it is precisely the determined embrace of this impossibility that confers a sense of urgency and resolve on the passion, a resolve as unconditional as it is uncompromising. Paradoxically, the "realism" of the appeal to the real consists in its militant opposition to "reality," whose parameters it seeks to suspend.

The century's engagement with the real is always a kind of wager that doesn't flinch when it comes to the use of force. In fact, the ready employment of violent means is the mark of its determination, the refusal to be restrained or limited in any way by the alleged pieties of the age, by its prevailing normativities.[4] The passion of the real is indeed very much sustained and driven by an enthusiasm and the willingness to exercise violence. "The theme of total emancipation, practised in the present, in the enthusiasm of the absolute present, is always situated beyond Good and Evil." In other words, "the passion of the real is devoid of morality" (63). "The absolute violence of the real" is, as he put it in an earlier formulation, "simultaneously lethal and creative" (52, 32). Not surprisingly, one of the principal arenas in which the encounter with the real is played out is war, which the book treats with the same kind of awe that characterizes its attitude toward the real itself. The twentieth century "unfolded *under the paradigm of war*" (34), more specifically still and, more shockingly, under the paradigm of total war and final struggle. This has to do with the fact that the century, as Badiou notes, not without relishing the frivolousness and shock value of his terminology, was given to "the idea —widely held in all domains of thought and action—that problems allow for an 'absolute' solution" (36).

As careful as he is to draw a distinction between the century's totalitarian fantasies of destruction and purification and his own notion of subtraction, also referred to as "active nihilism" or "affirmative negation,"[5] and as much as he indulges in the provocation of his unabashed fascination with the radical commitments of the past, what makes the wars of the twentieth century, especially the two world wars, such apt instances of the propagated real is precisely their radically antagonistic character, for Badiou's real is a figure of irreconcilable antagonism and conflict, situated in the gap, the disconnect between the end, the definitive destruction of something, and a new beginning, a commencement that one should not, as he insists, imagine to arise from the past in any dialectic fashion.

Unlike the notion of the real in Lacan, and in one of the most vocal advocates of Lacanian psychoanalysis in the late twentieth century, Slavoj Žižek, Badiou's conception of the real is, as his translator and commentator Peter Hallward put it, an "activist" one.[6] The real is very much something to be seized. It issues an appeal, an address or a claim that subjects ought to recognize and assume, calling for a break with the received patterns and parameters of action. Hallward writes, "The real is the element of action undertaken at precisely the unknowable point, action that converts the impossible into the possible. Action pursued on the 'level of the real' is action in its most inventive and most dangerous sense, a kind of rigorous improvisation pursued in the suspension of every moral norm and every academic certainty. Only such action can access the real in its structural sense. . . . The 'stasis' of the real—the real as that which always remains in its place—can be encountered, very precisely, *only* by moving it."[7] The real in Badiou's *The Century* is thus not, as one might expect at first, a neutral category aimed at capturing the unprecedented horrors that marked the "age of extremes." What it stands for is rather what appears at times as an urge, manifested in a number of different areas, at times as a certain type of maneuver or operation, performed time and again only to fail, yet at other times still an opportunity, as relentlessly sought as it is consistently missed. The real is taking the age of extremes, as I have said, at its most extreme—and this in order to embrace it. No wonder Badiou's invocation of this passion is so emphatically oblivious to the costs in human suffering exacted in its name. In fact, he quite explicitly defends the indifference in this regard, especially when it comes to the question of the individual.[8] Irrespective of continually missing the encounter with the real, to put it in a famous Lacanian phrase, for Badiou the passion of the real persists, and it has lost nothing of its allure.

The real stands for the will to engage in conflict and confrontation, not just in the twentieth century but also at the beginning of the new millennium, when the lessons and legacy of the avant-garde and of modernism, to which *The Century* pays belated tribute, have fallen into oblivion. Badiou's intervention itself is spurred by this passion, taking to task the malaise and lack of fervor that in his perception mark the present age. His own recapitulation can even be regarded as a symptom or last extension of what he describes, but the polemical and partisan character of Badiou's recalling of the real does not invalidate the term or the formula he proposes. It is precisely its vagueness and the slightly ominous ring that capture something about which the century itself may very well only have had the vaguest of ideas. The associations the slogan takes on in Badiou's elaboration, the sense of determination, finality, definitiveness, and violence, clearly resonate with the most extreme experiences and the most deadly engagements of the twentieth century, even if Badiou, in a sense, wants to turn them on their head. In its polemical thrust against approaches that view the century solely in terms of its aberrations and pathologies, Badiou's reappraisal is provocatively unequivocal, treating the passion of the real as a kind of inexhaustible and incorruptible resource, ostensibly unaffected by the excess to which it has given rise. The real is the name of a certain ruthlessness, impervious to the unintended consequences of its radical measures and interventions. In this sense it is both passionate and dispassionate; or, put another way, the passion of the real, "always situated," as Badiou writes, "beyond Good and Evil," is a sentiment that knows of no compassion, a passion without pity, so to speak.

The confrontations with violence and destruction at the center of the works on which this book is focused seem in many respects to instantiate the passion that is supposed to have animated the century, carrying its greatest ambitions and culminating in its greatest horrors. At the same time, their engagement with the real is far more equivocal than Badiou's evocative formula suggests. As we will see, they summon us before a similar configuration: the spectacle of suffering that they conjure up in the most vivid terms, urging our gaze to dwell on it. But the reactions this spectacle elicits are much more ambiguous, in some sense more painful. Rather than embodying a unified sentiment, the passion that is displayed in them is conflicted, strangely at odds with itself, torn, it seems, between exaltation and resignation. The passionate commitment that is at stake in the passion of the real is frequently undercut by, and gives way to, a sense of numbness and of stupor in the face of the intolerable. Given this uneasy amalgamation of affects warring with one another, I want to place the confrontations with violence and pain staged in the works studied here under a slightly different title and speak, instead, of *the pathos of the real*. Although in today's lexicon the term *pathos* has mostly pejorative connotations, it is a much richer notion than its Latin cognate, *passion,* and its associations of suffering and (erotic) desire. Of course, Badiou's own invocation of the "passion of the real" could be described as an attempt to recover and salvage the "pathos" of the twentieth century, the grandeur of its aspirations, now buried under the rubble of its failures. The flip side to such greatness is the sense of adversity, defeat, and devastation that is also implied in the notion of pathos. (As we will see, one important connotation of pathos is precisely the moment of grandeur in defeat.) The complex semantics of *pathos* is a better match for the elusive real and the twentieth century's engagements with it, not just because it implies a kind of dialectic of grandeur *and* defeat but also because of another prominent connotation it has to this day: the idea of *theatricality*.

Before recalling the rich semantics of pathos, I want to turn to the area in which the real first gained prominence and from which Badiou borrowed it: Lacanian psychoanalysis. Although the psychoanalytic notion differs from the later appropriation of the term by Badiou, it seems to have been charged with a certain pathos from the very beginning.

The Real after Lacan

As Hallward points out, Badiou's real is an activist, interventionist notion, one that is very much in keeping with the central concern of the philosopher's work, namely the question of the "event," which he has referred to elsewhere, in terms quite close to those used in connection with the real, as a kind of "deregulation of the logic of the world."[9] The Real—spelled with a capital *R* in English—is, of course, a key concept in the later Lacan, though it remains for all its prominence a fairly elusive term. It also figures very prominently in the work of Slavoj Žižek, one of Lacan's best-known and most congenial readers, who returns to the question of the Real time and again. As is well known, in Lacan the Real is one of the three registers shaping human experience and a crucial category in the Lacanian theory of the subject. The chief characteristic of the Real is its opposition and resistance to the two other registers to which it remains nonetheless bound, if negatively. (Badiou's passion of the real does largely without this orientation toward the Imaginary and the Symbolic.)[10] Though it is only one feature in a tripartite model and despite the interdependence of the three registers, famously illustrated by Lacan's Borromean knot, the Real, especially in late Lacan (and also in Žižek), clearly occupies a privileged position in relation to the other two.[11] Why this is so, however, is not immediately evident.

Perhaps the most salient aspect of the Real is its paradoxical and slightly ominous character. It is inaccessible, an absence or a void that defies representation, yet it is also characterized as excessive and violent. Where it appears, it is said to erupt or to break through, shattering representation and reality. Its impact is as intolerable as it is undeniable. Its "eruptions" cannot be ignored. The characterizations of the Real vacillate between a dimension that is somehow presupposed but utterly unknowable, clearly echoing in this respect Kant's noumenal *Ding an sich,* and a violent outburst, a traumatic encounter, a recalcitrant remainder that proves to be unassimilable by the psychic system. The Real is at times associated with primal organic matter of which we catch a glimpse wherever bodies are torn apart; it figures as the material, corporeal foundation of the subject from which we shrink in horror as from our own finitude wherever we are reminded of it—our unfathomable origin and end being the contingent facts of our existence that the Symbolic is unable fully to grasp. At times the Real is of a more phantomlike presence, immaterial and yet of a stubborn and quasi-lethal efficiency: something that cuts through, troubles, and disturbs the order of things. The term itself suggests a dimension irreducible to anything else, irrespective of the alleged interdependence of Lacan's three registers. There is nothing beyond or behind the Real, although picturing it in spatial terms is misleading, for the Real appears where the other registers cease to function, in the cracks of our Imaginary-Symbolic reality. The Real can be conceived of as what is lost as the subject enters the realm of the Symbolic, but it returns where this order reaches an impasse and breaks down.

While the domain of the Imaginary-Symbolic, of reality, is governed by laws or lawlike regularities, the Real belongs to the order of accidental cause, the Aristotelian *tuché,* invoked in Seminar XI,[12] the contingent trigger that sets in motion the very processes constituting the subject's Imaginary-Symbolic reality while separating us from and safeguarding us against this first "touch" or impact from nowhere, which set everything in motion: the finitude and contingency of our birth and death, the beginning and end, which are conditioned by our corporeal foundation. In this sense the Real can be said to be the intimate and yet excluded kernel of reality, its external center, occupying a position of "extimacy," as Lacan would call it.

But how does any of this account for the privileged status assigned to the Real? Though it is somewhat less explicit than in Badiou's case for the century's "passion for the real," there is a strong suggestion in Lacanian psychoanalysis that the Real holds an important lesson for those prepared to engage it. As in Badiou, the Lacanian Real is linked to violence and destruction. On the surface level this association has to do with the undoing of the Imaginary-Symbolic framework, for the Real is said to appear in the shattering of this framework. In its "extimacy" it both sustains and threatens reality, which is, in turn, both contingent on it and working to transcend the relation to its "lost" or "barred" cause. As it comes apart, reality gives way to the Real.

But there is more at stake in the engagement with the Real than this "surface vs. depth" or "appearance vs. hidden substratum" picture suggests. Getting in touch with the Real entails a profound reorganization or reorientation of the libidinal economy, which constitutes the chief concern of psychoanalysis. As much as the examples invoked in connection with the Real appeal to acts of violence and destruction, it shouldn't simply be equated with the spectacle of annihilation. Such annihilation may well be the index of the Real, but it does not spell out its real significance. It is true, the Real is invariably pictured as something horrible, a

Medusa-like sight that fascinates and disturbs us at the same time. But curiously enough, "tarrying with the negative" that is the Real is not in the service of placing us under the spell of horror, both thrilling and painful.[13] Tarrying with the Real is, rather, in the service of ridding the subject of another kind of spell, the spell, namely, of desire, the desire of the Other, that is. The most prominent example of this kind of liberation, which amounts to a disruption of the symbolic matrix informing our desire, is provided by Antigone, the paradigmatic figure of the Lacanian ethics of psychoanalysis.

To see the point of the psychoanalytic appropriation of Antigone, we should briefly recall that desire, in one of Lacan's famous dicta, is always the desire of the Other.[14] It is wanting to be desired by the Other, that is, wanting the Other to want me to desire her or him; desiring what the Other desires; and, finally, desiring in the same way as the Other desires. The Other's desire, however, is far from stable or clear, desire being, by definition, dynamic and volatile, metonymic, as Lacan says, moving from one object to the next, only to find that "this too is not it," never finding the object that would afford us definitive satisfaction.[15] Ultimately, desire proves to be about the impossibility of ever reaching full satisfaction while remaining bound to (the promise of) the Other's desire. It is being on a permanent flight for an ever-elusive object with no chance to extricate oneself from this dynamic.

What fascinates the psychoanalytic readers of Sophocles' play, not just Lacan himself but also his prominent Slovenian students and commentators, Slavoj Žižek and Alenka Zupančič, is Antigone's stubborn insistence on the burial of the desecrated remains of her slain brother. Dismissing the heroine's own claim, according to which the obligation to the dead trumps the *raison d'état* invoked by Kreon, these commentators emphasize her seemingly irrational insistence on performing the burial rites for Polynices. Her defiance of the Symbolic order, represented by Kreon, is so unconditional and fearless that it overrides her own survival instinct. Nothing affects Antigone's determination, neither the circumstances of the situation nor the consequences of her action. Downplaying both the fact that there is something excessive in Kreon's orders and that Antigone's act actually does have a rationale (that is, the duty to bury the dead), a Lacanian reading of the play sees her as a subject acting on a principle that has no other justification than itself; even the question of self-preservation does not perturb her. In the ultimate analysis, this principle is itself enigmatic, an opaque, incontrovertible "cause" more precious than life itself and in whose name, if there was one, the subject defies and asserts itself over and against the demands of reality. (It is this categorical appeal that explains Lacan's affinity for Kantian ethics.) In *The Ethics of Psychoanalysis* this intractable cause is called the Thing, though the term soon thereafter disappears from the Lacanian lexicon.[16] Elevating the unknown or unknowable cause to the dignity of the Thing is Lacan's definition of sublimation. Contrary to conventional wisdom, sublimation, on this account, does not consist in a kind of redirection or ersatz satisfaction of drives that would otherwise remain unsatisfied. Sublimation, Lacan insists, creates new values by suspending the Symbolic order. In sublimation the Thing is pitted against the reality principle, the Real against reality, creating nothing less than a space of freedom, even if the Thing appears to be a dark, ominous, foreign body within us, life-threatening even, as in the case of Antigone.[17] Another, more familiar, term for identifying this impenetrable hard kernel of the subject is the death drive, a drive that does not, as one might assume, propel us toward death but rather plunges us, like Antigone, into the space between two deaths, the space between biological and symbolic death. It is in "this domain of the undead: 'beyond life and death,'" as Žižek explains, "in which the causality of Symbolic fate is suspended."[18]

Here, too, the subject moves beyond desire, transcending the dependence on symbolic recognition by undoing its attachment to the desire of the Other that had forced it on its relentless and yet futile pursuit of (dis)satisfaction. In the register of drive, which can never be the drive of another nor a matter of one's choosing, the subject recovers in a sense its cause, its autonomy, despite the fact that the drive may be a much more exacting and cruel master than desire. The latter is always bound up with the law, the merciless injunction to enjoy that in reality can never be fulfilled. As much as it is triggered and driven by the rules and dictates of law, it never achieves enjoyment, *jouissance*. What would give it satisfaction always turns out to be illusory so that its real target is not satisfaction itself but, in fact, to remain unsatisfied. Lacan's name for that which thus systematically eludes our desire is *objet a;* desire is, by definition, not aimed at any specific object but chooses whatever the desire of the Other, *le grand Autre*, has put before us. Drive, by contrast, wants what we do not want but always get anyway. If the dynamic of desire is marked by variation—the place of *objet a* can be occupied by an infinite number of candidates—that of drive is repetition. It is in mindless repetition that we experience jouissance as that which we struggle to resist but cannot *not* enjoy. This is why such jouissance is painful and pleasurable at the same time: pleasure-in-pain. What insists in it is the dimension of the Real, that is, that which has not entered the Symbolic in the process of subjectivation. Unlike desire, which receives its directives and orientation from the transcendent field of the Other, the social symbolic structure by way of which we have split ourselves from, and have disavowed, our material, corporeal foundation, drive is purely immanent. It would be a mistake, however, to view this recovery in terms of reconciliation or a finally achieved peace with oneself. It is first and foremost a recognition of one's contingency. Analysis does not aim at completing the subject but rather seeks to confront us with our fundamental lack. It is not about the restitution of a lost whole but about the recognition of the subject's destitution. In Žižek's formulation: "when at the end of the psychoanalytic cure I 'traverse my fundamental fantasy,' the point of it is not that, instead of being bothered by the enigma of the Other's desire, of what I am for others, I 'subjectivize' my fate in the sense of its symbolization, of recognizing myself in a symbolic network or narrative for which I am fully responsible, but rather that I *fully assume the uttermost contingency of my being.* The subject becomes 'cause of myself' in the sense of no longer looking for a guarantee of his or her existence in another's desire."[19] But this contingency paradoxically coincides with the realization of one's freedom, or, as the title of the essay from which the last quote is taken has it, the "abyss of freedom."

The notion of the real, whether in Badiou's "passion of the real," in Lacan's conception, or in Žižek's explications of the latter, is hardly a unified one. In spite of its range and in spite of the various inflections it takes in these different thinkers, however, several commonalities emerge. It is true that, on the face of it, what is called the real in Badiou often appears as less elusive than that of the psychoanalytic account. This doesn't mean, however, that Badiou's real is a given. It is important to bear in mind that the real in the "passion of the real" is not conceived as some kind of thing, something that could be attained in some shape or form but, rather, as the driving force behind the century's highest aspirations. It is not the name of what is to be achieved but a certain stance vis-à-vis reality, namely a kind of detachment, an operation called "subtraction," that seeks to make room for radical innovation and the formation of a new type of (collective) subjectivity. In Badiou's parlance the real is what emerges when reality is made to cease to coincide with itself and when it gives way to what was thought to be impossible hitherto. Hallward is right to note that horror and disgust, key characteristics of a certain Real in the Lacanian repertoire, are not paramount in Badiou's "passion of the real." But violence certainly is. To be sure, Badiou is not entirely oblivious to the excess of violence that the "passion of the real" generated in the twentieth century. In some passages he seems to criticize the denunciation of the century's "barbarity" as reductive, suggesting that it is but one dimension or aspect of the "passion of the real."[20] But for the most part the proponent of the "passion of the real" unapologetically affirms the use of violence. Violence is not just a necessary means for the transformation that is to be achieved; it functions like a token of the faith and commitment to the cause of radical change. Recall how much Badiou is at pains to differentiate between right-wing "purification" and left-wing "subtraction," but while the latter suggests a different kind of move or maneuver based on a different vision of the transformation that is to be accomplished, it doesn't shirk violence either. Hallward points out that the Lacanian Real is more passive. What is missing from the psychoanalytic conception is the audaciousness and *élan* that the "passion of the real" is supposed to inspire; nor is there, at least not in Lacan himself, much of the sense of militant political engagement fueled by this passion. What prevails, instead, is a sense of mysteriousness and paradox. As we have seen, the Real forms a contradictory complex, a *coincidentia oppositorum*,[21] simultaneously inaccessible, nonsymbolizable, *and* aggressive, ominous, asserting itself in the most forbidding and irrefutable ways. It is typically described as exerting a Medusa-like effect on those who encounter it: irresistible and lethal at the same time. But there is also a Real that is less material than the one exemplified by the sight of "putrefied flesh . . . the disgusting substance of life."[22] This is the Real that is at stake, though not always in explicit terms, in the switch from desire to drive, in breaking away from the regime of the Symbolic (the notorious Big Other) and assuming the full responsibility for the utter contingency at the core of one's being. One of the difficulties of making sense of this shift consists in the fact that it is of the utmost violence, violence that the examples present as typically not only directed against the Other but also against the self: suicidal or virtually suicidal acts, the foremost examples being Antigone and Medea, which seek to "subtract" the subject from the domination of the Other and to suspend the power of the Symbolic order. Irrespective of the disastrous consequences, the (self-)destructive acts are hailed as the tokens of a fundamental reorganization of the subject's libidinal economy, revoking the effects of subjectivation to give birth to a subject embracing the dark, persistent dimension of the death drive at its very core. Again, this realization is a harrowing one, but the theorists of the real think of it as a price worth paying to undo our entanglement in the desire and demands of the Other.

The Real is what always returns to its place, as Lacan put it in *The Ethics of Psychoanalysis,* but its place is virtually impossible to localize.[23] It is the dimension of extimacy, of the inside-out, the unbearable kernel of the subject; elusive and stubborn, radically immanent, material, and yet spectral, illusory and yet persistent; haunting the order of the Symbolic, which can neither account for it nor rid itself of it. Its effects are similarly ambivalent, indeed double-edged: simultaneously disturbing and transformative, a sense of paralysis coinciding, paradoxically, with the possibility of a conversion to a state of pure immanence and autonomy, redrawing the coordinates of the given and forcing the subject to confront its own constitutive lack. It is as though we were asked to imagine the lethal gaze of the Medusa as awakening us to a different kind of existence, a different form of organization, both of the self and of the world, releasing us, as Eric Santner might put it, to a different kind of vitality.[24] Although the Real is accentuated slightly differently in Badiou, Lacan, and Žižek, it is privileged for similar reasons: for being antithetical to the reality principle and for being a kind of conduit for the undoing and radical recasting of the space of subjectivity and sociality.

Violent Images

As I have mentioned, Badiou develops what he calls the "passion of the real" by drawing on a number of different sources: philosophy, political theory, and, perhaps most surprisingly, modern poetry (Mandelstam, Pessoa, Mallarmé, Saint-John Perse, and a few others), art (Malévitch), and music (Webern, Schönberg). In spite of the examples provided, it is, however, not always easy to follow *The Century*'s trajectory as the author moves, rather effortlessly himself, through the different domains touched and transformed by the "passion of the real." While the formula is quite suggestive in the domain of the political, it is somewhat less evident in the arts, at least in the examples he gives. In what ways could the dimension of the real, unlocatable yet "always in the same place," this phantomlike power, have a place or be registered in works of art? Can there be such a thing as an aesthetics of the real? And if so, what would it look like? The works Badiou discusses in *The Century* typically instantiate the real not so much by way of their iconoclasm but by the operation of subtraction, by removing themselves from the regime of what is possible in order to reconceive and reconfigure the parameters delimiting the space of creativity and action. Abstractly put, one could say that the real is figured here not as disfiguration but as a form of displacement, indeed a shift in the terms of figuration itself. Among Badiou's favorite examples are Malevitch's *White on White* painting, as well as the puzzling line from Mallarmé's *Un coup de dés* "Rien n'aura eu lieu que le lieu."[25] For all the verve and momentum that comes to be associated with the "passion of the real," it is often presented in terms of a small gap, a minimal difference but one with far-reaching and incalculable consequences since this gap or difference is supposed to intervene in and change the very realm of what is imaginable itself.

In contrast to this picture the real figures in a much more ostentatious manner in the works at the center of this book, at least at first glance. For all their obvious differences, all the works discussed here revolve around spectacles of blatant violence and suffering, and they all seem to be about tarrying with this sight. In many instances the violence is evoked in strikingly visual terms, sometimes literally as a pictorial representation, sometimes *as if* it was an image before which we are summoned. The term *spectacle* should be taken in its proper sense of "given to be seen," of being arranged and staged for a spectator. The affinity between the focus on violence and excess and the appeal to images is one of the central puzzles of the texts' engagements with the real. As we will see, the scenes of pain and suffering are very much about the construction of, but also a challenge to, certain modes of spectatorship and of viewing. The arrangements often appear created expressly to expose onlookers to the deadening gaze of the Medusa, to place them and us before this absolute image. The real is what becomes visible in the spectacle of agony and pain whose affective impact the beholder cannot possibly escape. In fact, the works are not just about this impact; part of their ambition seems to be to reenact and produce it themselves, that is, to trigger visceral responses and induce quasi-somatic effects. Often the excess they draw into focus is both absorptive and paralyzing. What is glimpsed in the violence and agony staged in these works is the real of our corporeal existence as it comes into view only where it is caught at its limits.

But the sense of an insurmountable, unsublatable facticity experienced at the sight of horror is not the only register of the real in these works. True, in many instances the confrontation with violence is cast as an encounter with an erratic and irreducible presence. Violence appears as a matter that affects bodies, reducing them to things and exposing the human body in its fragile materiality; the agony and pain on display seem indisputable evidence of our finitude. But the spectacles can also have the opposite effect, creating the sense of unrealness, of a realm that appears at some remove from reality. At times there is a peculiar vacillation, then, between the sense of materiality, on the one hand, and a spectral, auratic immateriality, on the other. The latter results, in part, from a concentration on what one could call the phenomenal givenness, a focus on detail and appearance that can seem strangely oblivious to the agony before it. The real becomes visible in the often ostentatious exhibition of corporeal suffering and the creaturely materiality that eclipses the Symbolic order but also in the ways in which the gaze is drawn to and confounded by the peculiar phenomenality of the spectacles conjured up before it. Another way of getting at this split is to say that the fascination with the real is related to the ambition to produce presence, the irrefutable immediacy of powerful affect, brought about by the focus on the agonizing body, but also for the desire to capture the opposite, that is, a presence that is never fully realized, present only by way of its absence, in the mode of withdrawal, palpable precisely by remaining inaccessible, ineffable. The appeal to visual and pictorial representation is linked to this split. On the one hand, the framing, staging, and focus of the image removes whatever it features from reality, if only, as is often the case, to heighten its intensity, its presence. On the other hand, the real can never be the subject of representation in the first place. It is what disrupts the virtuality of the image. And in this respect it is what the texts bring into focus, not in their ostensibly unperturbed gaze at scenes of violence and pain but rather in the moments of the failure of representation, the nagging sense that the paintings, photographs, and other pictorial works encountered in the texts, are not about what they show but what they do not show, or what shows itself only in their destruction or disintegration.

No less important than the tension between these two different modalities of the real, however, is another kind of ambiguity: that between an experience of radical immanence and the search for the signs of transcendence. In fact, the response to the real, violence and suffering brought up close, resulting in an often unbearable degree of detail, is not limited to the sentiments of horror and awe. The remarkable preoccupation with the spectacle of pain, the way in which the works in question tarry with, and seek to immerse themselves in the sight of destruction and death, bespeaks a different kind of desire. The play between attraction and repulsion, the conflicting impulses of fascination and anguish in the face of the real, is sustained by the anticipation of some kind of insight. In ways very similar to the conception of the real we have seen in Badiou and Lacan (obvious differences between them notwithstanding), the confrontations with the real staged in the works on which this book focuses seem to hold the promise of a revelation and, possibly, a reversal. The contact with the dimension of ultimate negativity is to effect a transformation in which the sight of tormented, agonizing creatureliness shifts into a sense of sublime exaltation, the spectacle of disfiguration giving way to images of transfiguration. It is precisely the exposure and submission to a certain excess and radical alterity that are taken to culminate in a kind of elevation, finally overcoming and breaking the spell of the exorbitant real.

As I said earlier, the ambiguous reactions to which the confrontation with the real gives rise are best captured by a notion that doesn't have much purchase in our contemporary critical idiom. This notion is the notion of pathos.[26] As much as it may have fallen out of favor (colloquially, it is used in a largely pejorative sense today), the semantic complexity of the term matches the conflicting impulses and desires sustaining the engagements with the real that form the subject of the following chapters. Pathos is itself a complex and contradictory notion, not only in terms of its semantic scope—it can designate a painful event or the reaction to that event; it is one of the major effects of the tragic spectacle; it marks a register of speech associated with "high" or noble subjects; it is a proof of endurance under duress and a sign of distinction and nobility; it is the mark of theatricality—but also because of the tensions inherent to it, in particular the dialectics of devastation and elevation, of being overwhelmed and rising above it at the same time.[27]

Pathos

As a register of speech, pathos has given rise to the suspicion of its being employed for manipulative purposes from its earliest beginnings. Of the three means of persuasion discussed in classical rhetoric, πάθος (pathos) is the one in which the orator appeals to the emotions of his audience, often by foregrounding his own emotional response to the hardship or misfortune under discussion, making his case less by way of argument, *logos,* or through the authority of his character, his *ethos,* than by way of emotional appeal.[28] *Páthos* designates the moment when the speaker allows himself to be overtaken by his passion. Though in fact the opposite may well be the case, it is when the orator appears to be at his most spontaneous and impulsive, the most impassioned and stirring—a state of mind best induced, according to the standard recommendations, by evoking whatever causes the powerful affect as though one were in its presence, living through it oneself.[29]

The concept of *páthos* was central to Attic tragedy.[30] At the beginning of the *Poetics* Aristotle identifies the *páthê,* emotions, as one of the main objects of the mimetic arts (1447a). He later names *páthos,* typically translated as suffering, as a key element of the tragic plot (1452b), alongside reversal (*peripeteia*) and recognition (*anagnorisis*). Finally, the *páthê* play a crucial role in achieving the purpose of the tragic spectacle, which is both to "stir up the emotions" (1456b) and to relieve us of them (cf. 1449b). From the beginning the concept not only refers to pain and suffering as events but constitutes the affective reaction to these events as well. Put differently, it is something happening before and to a subject and is intended to prompt similar reactions in the spectators. Given that the sense of decorum prohibited showing violent death on the Athenian stage, *páthos* was present above all in the dramatic speech: in a discourse fueled and compelled by the passions and thought to be of a quasi-contagious appeal. It is the appeal of compassion triggered by the sight of suffering but also of awe in light of the self-possession on the part of those struck by misfortune. For as much as *páthos* stands for the irrepressible, spontaneous re-action in the face of suffering, by articulating their pain, the dramatic char-acters must have managed to remove themselves, at least somewhat, from the experience that threatens to overwhelm them. In this respect *páthos* also implies the distance and control somebody is able to maintain over his or her pain.

Since its first occurrence in the Greek lexicon, the term seems to have a remarkable capacity to span opposites: external and internal, trigger and reaction, spontaneous affect and reflective distance, being overpowered and asserting oneself anyway, instinctive compassion and staged emo-tionality, the grandeur of suffering and the recognition of its futility. The modern appropriation of the term concerns yet another polarity, that be-tween passivity and activity. In a seminal article Erich Auerbach has shown how the relatively neutral Aristotelian concept evolves from the Stoic con-demnation of the passions ("perturbatio animi") to the Christian idea of "passio," where the connotations of passivity give way to a more posi-tive and affirmative conception.[31] In the wake of Christ's "passio," suf-fering is no longer something that befalls us from the outside. Instead, "passion" takes on an active meaning. By taking the pain upon themselves, Christ and those following in his wake make suffering into a form of protest against the ways of the world: "what the Christian authors op-posed to the passiones was not the serenity of the philosopher but sub-mission to injustice—a Christian . . . should not withdraw from the world to avoid suffering and passion [as the Stoics would have it]; *he should tran-scend the world through suffering.* . . . The aim of Christian hostility to the world is not a passionless existence outside the world, but counter-suf-fering, a passionate suffering in the world and hence also in opposition to it."[32] Passion is the name of an engagement and intervention on behalf of conviction and faith, which prove their transcending powers precisely in submitting to and sustaining the pain. As in Greek tragedy, where *páthos* implies not just the suffering of painful events but also stands for the per-severance and dignity in the face of extreme calamity, the Christian pas-sion implies a certain distance from and a way of overcoming pain *in* pain. At times our modern usage of the term still bears out the same connota-tion, that is, the idea of achieving one's freedom from suffering in the very midst of it.[33] In a paradoxical turn pathos asserts itself by way of self-cancellation.

Pathos Formulae

Besides Auerbach's short article on the subject, the most prominent adaptation of the concept of pathos in the twentieth century is arguably Aby Warburg's idea of *Pathosformel* (pathos formula).[34] In keeping with the characteristic polarities of the category, Warburg's term encompasses the tension between the appeal to a certain affective excess and the need to get this affective overload under control, precisely by casting it into a form, by fixating this intense vitality in an image. Warburg's coinage also makes explicit another familiar opposition: that between the conventionality of inherited forms on the one hand and spontaneous expressivity on the other. According to his biographer Ernst Gombrich, Warburg's intuition about the persistence of certain motifs was first inspired by a remark by Jacob Burckhardt, who claimed that wherever pathos appeared, artists had to resort to the models provided by antiquity.[35] Warburg found evidence for this observation in the recourse by Renaissance artists, such as Botticelli or Ghirlandajo, to some of the pictorial templates they had come upon in the Ancients, especially in their treatment of movement and affect, "the forms used to express the highest degree possible of emotional involvement."[36] Warburg's own recourse to the concept of "formula" points to the means by which the expressive power of pagan antiquity becomes available to modern artistic creation. As much as pathos stands for eruptive, uncontrollable affect, to speak of pathos *formulae* is to remind us that the ostensibly spontaneous or natural gestures and movements through which the emotional turmoil manifests itself are part of a coded repertoire, even if what puzzled Warburg is precisely that these formulae can be employed in different contexts and can serve very different ends. In other words the formulaic character allows for a certain flexibility and adaptability of the pictorial motifs borrowed from antiquity. Finally, the notion of formula also implies the idea of a magic spell that allows the artist to capture the energy of violent affect *and* to keep it at a distance, deflecting its full force in quasi-apotropaic fashion. (Another means for tempering the surplus energy of the pagan figures without relinquishing it entirely is the *grisaille* technique, which also underscores the spectral character of these revenants from antiquity.)[37] In many instances the images of violence analyzed in the following similarly hark back to a certain iconic repertoire that they seek to reactualize. And, as in the model of Warburg's *pathos formulae,* they do so not only to activate the energetic impact of pictorial representation, the power of the image, its capacity to strike and startle the beholder, but also to avert and arrest this energy in the stillness of the pictorial form.

Bringing to bear the notion of pathos to the visions of agony and excess in the twentieth century on which this book is focused makes sense both in terms of the different references of the category and its inherent ambiguity. The works that we will look at zero in on scenes of violence and destruction, on pathos in a quasi-literal sense, featuring scenes from which the beholders cannot turn their eyes, spectacles that exert an irresistible and yet disturbing fascination. They owe their effectiveness to the strange compulsion to look and to be riveted by the sight of violence, irrespective of its staged character, in fact, the *mise en scène,* or rather *mise en image,* often appears to enhance the force of the appeal. Pathos, however, is not only what is at stake, in a quasi-literal fashion, in the exhibition of violence and suffering. It is also what is reflected in the reactions these spectacles elicit from those who behold them: ranging from horror and revulsion to disbelief and despair; from stupor and a sense of numbness to anguish and compassion. But beside the paralysis and pain, there is also the more ambiguous shudder in the face of an experience that is incommensurable, the notion of being in touch with another kind of reality or of witnessing the power of a force that is beyond one's control.

We could describe the tension within the complex semantics of pathos as that of a conflict between the effects and experience of dehumanization and the countervailing tendency, the reclamation of the very humanity that seemed to be forfeited. On the one hand, pathos is the name of unsalvageable pain and misfortune, radically immanent, that is to say, irredeemable creaturely suffering. It is the name of a pain that cannot be sublated or converted into something else, some higher meaning or cause, a pain, in other words, that shatters the symbolic economy that would allow us to make sense of it. As we have seen, the theorists of the real seem to be after something quite similar, except that they suggest that it is precisely by submitting to this experience of a radical immanence and by sustaining this numbness and shock that we push through to a different conception of subjectivity. But then, on the other hand, pathos is also the name of compassion. It is the means by which we relate to another's pain and by which the suffering other is recognized and affirmed as human, precisely at the point of radical crisis. The significance of pathos is split between a sight all the more overwhelming for being beyond recognition and empathy (this is where the theories of the real situate their subject) and a medium in which a shared humanity comes to realize itself.

The pathos that marks the encounters with the real in the works at the center of this book rarely appears in the latter sense. For the most part the preoccupation seems sustained and fueled by the expectation of some kind of reversal or conversion. In this respect the fascination with the spectacles of violence and suffering resonates with the notion of the "passion of the real" with which we began. At the same time, however, the anticipated conversion never occurs, and in this respect pathos marks the moment in which the exaltation of violence and suffering fails, leaving the beholders to contemplate the price of the alleged "passions" of the twentieth century while disallowing any attempt at transfiguration or absolution. They provide no cathartic relief or soothing sentiment of compassion. This is where yet another ambiguity of the notion comes to bear. Pathos stands for the loss of the very aspirations Badiou's passion of the real seeks to salvage. It also means a form of mourning that knows no consolation in the face of the destruction and suffering brought about by the failed encounters with the real.

There is something very bold in the gesture with which Badiou sums up the twentieth century as being driven by the passion of the real; at the same time, there is something rather blunt in the way in which he posits his terms. In part this bluntness has to do with the fact that *The Century* is as much about recapitulating what is behind us, the aspirations of the twentieth century, as it is about indicting the present for its sense of resignation and languor. The notion of the passion of the real may indeed capture the spirit of radical commitment that animated some of the major political and artistic movements of the twentieth century and their assault on the status quo. And it readily acknowledges, and in some sense even accepts, the excess of violence and destruction that came in their wake. But the bluntness of Badiou's programmatic intervention also makes him miss a good deal of the tensions and of the complexity of the terms he suggests and of the radical engagements of the twentieth century they are meant to elucidate.

While the philosophical and psychoanalytic accounts of the real, of its passion or rather pathos, provide the framework and foil for looking at a number of literary works that occupy a terrain of similar concerns, they do not inform the critical idiom guiding the following readings. The different confrontations with the sights of agony and pain that are the subject of this study do not follow the same script, and their contexts differ considerably. From the officer of Kafka's *In the Penal Colony*, who revels in the description of the bloody labor of the apparatus inscribing the law into the body of the condemned man, to Georges Bataille's excitement and horror before the photograph of a young Chinese man who is being dismembered alive at the turn of the century in Beijing; from W. G. Sebald's unease as he contemplates the panorama of the battle of Waterloo to Claude Simon's mirroring of his own traumatic experiences in World War II through the historical archives of war iconography; from Peter Weiss's minute descriptions of violent death on the Pergamon frieze and of the killing in the Nazis' torture chambers at Plötzensee to Heiner Müller's execution scenes and the apocalyptic fantasies of his so-called postdramatic texts—throughout all these we observe similar patters of appropriation and distanciation, of creating the semblance of immediacy, the attempt to let the violence conjured up become real *and* the urge to undo its spell. But rather than mapping the dynamic at work here on the theoretical expositions of the real and fitting all the texts in the same mold, the following chapters attend to the particularities of the works and discuss them on their own terms. That is to say, the individual chapters consist of close readings that proceed immanently, centering on problems and puzzles encountered in the texts themselves: the dialectics of attraction and repulsion in the face of a gruesome image in the case of Kafka and Bataille, for instance; the opposition to, and the appeal of, a certain iconography of pathos in Claude Simon, and in kindred ways in Peter Weiss; the apparent indeterminacy between the aporias and the apologetics of violence and terror in Heiner Müller; and, finally, the peculiar mixture of pathos and apathy in the paintings of Francis Bacon. All of them confront characters and readers (or beholders) with an exorbitant spectacle, the eruption of the real, and offer different attempts to come to terms with it. The works of the three postwar authors are concerned in a very immediate fashion with the catastrophic experiences treated in Badiou's *The Century*: the Spanish civil war, the two world wars, the death camps, and revolutionary terror. Compared to these authors, Kafka and Bataille, as well as Bacon, provide a more oblique reflection on the extremes that marked the twentieth century, though their preoccupation with violence has frequently been related to the century's horrors.

The first chapter compares Bataille's aesthetics of transgression with the "Chinese" cruelty of Kafka's *In the Penal Colony*. In many respects these two prominent engagements with the spectacle of suffering employ a familiar dramaturgy, of conversion and catharsis, transgression and transfiguration; but, at the same time, their ambition is to overturn the very logic, or economy, on which this dramaturgy is based so as to allow for a different order of experience. Ultimately, however, the fascination with violence and pain is based on two diametrically opposed visions. The encounter with the real, in spite of the ostensible similarity between these two dramatizations, rehearses different fantasies about the subject's relation to the space of the symbolic, its inscription in, as much as its possible extrication from, this space. Bataille's exaltation of violence and sacrifice aims at undoing the order of the symbolic, at least temporarily, whereas Kafka's fantasy of a machine inscribing the law into the body concerns the violence of that very order. Violence is not external to it but stands at its very beginning.

In the next chapter we move from the spectacle of public execution to the theater of war. The chapter begins with a brief discussion of the panorama of Waterloo (and other iconic battle pieces) in W. G. Sebald before turning to an author whose writing features the experience of the battlefield as that of a sudden disruption of the order of the symbolic and the imaginary, a conceptual and perceptual vertigo that does not subside. Claude Simon's attempts to make sense of his traumatic experiences in the Second World War are fueled, and hampered, by a constant onslaught and a constant flight of images, an excess of hyperprecise memories and their continual dispersal and dissolution. The visions of war are inevitably informed by an iconography of pathos, but the actual war experience is radically iconoclastic, the encounter with a real that shatters all the prefabricated images at our disposal. Simon's persistent return to the same episodes and events is part not only of the author's interminable efforts to render the "mindless fury of things," which was unleashed on him on the battlefields of the Second World War, but also of the attempt to account for his own fortuitous survival—which makes for the muted pathos that permeates this writing.

The third chapter looks at another survivor looking back on the violence he escaped, more or less inadvertently, and that does not cease to haunt him. Time and again, Peter Weiss's literary works, the plays *Marat/Sade* and *The Investigation,* as well as the novelistic trilogy *The Aesthetics of Resistance,* summon their readers before representations of destruction and agony, calling for what appears to be a paradoxical combination of anaesthesia and pathos, seeking to simultaneously desensitize and incense the beholder faced with the sights of devastation and defeat. Weiss's texts follow a contradictory poetics of numbness, or anaesthesia, and of militancy, shuttling back and forth between the resistance to pathos and the pathos of resistance.

The last chapter, on Heiner Müller, is about the painful contradiction, at least in the eyes of the author, between the inevitability of revolutionary violence and its inevitable "fallout," the excess that disavows the very project by which it was generated. My reading compares the playwright's so-called postdramatic work, shockingly graphic and grotesque collage-texts such as *Hamletmachine* or the ekphrastic prose poem *Explosion of a Memory,* with the surgical coolness that marked the "experiments" undertaken in some of his earlier works, the series *Versuchsreihe* (*Philoctetes, The Horatian, Mauser*), and its challenge to fully assume the aporias of violence exercised in the name of radical change. The pathos advocated in the earlier texts is not that of compassion for the victims, sacrificed for the sake of an unrealized cause, but rather that of embracing the monstrous real of indiscriminate and presumably unavoidable destruction.

The real is, almost by definition, an elusive and rather abstract category. The chapters of this book seek to counterbalance this seemingly inevitable abstractness of the term by engaging as closely as possible with the texts. Their investment in visions of violence and excess may be viewed as a testament to the "passion of the real" that fueled some of the grand aspirations of the twentieth century, as well as the disastrous aberrations they entailed. It also bears testimony to the ambition of achieving, by aesthetic means, the impact of the real, of (re)producing its characteristic sense of excitation and disturbance. At the same time, the confrontations with the real, staged in a number of different guises and settings, provide a different and more nuanced account of the fascination and the disquiet the last century's excess in violence caused those willing to face it.

CHAPTER ONE

In Praise of Cruelty

Bataille, Kafka, and *ling'chi*

A Photograph

The photograph shows a young man who is being dismembered alive. Two large gaping wounds in his chest are bleeding profusely. It looks like his arms are bound behind his back but in fact they have been cut off. There is no scaffold or stage, only a structure of poles keeps him upright while three executioners, surrounded by an onlooking crowd, are busy cutting him into pieces. It is difficult to describe the expression on his face. While the executioners seem absorbed in their task and while the spectators appear riveted to what the men are doing, the young man's eyes are turned upward. As a result, two diametrical visual axes divide and organize the image. Both the gaze of the crowd and that of the henchmen converge somewhere in its lower center; the victim's gaze points into the distance. The picture juxtaposes a moment of concentrated absorption with a view of rapture, the intensely focused onlookers form a sharp contrast to the blank expression on the young man's face.

The photograph features *ling'chi* [or *leng-tch'e*], the "torture of the hundred pieces." It is part of a series that documents the successive dismemberment of a young man at the beginning of the twentieth century in Beijing. Starting with the chest, the executioners would typically proceed to severing the forearms and the lower legs, and finish by cutting off the head. Usually, the victim would die before the procedure had reached its end. The final image features a truncated body that is hardly recognizable as human. The moment of death must have occurred somewhere between the second and fourth image.[1]

Although the punishment of ling'chi dates back to the tenth century, according to legal historians of China's judicial traditions, it was a relatively late addition to the Chinese penal code (it was only codified in the thirteenth or fourteenth century). Controversial as long as it was in effect, the punishment was abolished in 1905. Apparently, there is a large number of pictures of Chinese executions, taken by Western travelers at the threshold of the last century. In fact, the one described above was presumably taken in early 1905, the year the punishment was abolished. These photographs would figure in scientific and pseudoscientific treatises, in travel narratives about the Far East, and they would even circulate as postcards, catering, not unlike pornographic images, to a certain "orientalist" voyeurism.

In the past couple of years the discovery of a great number of pictures of ling'chi has created a lot of interest in the images and their history. A conference took place in 2005, its proceedings yet to be published; a collaborative study appeared in 2008; and there have been exhibitions both in Cork, Ireland, and in France at the Musée Nicéphore Niépce in Chalon-sur-Saôn.[2] A Web site run by the Institut d'Asie Orientale in Lyon (a division of the Institut des Sciences de l'Homme of Lyon) documents this remarkable increase in scholarship and research, providing detailed bibliography, articles, and other information.[3]

For the longest time the photographs owed much of their notoriety to Georges Bataille, who reproduced four of them on the final pages of *Tears of Eros* and whose claims about (and on) these pictures have, until recently, dominated discussions about them to a very large extent. At once "ecstatic and intolerable," as Bataille called them, they were supposed to illustrate the "ambiguity of the sacred," a key notion in the author's theory of culture and religion, derived from the religious anthropology of Emile Durkheim and Marcel Mauss. As a consequence of their appropriation by Bataille, the pictures have become something of a token of the French writer's aesthetics of transgression, arguably one of the most ambitious and prominent attempts in the twentieth century to place the sight of suffering and pain at the center of aesthetic reflection and experience, an attempt that has had significant resonances in a number of areas.[4]

In an article originally titled "The Most Intolerable Photographs Ever Taken," the art historian James Elkins has taken issue with contemporary art theory's investment in "transgression" and the "informe," both prominent concepts in Bataille, by confronting the recent appropriations of these terms with the photographs of ling'chi.[5] In Elkins's view the pictures of Chinese torture make artistic strategies of "transgression" seem thoroughly out of place. The primary target of his criticism is *Formless*, an exhibition catalogue accompanied by a programmatic essay by Yve-Alain Bois and Rosalind Krauss that seeks to recover Bataille's contribution to the theory and practice of modernist and late modernist art.[6] According to Elkins the images of Chinese torture are not only counter-examples to the claims of the breakdown of representation operated by transgression (and its alleged culmination in the formless); they also make the provocative gestures of a transgressive aesthetics look perfectly innocuous, if not "silly."[7] The ling'chi pictures themselves instantiate the very transgression called for by Bataille and those working in his wake—"They are the unsurpassable evidence that pure visual transgression is possible"[8]—but it is a transgression that overpowers and renders obsolete its contemporary theorizations. "Intolerable for art history," Elkins writes, the images "ruin" the "interest in the ruin of system and sense" so important to Bois's and Krauss's "reworking of surrealist theory."[9]

It is true that the initial effect of the ling'chi pictures is visceral. They are too *real*, too savage and forbidding to be subsumed under any aesthetic program or practice, even if the point of that program or practice is the disruption and displacement of the very categories and terms in which artistic production is conceived. The images unsettle the framework of art theory and "ruin" its conceptual distinctions and topologies. They situate themselves beyond the opposition between figuration and its transgression on which the notion of formlessness appears to depend. They are of the order of the real that suspends the difference between reality and representation, illusion and truth. Their "reality-effect" overrides the operations of "l'informe" propagated in Bois's and Krauss's catalogue. Their *punctum*, to use Roland Barthes' term, "punctures" and wounds the beholder, denying us the distance of *studium* and the pleasures of detached, "disinterested" involvement.[10] Akin to photographs of lynching, they immediately change the terms of the debate, shifting the framework away from the perceived limits of representation to questions of force and affect, of an affective impact that contemporary art is virtually incapable of achieving, no matter how aggressive its gestures.

Although Bataille had close personal ties to Lacan, and his work surely had some influence on the latter's thought, the real is not a concept in Bataille. But it is not difficult to see that his reflections on violence, death, and sexuality are related to the dimension designated by this term. Bataille's fascination with the images has to be seen in connection with his speculations on the sacred, on excess and transgression. Although Elkins is aware of the religious and anthropological dimension of Bataille's interest in the images, the art historian largely disregards it, in spite of the fact that he himself criticizes Bataille's students for failing to take into account this aspect of the writer's thought. By contrast, Elkins himself seems unaware of the fact that "l'informe," the idea of the formless, and transgression belong to different phases of Bataille's development and, in fact, stand for different views of violence and destruction. The formless is coined in the "Dictionnaire critique" of the short-lived art journal *Documents* (1929–30), while transgression only becomes prominent in the writings of the 1940s and 1950s and evolves along with Bataille's interest in the sociology of the sacred. The "antiaesthetic" editorial politics of *Documents* launches an attack not only on academic notions of beauty but also on the surrealist celebration and aestheticization of violence, best encapsulated perhaps by André Breton's famous dictum "La beauté sera convulsive ou ne sera pas" (Beauty will be convulsive or will not be at all). The notion of the formless, though in some respects violent in itself, undercuts the surrealist association of violence and beauty, pain and sublimity. (The visual material featured in *Documents*, such as Eli Lotar's well-known slaughterhouse photographs, focuses on the squalor rather than on the splendor of death.) The later reflections on transgression, however, and the examples that Bataille gives of it, typically present the experience of violence and pain as both exalting and destructive, simultaneously shattering and reinvigorating. Obviously, Elkins's association of the ling'chi pictures with the idea of the formless is based in the fact that the images feature, quite literally, the destruction of a human torso, formlessness *in vivo*, so to speak. But while the tongue-in-cheek iconoclasm practiced on the pages of *Documents* targeted the Surrealist infatuation with the beauty of convulsion, Bataille's own rapture before the images exhibits a pathos in the face of the real that is paradigmatic of his later positions.[11]

In the wake of the recent academic and curatorial interest in ling'chi, a lot more information about the pictures has become available, and Bataille's engagement with the images has been put into perspective. It is, as we will see shortly, more in tune than one might suspect with a certain pattern of Western responses to Chinese executions. In this respect the recent research has gone some way in demystifying Bataille's seemingly unique appropriation of the images. But such similarities notwithstanding, the kind of experience and insight that Bataille seeks both to document and to demonstrate by showing the pictures is based on an altogether different economy of suffering and pain than the one operative in the Western "protocols" of viewing the spectacle of cruelty. The improved understanding of the legal and cultural circumstances in which to situate the pictures provides an opportunity to look at Bataille, looking at the pictures, against the backdrop of other contemporary reactions to ling'chi, on the one hand, and in relation to his own theories about transgression, expenditure, and the sacred, on the other, which the art historical debate about the images has failed to take into account. But the latest research does not only invite this kind of contextualization of Bataille's relation to the image; it has also made it possible to make different connections, and I would like to bring some of its findings to bear on one of the most egregious accounts of an execution in twentieth-century literature, a narrative that, like few others, has made the description of intolerable violence its centerpiece: Franz Kafka's *In the Penal Colony*. The idea of relating Kafka's story to the pictures of Chinese torture originated in what appeared to be a historical connection. It was Robert Heindl, the author of *Meine Reise nach den Strafkolonien* (My Visit to the Penal Colonies), generally regarded as one of the major sources of Kafka's famous narrative, who first published the photographs of ling'chi in some of his works, though not in the travelogue Kafka had definitely read.[12] Although it is not certain that Kafka had any familiarity with the images, there are some striking parallels between the "spectacle" at the center of the story and the Western accounts of Chinese executions. But the point of reading the story in light of the new research on ling'chi is not to speculate about sources and influences but rather to regard it as another instance of a certain poetic investment in the sight of extreme suffering and excess, a dramaturgical experiment on the boundaries between the somatic and the symbolic.

For all the obvious differences in temperament and style, Bataille and Kafka both quote and undercut a certain conception of pain and violence to supplant it with diametrically opposed models. As we will see, Bataille's vision of this excess aims at shattering the symbolic order and transgressing the bounds of subjectivity set by it. The violence he advocates is supposed to give access to the fluid continuum of cosmic forces, held in check and kept at bay by the prohibitions and laws organizing and delimiting the realm of everyday experience. Violence, excess, and transgression are about undoing the symbolic processes of differentiation. Their goal is a quasi-Dionysian sense of dissolution—a dissolution that the subject experiences as a reunion with undifferentiated primal forces and that Bataille defends with a great deal of pathos, that is to say, by staging how he himself is overwhelmed by the image of the young Chinese man. Kafka's *In the Penal Colony* achieves a peculiar amalgamation of elements, adapted from the traditions of tragedy, the Passion story, and the Judaic conception of law. Many of these elements are employed in a parodistic manner, and the story's unabashedly voyeuristic account of violent death is counterbalanced and to some degree attenuated by its comic effects. The violence it features so prominently does not point beyond the symbolic order but is what is at work in the subject's very inscription in that order. Although hardly any register could be further from the mood of Kafka's fiction than that of pathos, *In the Penal Colony,* "not just one particular story but Kafka's master narrative,"[13] evinces a certain pathos, not only in terms of the suffering it evokes so vividly but also as a reflection on writing and death, of the impossible transfiguration and unachieved death writing affords.

The "Supplice Pattern"

If our first reflex before the image of torture is to cringe and recoil, both Bataille and Kafka seem to have made a point of suspending this very reflex, forcing our gaze onto the extraordinary spectacle put before our eyes. For a better sense of the terms and implications of the mechanisms on which they capitalize for doing so, if in different ways and with different ends, I would like to draw on the work of Jérôme Bourgon, a cultural historian and specialist of Chinese penal law, who has compared the accounts of Chinese executions by European travelers with those of native observers.[14]

According to Bourgon, whose research is based both on textual and on pictorial testimonies, the European perspective is invariably inflected by what the author calls the "supplice pattern." This model has three salient features: (1) the public execution is based on a legal verdict, and it is implemented by judicial authorities; (2) it is staged as a public spectacle; and (3) the event follows a subliminal religious script that sets up the different roles and determines the procedure of the execution. It foresees a kind of conversion on the part of the condemned, while the executioner, embodying cruelty and mercilessness, is assigned the part of the Devil. The ultimate target of the procedure is the audience: the condemned person's repentance and dignified acceptance of death aims at arousing the public's compassion; suffering is supposed to invoke the pain of Christian martyrs, leading to a form of catharsis on the part of the spectators. "The ultimate aim of all executions was to create or revive a strong feeling of communion among all participants."[15] The spectacle of public execution thus takes its course according to a plot that fuses legal, aesthetic, and religious elements, forming, as Bourgon puts it, a "'penal artistic' complex."[16]

The proposed pattern is admittedly typological. But the schematic character of Bourgon's model helps throw into relief the distinctive features of Chinese executions. For the differences between European and Chinese conceptions of punishment that Bourgon identifies are indeed remarkable. They concern especially the last two features: the staged character and the religious subtext of the spectacle. The most striking of these differences is the absence of any stage or structure that would elevate the event so as to make it more visible for an audience. Ling'chi does not have the character of a spectacle; high visibility, so characteristic of the "supplice pattern," does not seem to be among the principal objectives of the procedure. Onlookers stand around the happening, closely gathered, obviously making an effort to see, but the execution is not staged for them. A further conspicuous feature, invariably noted by European witnesses, is that the participants typically don't seem to display any strong emotions; at least, none are to be seen either on the part of the executioners or on that of the person about to be killed. More than anything else this absence proved utterly disturbing to European observers and contributed considerably to the widespread cliché about innate Chinese cruelty. Given that the executions were performed largely in silence and without much ado, governed, as it seemed, by a preoccupation for technical and procedural accuracy, the event also manifestly lacked the plot so central to the Western conception of punishment. It didn't seem to aim at arousing the audience, at stirring and orchestrating its compassion and releasing pent-up tensions to effect a feeling of communion among the spectators. According to Bourgon's careful reconstruction what mattered to the Chinese legal tradition was the conformity of the execution to the punishment as it was codified in the law. It looks like the procedure was governed by a certain concern for literalness, for, as Bourgon puts it, the "readability" of the law: "the execution is only the realisation of a legal message, stressing the equivalence between the 'name' of a crime and the 'punishment.'"[17] The public display of pain and suffering would have diverted from that purpose. Besides, what made ling'chi into one of the most severe punishments available was not so much the pain inflicted on the person sentenced but rather the partitioning of his or her body. This is what constituted the particular horror of the procedure in the eyes of the Chinese. It was not about extracting the truth and bringing about repentance on the condemned's part. Once the trial had ended, the validity of the sentence was beyond doubt. It didn't require the consent or confirmation of the condemned person; his or her emotions were irrelevant to the execution, whose object, simply put, was the body, not the soul.

Because the dramaturgy, the legal underpinnings, and the underlying economy of pain are so different in the Chinese penal system, Bourgon's findings provide a useful template for understanding how the dramaturgy and the affective economy that has informed the spectacle of violence in the West—even long after the religious script has lost its purchase on the Western mind, though apparently not on our imaginary—continues to be operative but is also contested and displaced in Bataille's and Kafka's scenarios of exaltation and transfiguration before the real of an unimaginable violence.

"At Once Ecstatic and Intolerable": Georges Bataille

Ohne Grausamkeit kein Fest.

—NIETZSCHE, *ZUR GENEALOGIE DER MORAL* II, 6

Obviously, Bataille had no awareness or, apparently, much interest in the circumstances of what he saw in the pictures. Unlike the foreign observers who witnessed the executions, he paid little attention to the sequence of the procedure, nor did he seem to be looking for its "plot." *The Tears of Eros* features four pictures, but Bataille tends to single out just one: "this" photograph. It appears as though all considerations, all questions one could pose, are suspended before the image. There is no effort to supplement the spectacle with a narrative and to thereby mitigate its effect. On the contrary, the power of its impact is all that counts. The ostensible absence of a framework or of any clues that would allow him to figure out the rationale of the event doesn't seem particularly disturbing to Bataille. And yet, like the foreign observers of the actual executions, what he ends up seeing are the signs of a convergence and a reversal in "that instant where the contraries seem visibly conjoined." "Divine ecstasy and its opposite, extreme horror," coincide on the image, he writes, revealing "an infinite capacity for reversal."[18] As much as it recalls the iconography of martyrdom, however, the significance of this reversal, of the oscillation between agony and ecstatic rapture, is not based on a dialectics of guilt and forgiveness, of sin and redemption, debt and relief. The paradoxical conjunction of opposites exposes a different kind of dynamic, one that is difficult to grasp and yet, in Bataille's view, evident in our fascination with violence and transgression. There is something revelatory, perhaps even epiphanic, in this sight, but it is not put in the service of a communion.[19]

While Bataille was clearly not preoccupied with making out the dramatic plot that is possibly underlying and organizing the horrific spectacle featured in the pictures, his own presentation of the photographs of ling'chi involved a certain degree of staging, in a double sense even, that is, literally and figuratively speaking. Figuring at the end of the last book published during his lifetime, the picture and the commentary that accompanies it became a kind of testament—the conclusion and culmination not only of this particular book but of Bataille's life and work. But this legacy doesn't come in the form of a will, a written testament, but rather as a performative instantiation of what much of his work had sought to illuminate and to bring into view for almost four decades. In his possession since 1925, "this photograph," he writes in 1961, "had a decisive role in my life. I have never stopped being obsessed by this image."[20] Given the significance attributed to the pictures, the commentary that actually comes with it is surprisingly sparse. This may simply be a consequence of the author's declining health,[21] but it is more likely indicative of the desire to let the pictures speak for themselves. Their late publication "stages" a kind of assault on the readers, a confrontation that would make them realize, with the full force of a punch in the stomach, as it were, some of the difficult truths about the "attraction and repulsion" experienced at the sight of violent death. In the late 1930s, in an essay that bore that title, Bataille had written, "I believe that nothing is more important for us than that we recognize that we are bound and sworn to that which horrifies us most."[22]

As he mentions himself, his relation to the image dates back to the 1920s, and it is actually not the first time it appears in his writing. In an earlier work, the unfinished *Somme athéologique,* Bataille had given several brief and rhapsodic accounts of the overwhelming effect the picture had on him. "An image of torture falls under my eyes; I can in my fright, turn away. But I am, if I look at it, *outside myself. . . .* The sight, horrible, of a torture victim opens the sphere in which is enclosed (is limited) my personal particularity, it opens it violently, lacerates it."[23] The pictures had served as a kind of stimulant for a self-induced vertigo, a temporary suspension and ecstatic transgression of the bounds of subjecthood—a technique reminiscent of meditative exercises in the mystic tradition called "dramatizations," which consisted in conjuring up images of the crucifixion so as to make present, and available for participation in, through a form of imaginary, hallucinatory reenactment, the suffering of Christ.[24]

As in the climactic structure of the "supplice pattern," Bataille's own dramaturgy conjoins the sight of suffering with the revelation of truth. But it is a delirious kind of truth, one best grasped bodily and affectively, and one that lacks any dimension of transcendence or any sense of progression. For all the apparent similarities, both the early "dramatization" and the later "staging," at the end of *The Tears of Eros,* were meant to instantiate and seek to impart a conception of pain and violence that is at odds with the Christian economy of redemption and salvation. It was based on often wide-ranging speculations regarding the nature of the sacred and of transgression, elaborated in a series of books written, for the most part, in the 1950s[25]—studies indebted, above all, to Roger Caillois' ideas about the festival and to Marcel Mauss's famous essay on potlatch —and grounded in a rather eccentric vision of the movement and circulation of energy on earth.

According to this peculiar "cosmovision," as one reader has called it, the human economy is only a subset to a more comprehensive system, the so-called general economy. Unlike its opposite, the "restricted" (that is, the human) economy, wrongly regarded as the model of all economy, the "general economy" is as much about expenditure as it is about production. Solar energy seems to provide the underlying model for these speculations. "The origin and essence of our wealth are given in the radiation of the sun, which dispenses energy—wealth—without any return."[26] All organic matter is bound up in the ceaseless circulation of energy emerging and subsiding. The general economy gives all and takes all in the unending movements of its cycles. The relative stability of the human world is wrested from (and needs to be shielded against) this excess of energy in a continual effort, which we fail to recognize for what it is. Humans manage to contain this excess for a while and to transform the surplus into the "things" that make up the "discontinuous" reality of their human world, the world of work and reason. But the lure of the general economy continuously threatens to draw human life back into its orbit. In fact, there is a secret longing to return to the "primal continuity" (the perpetual destruction and regeneration of organic matter, of life) that is the mark of the universe. Religious sacrifice and eroticism allow for a temporary and controlled reconnection with the destructive and yet alluring forces of the general economy. Sacrifice undoes the logic of profit and suspends an order based on utility, on "instrumental reason." "To sacrifice is not to kill but to relinquish and to give."[27] It relinquishes the regime of "things," returning the victim to the play of cosmic forces, of which it affords the participants a passing glimpse in the act. The opposite of accumulation and productivity, "unproductive expenditure" aims at shattering the world of human artifice and "things," a critical term throughout Bataille's later writings.[28]

The advocacy of such profitless expenditure is very much a response to the idea of reification. But as much as he seemed to call for a destruction of the world of "things," a temporary relief or suspension of the barriers that keep human sexuality and our violent impulses in check, Bataille was keenly aware of the necessity of the taboos and prohibitions that keep the onslaught of destructive urges, from without as much as from within, at bay. This emphasis on the mutual dependence of transgression and taboo, "opposite and complementary concepts,"[29] is well known. In many ways it counts as one of the central tenets of his work. But this key insight about transgression does not only concern the dialectical configuration of interdiction and violation (influenced without a doubt by Kojève's famed lectures on Hegel's *Phenomenology*, which Bataille attended religiously)[30] but, more importantly, its relation to the unrecognized forces animating and sustaining the cycles of life. The purpose of prohibitions on the sacred is not to rein in the violent impulses susceptible to the pull of these very forces but rather to provide a mechanism to act them out. "Taboos are not imposed from without."[31] They are not instituted to repress violence. Instead, they serve to acknowledge its persistence and inescapability, indeed to allow it to manifest itself in a controlled manner. This is why "sacrilegious acts are held to be as ritual and holy as the very prohibitions they violate."[32] At the same time, "the profound complicity of law and the violation of law" ensures that transgression "suspends the taboo without suppressing it."[33]

At first, Bataille's deployment of the pictures of Chinese torture could appear as a somewhat gratuitous act of exposing us to the sight of intolerable suffering; in fact, however, it is informed and sustained by an elaborate, if often eclectic and indeed eccentric, set of ideas. While Bataille's ecstatic gaze at the young Chinese is certainly as much of a projection as the contemporary European accounts of Chinese executions, and while the French writer's own "dramatization" of his encounter with the pictures seems in some respects reminiscent of the "supplice pattern," Bataille's story is actually quite different in that it is one in which suffering does not become converted into something else, nor does the violence suffered and celebrated point to imminent salvation. The dynamic of transgression and taboo cannot be integrated into a narrative of progression, nor can the Bataillean model of sacrifice be accounted for in terms of exchange, of debt and relief—as in the notion that Christ died *for* us and thereby delivered humankind from its sins. On the contrary, it is first and foremost without any recompense, suspending the logic of economic transaction and profit in order to allow the dormant forces of the "general economy" a periodic outlet so as not to be engulfed by them.

The reproduction of the pictures of the Chinese torture victim on the last pages of *The Tears of Eros* is, of course, itself a stark violation of aesthetic protocol, a transgression of the modern taboo on the unmediated representation of violence and pain. The impact of this violation is further increased by the unapologetic gesture with which the reader is confronted with the pictures. In his assault on our aesthetic sensibility Bataille is mobilizing a pathos with which we are no longer accustomed, both in the exposure to the spectacle of pain that does not seem to allow for transcendence or sublation and in his own entrancement before this spectacle. It is not exactly the Christian pathos of overcoming suffering through suffering, in the wake of the crucified son of God, but it is a pathos informed nonetheless by a strong sense of a revelation achieved through pain. This revelation is not that of the Gospels but of a more archaic "truth" about expenditure and self-loss at the center of Bataille's later thought.

Kafka's "Chinese" Cruelty

Looked at with a primitive eye, the real, incontestable truth, a truth
marred by no external circumstances (martyrdom, sacrifice of
oneself for the sake of another), is only physical pain.
—FRANZ KAFKA, *DIARIES*, FEBRUARY I, I9I2

The eyewitness accounts of *ling'chi* that form the basis of Bourgon's analysis of European reactions to the "punishment of the hundred pieces" cannot fail to bring to mind what is perhaps the most prominent text centering on the spectacle of pain and punishment in the modernist tradition: Franz Kafka's *In the Penal Colony*. As in Bataille, there is something breathtaking in the narrative's depiction of the famous apparatus at its center, above all in its combination of gruesome details and detachment. Kafka clearly relishes the matter-of-fact account of the cruel mechanisms of the machine and the justice system of the colony's "Old Commandant." It is undoubtedly the narrative's ostensibly dispassionate account of a passionate yearning and failed search for transcendence that creates its strange effectiveness, alternately chilling and hilarious. Not unlike Bataille's enlistment of the images of violent death, *In the Penal Colony* appeals to, and denies us, some of our instinctive reactions when confronted with the spectacle of extreme pain. Kafka's story, however, is not sustained by the same kind of wide-ranging anthropological speculations as those informing Bataille's case for an aesthetics of transgression. Nor is it very obvious what kind of "case" is actually being made in the story at all. To be sure, on the face of it *In the Penal Colony* is about the confrontation of two conceptions of justice and punishment, archaic and modern. But not only is the opposition between these two different orders unstable; different visions of violence intersect and collide in the gruesome spectacle at the center of the story: clichés about Chinese cruelty; the Christian script of the "supplice pattern"; the image of the Jewish God inscribing his law in the hearts of his people (Jeremiah 31:33); and, finally, the promise and peril of writing itself, its lethal and life-giving, in other words, its trans-figurative power. In what follows I look at Kafka's story as an implicit commentary and reflection on the ling'chi pictures, as yet another, more oblique, perspective on this strange "theater of cruelty." To some degree *In the Penal Colony* is about achieving the same kind of nauseating immediacy that had thrilled and stunned Bataille before the image of the young Chinese. As we will see, the officer's vivid depictions of the apparatus invoke the Christian drama of illumination and transfiguration through suffering. At the same time, the "image" that the story projects gives rise to conflicting reactions and an "agon" that ends in what looks like an utterly inglorious and prosaic death. In this struggle no party seems to prevail, and no position is vindicated. On the contrary, the distinction between archaic and modern is brought to collapse. I begin by recalling the story's emphasis on the visual, on seeing and on being transformed by a vision, the vision, in fact, of a violent death coinciding, presumably, with a transfiguration. This is followed by a closer look at the story's "fractured dialectics" and its theatricality.[34] As we will see, the narrative's drama-turgy undercuts the luminous spectacle it evokes, making it virtually impossible to decide the meaning of the excessively cruel procedure at its center.

Kafka has made no secret of his fascination with violence and pain. In a letter to Milena Jesenská he writes, "Yes, torture is extremely important to me. I am interested above all in being tortured and in torturing."[35] This preoccupation is evident in his work, whether it is the colorful wound in *A Country Doctor* or K.'s execution by knife in *The Trial*. The torture scene featured in *In the Penal Colony* focuses on an apparatus that is designed to prolong the torment ad infinitum. But the imaginary spectacle of horror at the center of the story, the pathos it promises to stage, is continually eroded by a sense of ridicule and disgust. Rather than inspiring compassion or pity, the scene gives rise to a pedantic curiosity, on the one hand, and a sense of embarrassment, on the other (perhaps two of the most common dispositions in the affective repertoire of Kafka's characters). As I said earlier, there could hardly be anything more foreign to Kafka's po-etics than the register of pathos. Winfried Menninghaus has shown in great detail how Kafka's fascination with physical pain and violence tends to-ward the dimension of the abject, toward the human body in its frailty and even repulsiveness.[36] In *In the Penal Colony* this body is a site of inscription—of the law transforming the human animal into the *animale rationale,* and the onlookers into a community—and of a transfiguration—transforming life into writing, into literature. In this sense the apparatus is not just a device in the service of deconstruction, a parody of pathos, but an allegory of a metamorphosis that keeps failing.

VISIONS

Franz Kafka's *In the Penal Colony* is not inspired by, nor does it try to recreate, any image, at least not in any direct fashion. And yet the strong emphasis on the visual, on looking, hardly escapes the notice of any reader.[37] Everything in the story seems to work toward making present, in the most vivid terms, what it describes, above all the peculiar apparatus at its center. A vivid choreography of gestures and looks unfolds before the reader's eyes; indeed, the story consists very much of staging a scene of seeing.

The officer, busy setting the stage, urges the explorer to take a seat so as to enjoy the spectacle from the most comfortable vantage point. Throughout, he is at pains to retain the traveler's attention and to focus his gaze. His preparations of the execution are accompanied by technical explanations and praise of the technological sophistication of the apparatus. In fact, as he continues to evoke (and anticipate) the workings of the machine, he also stresses repeatedly that viewing the apparatus in action will take care of any doubts, hesitations, or possible questions.[38] Trying to dispel the impression that he was attempting to affect (or manipulate) the explorer's view of the matter ("I wasn't trying to play on your emotions"), he notes, "in any case, the machine still works and is *effective in its own way.*"[39] His praise concerns, before all else, the apparatus proper because everything else will fall into place, once the machine is set into motion, once the mechanism is allowed to demonstrate its efficacy. Very much in the rhetorical tradition of *ekphrasis,* the speaker does his best to foreground the object and tries to draw attention away from the words that evoke it. This tendency is also very much in keeping with the officer's pronounced contempt for judicial procedures based on question and answer and the "confusion" in which they inevitably result. As is quite evident, his own speech will be a case in point. It gives rise to questions on the

part of the explorer that divert attention from the real object of the officer's efforts. Hence the officer's short and matter-of-fact rebuttals of the
objections implicit in the visitor's queries. It appears that in the officer's
view these questions, posed from the outside and in ignorance of the apparatus, miss the point.[40] That is why in the beginning he doesn't even
appear to bother to refute them in an elaborate defense but rushes on to
complete his description so that the execution can take place and *speak
for itself.* The explanation of the sentencing procedure, given with a sense
of embarrassment at the naiveté of the question, is cut short—"but time
flies" (41)—to redirect attention to the execution's own procedure.

The officer's speech aims at making the apparatus appear in all its splendor and "self-evidence." The spectacle that the apparatus gives to see is
one, as we know, that immediately addresses itself to the senses. It brings
"illumination" first to the condemned, who reads his sentence with his
wounds, and then, by some sort of contagion or osmosis, to the onlooking community. While the immediacy of access and participation through
the senses (as opposed to speech), especially through vision, is stressed
throughout—the execution is a mass spectacle with crowds scrambling
to get a good view—at the height of the event some of the onlookers are
said to close their eyes, as if, we might speculate, to enjoy the realization
of justice in the intimacy of an inner vision.

The apparatus is supposed to perform a paradoxical operation: it is
on the disfigured body of the condemned that it makes justice present. At
the same time, for justice to become visible, if only to the inner vision,
the writhing, tormented body under the Harrow has to disappear, has to
give way to something else. The formula for this metamorphosis or conversion is transfiguration. That is indeed the term used in one of the story's
climactic moments: "How we all took in the expression of transfiguration from his martyred face, how we bathed our cheeks in the radiance of
this justice finally achieved and already vanishing" (*P,* 48). The German
reads: "Wie nahmen wir alle den Ausdruck der Verklärung von dem
gemarterten Gesicht, wie hielten wir unsere Wangen in den Schein dieser
endlich erreichten und schon vergehenden Wärme" (*S,* 228).[41] Literally,
taking off the expression of transfiguration from the sufferer's face, the
scene recalls a well-known Christological topos. The term *Ausdruck*
evokes its cognate, *Abdruck,* and the gesture of "abnehmen"—as in taking off a mask from somebody's face—reinforces the association with the

face-cloth bearing the features of Christ's face, which would become famous as "vera icon," the "true image of Christ." Basking (or "bathing," as Corngold translates this passage) itself in the light of justice, the community regenerates itself ("bathing" would suggest—by no means infelicitously, I think—a baptism and rebirth in the water).[42]

REFLECTIONS AND REVERSALS

As evidently as Kafka's story rehearses, at its pinnacle, key elements of the European "supplice pattern" (notably the communion of the spectators—parodied by the officer's embrace of the explorer), it also dismantles the Christian script governing the spectacle of the execution. The disturbances that Kafka introduces into the drama of death, redemption, and transfiguration are best grasped by turning to another constitutive feature of the story. *In the Penal Colony* is not only a text about a certain kind of spectacle, of spectatorship, and indeed of spectacularity. It is not only a "spectacular" but also a specular text, a text about specularity, in other words, a work that echoes, mirrors, and doubles is own elements and procedures. These reflexive and self-reflexive characteristics of Kafka's *In the Penal Colony* effect a kind of refraction, displacing and dismantling the spectacle of suffering and the positions held by its protagonists and observers, its proponents and its opponents. In other words, in the process of mirroring or reflecting it, the matrix of such spectacles, the "supplice pattern," gets twisted and distorted.

Doublings and mirror effects are at work on several levels of the narrative. The most obvious is the doubling of the two main protagonists by the story's other "pair," the condemned man and the soldier whose actions and reactions seem to mirror and mimic those of the explorer and the officer. At times these "mirror images" are inverted or slightly off. The explorer's ostensible disinterest, for example, has its counterpart in the condemned man's eagerness to see what the officer is demonstrating with such enthusiasm. In turn, the condemned man's searching gaze, seeing and understanding nothing, anticipates the explorer's embarrassment and cluelessness before the Old Commandant's written instructions. A peculiar confraternity emerges between the Chaplinesque couple of the condemned man and the soldier (bringing to mind similar pairs in other Kafka texts: think of the two bums, Robinson and Delamarche, of *Der Verschollene,* or the strange twins of *Das Schloß*). The solidarity between the two "natives," who are sharing the prisoner's "last supper" of rice pap, contrasts with the "agon" evolving between the officer and the explorer.

The most crucial series of reflections and inversions takes place, of course, between the latter two. Their interaction can be characterized as governed by a set of symmetries and asymmetries. Despite the noted divergences and differences in their views, demeanor, and actions, their trajectories seem to converge. In some sense they even appear to switch positions in the end. Here are some examples.

The officer's eloquent and passionate plea for the apparatus stands in marked contrast to the traveler's guarded silence. The inexhaustible flow of praise on the part of the officer, advertising his "product" like a salesman (the German original actually once refers to him with a term connoting just that, calling him a "Vertreter"), is met with monosyllabic reticence on the part of the explorer. Of course, the outward detachment of the latter conceals a growing inner agitation, a kind of running commentary on what he is made to see and hear and a silent debate on what to do. The voyager's thoughts, unspoken for the longest time, this inner voice is crucial in shaping and inflecting the readers' views, thus succeeding in the very task all the officer's eloquence failed to accomplish. In the end, however, the officer has more or less stopped talking. While not matching him in terms of eloquence, the explorer finally speaks his mind, and his verdict is as apodictic and firm as the officer's unshakable belief in the redemptive power of the machine that had made any objection seem utterly obsolete.

There is another reversal of the two positions. Determined to make his point, the officer proceeds to lay himself on the bed, yielding, one can't help thinking, to an old temptation, namely "to lie down . . . under the harrow" himself (45). The promptness with which he accepts his verdict exemplifies and asserts his earlier credo in the futility of argument. But of course the officer's silent compliance with the sentence is also a last attempt to demonstrate, *in actu* and in the flesh, the virtues of the apparatus that his speech had failed to convey.

Meanwhile, the carefully guarded detachment of the explorer, whose "neutrality" for a time seemed dangerously close to tacit complicity, is on the wane. It has given way to a gradual approximation to the officer's position. The explorer, steadfast in his resistance to the officer's rhetoric of persuasion, is taken over by curiosity. It is unclear whether this curiosity is piqued by the promise of technical perfection or that of the machine's redemptive, transfigurative power. (Obviously, for the officer these two aspects are one and the same. The "Vollendung" of the apparatus, mentioned early on, connects aesthetic perfection, technological achievement, and the notion of completion as in the fulfillment of a prophecy.)[43] He approves of the officer's self-immolation (telling himself that he would have done the same!) and thereby seems to tacitly consent to the position he had refused to acknowledge all along. At the end of the story he appears visibly disappointed not to detect even a trace of the promised transfiguration on the dead man's face. The breakdown of the machine had seemed to vindicate him, but there is a hint of regret and disappointment here, too. It is, in fact, only the malfunction of the apparatus that finally prompts him to interfere in the violent death of his friendly cicerone. This is not torture, as intended by the officer, but murder, he is thinking to himself.

In a curious twist on the mirror structure of the commandant's system of punishment, which maps the violated rule onto the violator's body, the explorer seems to have adopted the very method against which he had pronounced his verdict. In the "old" system the punishment consisted in writing the law that had been transgressed on the body of the condemned man. The point of contention, the apparatus, whose dignity and efficacy the explorer was so determined to deny, becomes the instrument of executing the very justice its previous use is supposed to have violated.

The similarity between the position of the explorer and of the officer is notoriously manifest in the word *zweifellos*, which underscores the immutability of their respective convictions. The officer had perplexed his counterpart when he decreed, "the guilt is always beyond all doubt" (die Schuld ist immer zweifellos). But this verdict is echoed by the explorer's own judgment, "The injustice of the procedure and the inhumanity of the execution were beyond all doubt" (46), first uttered to himself and then, at the prompting of the officer, made public. "From the very beginning the traveler had no doubt about the answer he had to give" (53). This is perhaps the most remarkable reversal of roles, for it turns out that while the officer was trying to make his case for the apparatus, it was in fact he who was being judged. And the more compelling his case for the machine, the worse matters became for him. Like the condemned man, he is being tried without realizing it and by a court that has determined his guilt "from the very beginning."

The narrative does not only reconfigure the positions occupied by the characters; it also, in classic *mise-en-abyme* fashion, mirrors the various trials it stages in one another. And remember that the officer does not only put all his effort in painting, in the most vivid terms, the miraculous machine; he also evokes, with remarkable theatrical talent, the trial that he, in turn, hopes to stage on behalf of the apparatus. It is for this that he wants to enlist the traveler's help. He imagines their appearance at the public meeting as a carefully orchestrated and triumphant drama that will end with the resounding defeat and public humiliation of the current governor to finally restore the apparatus to its rightful place. In fact, it is a spectacle to finish off the "spectacles" (51) of the meetings that have replaced the splendors of the execution with discourse and ladies bent on distracting men from their mission. With dramaturgical ingenuity, the officer even envisions two different scripts of how to bring about this sea change in the colony. One has the explorer clamoring the "truth": "Don't hold back in your speech, raise a big ruckus with the truth . . . , roar, yes indeed, roar your judgment, your unshakeable opinion at the commandant" (52).[44] In the other, he is to pronounce his "verdict" with more understatement leaving the rest to the officer.

In spite of their gradual approximation and partial congruence, there remains an insurmountable disconnect between the two views of justice, punishment and law, clashing in Kafka's story. From the very beginning the officer is concerned with the momentary revelation that occurs as the execution takes place. His focus is on the technical means that bring about this moment. The apparatus comes to stand for the epiphanic effect, whose dazzling light eclipses all other considerations, even making them seem utterly irrelevant. Remember the officer's genuine embarrassment at the explorer's interjections noted repeatedly in the text.[45] The discrepancy between the explorer's questions and remarks (presumably shared, at least for the most part, by the reader) and the officer's reactions is often hilarious. At what is perhaps the turning point of the story, the disconnect is particularly evident. "It did not seem that the officer had been listening. 'So the procedure has not convinced you,' he said to himself [!] and smiled, the way an old man smiles at the nonsense of a child and keeps his own true thoughts to himself behind the smile" (53). That the officer should compare his counterpart (and, by extension, the reader) to a child is no coincidence. For in some way the execution is meant for children, who are granted privileged access to the spectacle.

Although he can't suppress his curiosity, piqued after all by the technological sophistication of the apparatus, the explorer, by contrast, is concerned with the procedural aspect, with questions of evidence, defense, guilt, and so forth—in other words, with "due process." But then so is the officer. His disaffection with the new administration stems from their obvious disrespect for the old ways. Now, it is precisely the priority given by him, his inordinate devotion to the technical dimension of the process that appears cruel and excessive. It is not a sadistic cruelty, though, but one that is above all marked by the absence of compassion. The ostentatious disregard for the suffering of the condemned man is not only the most egregious but perhaps also one of the most comic effects of the story, especially as it comes coupled with a sense of nostalgia, an attachment to a sentimentalized past that reaches a peak when the officer evokes how he would watch, up close and with two children in his arms, how "understanding" or "enlightenment" would dawn even on "the most dull-witted."[46]

Instead of pointing out the "humaneness" of the penal system, as could be expected in a situation like this one, "its sole advocate" goes the other way, detailing the exceptionally painful procedure of the colony's punitive measures. Instead of reducing the pain of the condemned man to a minimum (the declared agenda of penal justice ever since the guillotine), the officer boasts a mechanism that prolongs it, achieving the maximum of pain over an extended amount of time. It is clear, though, that this pain is not an end in itself but rather the necessary condition for the transfiguration that it is meant to achieve. Pain is not inflicted, as in the supplice pattern, to extort the kind of public confession of the criminal that, in turn, would allow for his absolution. The condemned man doesn't know his crime or his punishment. "It would be pointless to tell him. After all, he is going to learn it on his own body," as the officer explains early on (40). Nor is there any need for him to recognize the authority of the court and, as a consequence thereof, the divine order, from which the court derives its legitimacy. As much as the illumination and transfiguration at the vanishing point of the procedure are reminiscent of the supplice pattern underlying executions in Europe from the Middle Ages to the nineteenth century (and beyond), no confession, no repentance, no absolution organizes the cruel spectacles of punishment in whose "splendor" the community of the Penal Colony "basks" itself.

Of course, compassion is not exactly what drives the explorer's attitude either. Whenever his gaze falls on the condemned man, he notes his animal-like features and bearing. In a mental note to himself, preparing his case against the apparatus before the new commandant, he points out that the condemned man is not "a compatriot, and he certainly did not arouse pity" (46). The traveler's reluctance to speak his mind, his preoccupation with decorum, and the continual attempts to find rationalizations for his own "neutrality" cast a rather negative light on the moral superiority claimed by the enlightened stance he represents. Indeed, the apodictic nature of his own verdict makes the man "conditioned by European points of view" (49) rather suspect.[47]

The reflection of the supplice pattern that the story gives us is a distorted one. Kafka adopts certain elements of the pattern while eliminating others. But these "missing" parts are nonetheless present, or they return in unexpected ways. One last example: in the officer's account of the execution, the "drama" ("das Spiel") never takes on the semblance of a martyr play.[48] As we have seen, the condemned man's attitude has no (or at least very little) bearing on the success of the "performance." Just as there doesn't seem to be any differentiation between crimes (the punishment is always the same), the identity of the victim is irrelevant for the procedure. The condemned man is as replaceable as any "extra." By contrast, the officer's unhesitating acceptance of his "sentence" recalls, rather overtly, the martyr's ultimate proof of faith. On the face of it—unlike the martyr who doesn't abandon his faith—the officer seems to acknowledge his "guilt." But once again, in a paradoxical conflation of opposites, by submitting to the sentence ("Be just!") without a word of protest, he demonstrates that the system, charged with meting out justice arbitrarily, has no room for exceptions, in other words, that it is not arbitrary. Applying its own "logic" as rigorously to its "sole advocate" (in other words to itself) as to anyone else, it disproves the charge and puts its adversaries to shame.

METAMORPHOSES

But what is "Chinese" about Kafka's cruelty? The "Chinese" character of the cruelty in *In the Penal Colony* resides, above all, in the disturbing relation to pain that the story puts on display.[49] The officer's egregious indifference vis-à-vis suffering is simply unassimilable to a perception that remains profoundly tied to the "supplice pattern." As in *ling'chi,* the suffering is subordinated to the law, whose "visibility" or, in Jérôme Bourgon's terms, "readability" takes absolute priority.[50] One might object that, different from the characteristic absence of any signs of transcendence in ling'chi, the working of the apparatus in Kafka's story is converted into a drama of transfiguration. Ultimately, however, "the promised redemption" does not take place. The apparatus has collapsed. Instead of the illumination that was to transpire on the dead man's face, the look of the dead officer is "as it had been in life." The last, haunting image of the dead officer resumes, albeit *ex negativo,* the vision of transfiguration at the climactic moment of the story. But a closer look into the open (presumably empty) eyes of the officer reveals yet another picture, one that undoes the ostensible opposition between—and mutual cancellation of—the blank gaze and the vision of redemption. The last image of the officer features a hybrid creature—half-mythic, half-saintly. The great iron spike protruding from his forehead evokes the horn of the unicorn as much as the crown of thorns.

The reading presented here has concentrated on two specific features of Kafka's story: its ekphrastic ambition, its *mise en image,* on the one hand, and, on the other, the narrative dramaturgy, the unexpected twists and turns in the "script" of the story, intended, it seems, to displace and dismantle this very image. Like the pictures of ling'chi, as reflected in the Western gaze, the image appears to hold the promise of a reversal, from extreme suffering to redemption and regeneration. Yet no such reversal occurs. The last image is one not of redemption or relief but of stasis and suspension. Impaled on the spike and dangling above the pit, the officer appears suspended between life—again, the expression of his face is said to be as it was in life—and death. While the anticipated reversal does thus not transpire where it was expected, the dramaturgy the story unfolds is one of continual turning points, inversions, and reversals. In a recent essay Alexander Honold has pointed out that *In the Penal Colony* conforms remarkably well to the Aristotelian conception of the tragic plot based on two types of reversals. *Anagnorisis,* or recognition, marks a turning point in the protagonists' knowledge, *peripeteia* one in the dramatic action.[51] As Honold notes, Kafka's narrative creates an eager anticipation of turning points, not only in the officer's description of the reversal that is to occur on the face of the tormented man but also, of course, in the readerly expectation of the traveler's response and intervention, which leads, in turn, to another, utterly unexpected turn of events, the officer's self-immolation. Honold does not mention the third element of Aristotle's theory of the tragic plot, *pathos,* which in a way forms the centerpiece of the story, even though the story's dramaturgy of continual shifts and turning points transforms the image of such pathos into its opposite, giving way to a mixture of ridicule and horror. The plot of the Christian "supplice pattern" has served us as a foil for measuring the twists and displacements that make up the "script" of *In the Penal Colony,* its evocation and revocation of pathos.

Obviously, the notion of "script" has a much more literal presence in the story. Thus far we have focused on violence as image and spectacle and on the "agon" over its possible justifications. But it is, of course, intimately linked with the idea of writing and, more specific still, with the idea of the law. The nexus between violence and writing and violence and the law opens up two additional perspectives on the question of what kind of "case" it is that is being made in *In the Penal Colony.* One points to Kafka's vexed relation to his Jewish heritage, more particularly to the Jewish law, the other to a certain ambivalence with regard to his own writing. On the first view the machine inscribing the law onto the body is an instantiation of Jeremiah 31:33, the Lord's promise (or threat) to the people of Israel to put his "law in their inward parts, and write it in their hearts." Like the law of the Old Testament the law of the "Old Commandant," who the commentators have been quick to associate with the God of the Hebrew Bible, has no need to justify itself, demanding unconditional obedience. In its mechanical mindlessness the apparatus echoes the inscrutable demands of Yahweh. The machine recalls a "view of Judaism," as Eric Santner has put it, "as a legalistic religion of radical subjection to the pure heteronomy of divine jurisdiction," which proved both fascinating and deeply troubling to the generation of German-Jewish writers of which Kafka was, in many respects, one of the foremost representatives.[52] In Jeremiah 31:33 the inscription of the law on the hearts is a part and a continual reminder of the covenant between God and his people. The publicly staged inscription of the law in *In the Penal Colony* serves a similar purpose: the illumination that is supposed to come over the tormented body affects the entire audience, reconstituting in it a feeling of community. According to a famous remark in Nietzsche's *Genealogy of Morals,* pain is the precondition of memory.[53] It is through the infliction of pain that the human animal becomes the animal that is capable of making promises and hence of committing itself to and maintaining (nonviolent) social relations. The procedure the machine is supposed to perform echoes not only the inexorable law of the Jewish God but also the failed process of humanization, variations of which one finds at the center of a number of Kafka's stories.[54] If the apparatus worked, it would bring "illumination to the most dull-witted"; it would hence transform the condemned, who is characterized throughout as a mindless, animal-like creature, into an *animale rationale,* in other words, into a human being and, by the same token, reassert the collective order and reinforce the communal bond. But it doesn't work, and the supposed inscription in the order of the symbolic actually destroys the subject or, rather, leaves it suspended in the strange dimension between life and death, manifest in the bizarre expression on the officer's face. As in the images of ling'chi, the violence invoked in the officer's nostalgic account of the penal colony's punishments is an expression of strict, mindless legality, not, as Bataille would have it, a celebration of transgression and the suspension of the law, a temporary release from the constraints of the symbolic order, but rather the violence tied to the instauration and reaffirmation of that very order.

As numerous commentators have noted, *In the Penal Colony* is not just about Kafka's conflicted relation to Halachic law but also about his ambivalent feelings vis-à-vis his own writing.[55] As in the ecstatic vision of the tormented body, which the apparatus is supposed to produce, writing can be an experience of exaltation and provide access to a higher order of being. But it is also a matter of bad conscience, of guilt vis-à-vis a life entirely subordinated to literature and hence not really lived. Kafka has recorded the feeling of exaltation that successful writing can afford the writing subject in his account of the night in which he wrote "The Judgement," a night that he famously described as the moment in which he was born as a writer. Mark Anderson has pointed out the remarkable parallels between Kafka's description of this night in a diary entry (September 23, 1912) and the description of the punishment in *In the Penal Colony.* "The essential elements are almost identical: the duration of the writing (twelve hours in 'In the Penal Colony,' an entire night for 'The Judgement'); the passive reception of the text; disappearance of pain halfway through the process as the body passes from a temporal to a spiritual order; the 'opening' up of body and soul; and finally the luminous eyes as the sign of transfiguration."[56] The transformation of life, and especially the body, into literature is a topos Kafka shares with other writers, especially his beloved hero Flaubert.[57] The creative process dissolves the body into writing, preserving it in a sublimated and heightened form. But this peculiar transubstantiation is also destructive of the body, draining its vitality and forever transfixing the subject on the threshold of life, which it can only observe from a distance. Recall Kafka's famous characterization of his writing as the hesitance before birth, "das Zögern vor der Geburt." Like the inscription operated by the apparatus, writing is thus a means of transfiguration and of torture. It is guilt-ridden, and if it stalls, as it had when Kafka wrote *In the Penal Colony*, it becomes a painful reminder of the strange position of the subject engaged in this life-inimical activity, stuck, like the officer, in the writing machine and suspended between life and death.[58]

Bataille's pathos before the image of the Chinese torture victim is one of ecstatic self-loss. What manifests itself in the sight of this suffering are the violent rhythms of the general economy that threaten to engulf the beholder. Bataille's engagement with the images of *ling'chi* does not only stage this force but seeks to transmit its impact to the viewer/reader of his work. The forces of the general economy can only be glimpsed as the protective shield of the symbolic order gets suspended. Bataille's writing is an attempt to regain access to this lost and disavowed dimension of human experience. Much of his political engagement of the 1930s and 1940s can be viewed as being part of the same endeavor, though the terms shift a bit over time. In the later phase of his work, the speculative economic and anthropological writings of the 1950s, the activism recedes and is replaced by theoretical elaboration, on the one hand, and amassing of evidence for his thesis concerning the nexus between sexuality and death, on the other. Along with the book on the cave paintings of Lascaux, *The Tears of Eros* concludes this labor and constitutes something like Bataille's last dramatic attempt to communicate his insights or "revelation." Bataille's aesthetics of transgression, which has had repercussions in numerous areas, is epitomized by the dramatization of somatic vertigo before the lacerated and truncated body of the young Chinese man. It is the pathos of the real at its purest but also in its characteristic ambiguity between the desire of somatic immediacy and traumatic transformation, on the one hand, and theatricality and posing, on the other.

It is far more difficult to explain the peculiar fascination with the spectacle of violence that is at work in Kafka's *In the Penal Colony*. The story's dramatization of the scene systematically confounds the positions and views taken. It is true that the imaginary vision of the tormented body is treated with considerable irony, and the pathos of this vision is continually undercut by the theatrics of the narrative. But the violence that pervades the story is not simply a laughing matter. In fact, it is deeply ambivalent. On the one hand, it can be viewed as the violence of inscription, the painful initiation of the subject into the symbolic order, whose erratic, inscrutable laws form and deform it at the same time. On the other hand, it can be viewed as being about the transformative power of writing in both its redemptive and destructive aspect. It promises a different kind of existence, an existence in the space outside of the symbolic order or on its threshold, heightening and transfiguring the writing subject. But ultimately it traps the subject between life and death. This is the secret pathos of Kafka's story.

CHAPTER TWO

Fragmentary Description of a Disaster

Claude Simon

[Show one who] shields his terrified eyes with one hand, the palm turned outwards toward the enemy, and the other hand resting on the ground to support his half raised body. Show others shrieking, open-mouthed and in flight. Show various kinds of weapons between the feet of the combatants such as broken shields and lances, broken swords and other similar things. Show dead men, some half and others completely covered with dust. [Show] the dust, as it mixes with the spilt blood turning into red mud, and the blood picked out by its colour, running its perverted course from the body into the dust.

—LEONARDO DA VINCI, "HOW TO REPRESENT A BATTLE"[1]

Two Battlefields

In the course of his peregrinations in the tracks of destruction, the unnamed narrator of W. G. Sebald's *The Rings of Saturn* comes upon the battlefield of Waterloo. The official monument of the memorial, a lion atop a pyramid, strikes him as tasteless, and he observes to his astonishment a small group, costumed as Napoleonic soldiers, moving about, seemingly without purpose, between a few stalls at the edge of the battlefield. "For a while I watched these mummers, who seemed to be in perpetual motion, as they disappeared amongst the buildings only to re-emerge elsewhere."[2] The sight of such pointless theatricality and the sensation of attending a production that seems to make do without an audience quickly give way, however, to the opposite impression: the battle panorama, which the narrator visits in the nearby rotunda, is emphatically intended for viewing. Quite different from the forsaken music troupe, which seems to embody Marx's observation that history recurs as farce, the panorama purports to provide a comprehensive view of events. It simulates contemporaneity, immediacy, and overview. Its presentation strives to make the events depicted entirely present, even to overwhelm the viewer, visually and affectively. This effect is achieved technically through *trompe l'œil*, dramaturgically through the transgression of one of the central conventions of pictorial representation: literally drawing the picture beyond its boundaries, the panorama does away with the lateral frames of pictorial representation. The events portrayed extend continuously 360 degrees around the observer's line of sight, stretching above to the sky or the horizon. The space surrounding the viewer is fitted out with objects and figures from the painting, aiding in the simulation of continuity between the pictorial world and the world of the observer—even when, as in the case of Sebald's narrator, this strategy misses its mark. The arrangement in the foreground of the panorama strikes him as "a sort of landscaped proscenium" (124), and the view to the horizon fills him with unease. "This then, I thought, as I looked round about me, is the representation of history. We, the survivors, see everything from above, see everything at once, and still we do not know how it was" (125).[3] To the observer of the late twentieth century, the panorama comes to stand for a naive and uncritical concept of history and its representation. Its pretensions to totality and coherence seem presumptuous, its trust in the availability of past experience naive, its suggestion of immediacy suspect. The battle panoramas are the expression of a monumental mode of historiography, purporting to bring past triumphs to life before the eyes of posterity.

The rejection of the claim to immediacy, perspicuity, and totality epitomized by the panorama of Waterloo is resumed and extended in an episode from *Austerlitz* that presents us with the description of another battle delivered by the title character's history teacher, the eccentric André Hilary. In his rendering of the historic battle of Austerlitz Hilary—far from limiting himself to description in the narrow sense of the term—conjures up moments of the battle in a quasi-dramatic fashion that is as virtuosic as it is ironic. The vividness of his "dramatic descriptions,"[4] which his audience claims to remember in the greatest detail even years afterward, seems only to be increased by the fact that "very often, probably owing to his suffering from slipped disks, he gave them while lying on his back on the floor" (70). The immobility of the narrating voice and the dynamic action of the narrated events form a compelling contrast. As a narrative counterpart to the battle panoramas, Hilary's description strives toward incommensurate ideas of representation: the bird's-eye view—"surveying the entire landscape of those years from above with an eagle eye" (70), as Hilary characterizes his own reconstruction of events—and the suggestion of being on the scene, in the immediate presence of the event. Before the students' eyes arises "a picture" (71) that is at once concrete and abstract in equal measure. The movement of the different regiments in their colored uniforms gives them an image of the battle as a kaleidoscopic play of patterns; the acoustic and atmospheric depiction of the clash of opposing cavalries and "whole ranks of men collapsing beneath the surge of the oncoming force" (71) brings a sinking feeling to the pits of the captivated listeners' stomachs. But Hilary perpetually undermines his own virtuosity. He remarks that no rendition, no matter how systematic or complete, can do justice to the actual events:

> All of us, even when we think we have noted every tiny detail, resort to set pieces which have already been staged often enough by others. We try to reproduce the reality, but the harder we try, the more we find the pictures that make up the stock-in-trade of the spectacle of history forcing themselves upon us: the fallen drummer boy, the infantryman shown in the act of stabbing another, the horse's eye starting from its socket, the invulnerable Emperor surrounded by his generals, a moment frozen still amidst the turmoil of battle. Our concern with history, so Hilary's thesis ran, is a concern with preformed images already imprinted on our brains, images at which we keep staring while the truth lies elsewhere. (71–72)[5]

Hilary's hesitation gives weight to the fundamental difficulties of depiction. On the one hand, the problem is to some extent quantitative. "It would take an endless length of time," the history teacher explains, "to describe the events of such a day properly" (71). On the other hand, there is the more qualitative problem of accuracy and authenticity. As the narrator of *The Rings of Saturn* had noted, no matter how much we are given to "see," "we do not know how it was." But not only is there an inevitable gap between the event and its later representations; there is also the intrusion of "preformed images already imprinted on our brains." This realization is, in fact, something of a quote. It is based on a famous observation by Henri Beyle—that is, Stendhal—regarding the derivative and hence unreliable character of our memory: what Beyle believed to be deeply inscribed and exact memories of Napoleon's journey across the Alps was in fact based on an engraving.[6] It is certainly no coincidence that the same Stendhal is invoked at the end of the Waterloo episode in *The Rings of Saturn*. There the narrator concludes his own views about the impossibility of "picturing" an actual battle, by recalling what is probably one of the most famous descriptions of a battle in modern European literature: the Waterloo episode from Stendhal's *The Charterhouse of Parma,* which is precisely about the impossibility of obtaining a view of the battle from any single standpoint but also about the discrepancies between the battle paintings and literary descriptions that inform the charmingly hapless hero's expectations and his actual experiences on the battlefield. Ironically, the insight in the inevitable overdetermination of memory and the imagination with prefabricated images and clichés takes itself the form of a literary reminiscence.

Sebald's own writing can be viewed as an antidote against the ideal of transparency and against the pathos that characterize the panorama and its precursor, battle painting. In its nineteenth-century incarnation the genre of battle painting provided the paradigmatic case of a view of history that conceived of change as a fateful struggle between nations, led by heroic individuals and determined in decisive battles whose turning points the battle painters sought to capture, thus transforming carnage into iconic and ideological capital.[7] The twentieth century also "unfolded *under the paradigm of war.*"[8] But clearly, much of the art and literature of the twentieth century broke with the assumptions informing the iconography and ideology of the nineteenth-century art form, even as the idea that history unfolds under the sign of violence became ever more compelling. Sebald's oeuvre is a case in point, both in the ways it represents and reflects (on) the historical experience of the twentieth century and in its view of history not as a matter of progression and progress but as a series of catastrophes. In his books the apparent transparency of the panorama gives way to *bricolage,* a semifictional and semidocumentary patchwork of stories and histories; and the pathos of battle painting is replaced by melancholy. Like the Benjaminian rag picker, Sebaldian narrators sift through the rubble and debris of history, tracking what Sebald has called the "natural history of destruction," gathering evidence of a sweeping and yet largely misunderstood process of disintegration, the flip side, as it were, to the story of progress and civilization. Still, Sebald's own works do not actually deal with the experience of war proper, despite the fact that he has criticized the German literature of the second half of the twentieth century for its failure to deal with one of the worst aspects of World War II, namely the air raids on German cities.[9] The violence and destruction Sebald's works register is in some sense both more universal and more obscure. It is what is deposited and "sedimented" in the various archives, landscapes, and settings that make up the world of his texts but also, and especially, in the life stories of the characters that his narrators encounter and whose biographies, whether fictional or nonfictional, they reconstruct. In the words of one recent commentator, what Sebald seeks to capture in his strangely documentary fictions is "the persistence of past suffering that has . . . been absorbed into the substance of lived space, into the 'setting' of human history."[10] This is why in Sebald's "natural history of destruction" violence often figures in rather oblique ways. It is manifest not as a dramatic, eruptive force, though frequently the author mirrors man-made and natural disasters in one another, but mostly in more muted forms. Think, for example, of the violent acts with which the four protagonists of *The Emigrants* end their lives, belatedly implementing, it seems, the very annihilation for which the Nazis had singled them out and that they had escaped fortuitously. With very few exceptions the experience of war is not featured directly.[11] It typically has a rather more subliminal presence, as for example in the mounds of rubble that the narrator, as a child growing up in Germany in the late 1940s and early 1950s, for the longest time took to be a "natural" element of the cityscape. Sebald's oeuvre is very much a meditation on how the violence of history has settled and "sedimented" in various repositories, both material and symbolic, from which it keeps unsettling and haunting the present.

Ekphrastic Writing and Iconoclasm: Picturing the Real

If war, as Alain Badiou has claimed, is one of the defining characteristics of the twentieth century, if indeed, as he puts it, "the passion of the century . . . is nothing other than war," and more specifically still a "definitive" war, that is, "a total and final war to end all wars"[12]—if this is the case, then which are the forms that have taken the place of the paradigmatic nineteenth-century iconography of battle painting and the panorama? How did those swept up by this "passion of the century," those drawn into it, whether willy-nilly or enthusiastically, account for their experiences? Which manner of representation could match the extremity of this experience? What are the modalities under which one could render the excess of the twentieth century's "definitive," "total," and "final" war? As I have said, even though the aesthetics and ideology of battle painting serve as a foil for Sebald's poetics of the natural history of destruction, war itself is not his proper subject. For an answer to these questions I therefore turn to an author whose writing consists of one unending effort to find a way to speak of this experience without succumbing to the illusion of transparency and the lure of pathos epitomized by the aesthetics of battle painting. The very difficulties cited by the Sebaldian narrators in their reflections on the representation of war are indeed reflected in an oeuvre that seems to have spent, in the words of Sebald's André Hilary, "the endless length of time it would take to describe the events of such a day properly," while grappling with the very questions raised apropos of battle painting.

Writing about his own experiences in World War II, Claude Simon has always insisted on the radical disorientation experienced under fire and the difficulty, noted by Stendhal, of doing justice to it retrospectively. For any retrospective account that presumes to show, to make us see "how it must have been,"[13] performs the very operation that had become unavailable in that moment. Any subsequent attempt to render the radical displacement of the coordinates of perception and cognition has to restore to some degree what was lost during the moment of crisis. In this sense any rendering, precisely by virtue of being a rendering, changes the very thing it seeks to convey. Like the Sebaldian narrators, Claude Simon takes issue with the notion that the war experience is accessible and available to any straightforward rendition. His writing is very much about the inaccessibility and elusiveness of this experience, both then and now, that is to say, both on the battlefield and in the laborious process of recollection and reconstruction. The difficulty of access to and apprehension of that experience is further compounded by the other difficulty touched on in Sebald's discussion of the panorama and the narrative depiction of battle: the fact that both the memory and the imagination are beset and distracted by the continual interference of large numbers of stock images. In Claude Simon, who, incidentally, has invoked the same Stendhal episode about the writer's faulty memories of his participation in the Napoleonic campaigns, the steady interference of images becomes a key part of writing about the war experience, even if this writing consists, to no small extent, in countering that interference. Resisting the notion that the past is a given that simply needs to be described, put before the reader's eyes, as it were, the novels' ongoing efforts to convey a sense of "how it was" take the form of a struggle with, and against, the images that continually impose themselves.

"Fragmentary Description of a Disaster" was the alternative title for Claude Simon's best-known and most successful novel, *La route des Flandres* (translated into English as *The Flanders Road*). The book continues the tradition of battle painting and rewrites it in a quasi-iconoclastic manner. In this sense Simon's writing could be characterized as a form of battle painting by other means, not only with respect to its reservations vis-à-vis the ideal of transparency, of ever actually being able to say, "Look, this is how it was," but also in the way it quotes and revokes the pathos of the genre. Pathos is in play on different levels of the novels. It figures most prominently perhaps in a certain heroic iconography in which the narrative tries to mould the war experience. Scenes and episodes are assimilated to a host of standard configurations, poses, and gestures, drawn from a shared iconic repertoire and producing strange effects of déjà vu. But the desire to endow the experience with a kind of mythic and ennobling aura by inscribing it in a certain iconographic lineage is typically undercut by somatic memories that are so powerful, indeed so traumatic, that they quickly undo any such idealizations. For the most part, however, the appeal to certain iconographic formulas is driven by a sense of sarcasm and disbelief in the first place. For all the hesitation and doubt that mark their efforts to reconstruct what they have experienced, the Simonian narrators speak of their war experience with some degree of derision for the apparent need of such idealizations, their own as well as that of others. It could therefore appear as though pathos had, for the most part, merely a negative, polemical presence. But there is a less tangible and less visible pathos that sustains the unending search for understanding and, more broadly, Simon's writing as a whole. To put it briefly: the experience of war is the experience of death, of the subject's utter destitution and reduction. What the protagonists try to recount is the experience of having been reduced to a being selected and bound to die. In some sense it is the fortuitous, contingent survival that forms the impenetrable and opaque center of Simon's novels and makes for the mute pathos that holds together his "fragmentary description of disaster," his "iconoclastic" battle paintings.

In the following I analyze the apparent tension between the insistence on the elusive experience at the center of Simon's novels—an experience in excess of any representation because it is the experience of the radical crisis of representation itself—and the remarkable presence of images and visual representation in the text. I argue that the investment in images, in visual representation and the visual as such—the *mise en image* that is the key operation of this writing—not only originates in but is also conditioned by the peculiar sense of disorientation and disconnect experienced during the war and that the continual transformation of scenes—seen, remembered, or imagined—into images speaks to the insistent desire to discern the meaning that is so patently absent from that experience. Another way of putting this is to say that, on the one hand, *mise en image,* the proliferation and continual displacement of images, is precisely a way of getting at, or at least registering, the traumatic real of the war experience, its nagging persistence and its elusiveness, while, on the other hand, the pictorial templates the writing mobilizes in such great numbers indicate the urge to overcome the ostensible absence of sense. But just as the insistence on the incommensurability of the experience gives way to ever-renewed attempts to detect some kind of necessity at the core of an experience marked by contingency, the search for the significance of what occurred fails; the insights the images seem to promise are never realized. I flesh out these assertions about the operations of *mise en image* in Claude Simon by analyzing the role played by the visual representation and the visual arts on a number of different levels: first, in the author's poetics, grounded in what one could call the missed encounter with the real, that is to say in an experience as impossible to assimilate as it is to forget; second, in his deployment of verbal images, the metaphors and comparisons pervading the texts; and, finally, in his descriptions of a few actual artworks.

Marking his opposition to a certain notion of realism, Simon's programmatic appeal to the visual arts is, above all, an appeal to the principles of their organization that, in the author's view, are antithetical to the logic of narrative and plot. As such this appeal goes some way in explaining the structure of his own novels: the tension between the ostensible incoherence on the texts' surface level and the assertion of their inner consistency and cohesion. The interest in the visual arts, in particular in modernist nonfigurative art, is also tied to the perceptual vertigo experienced under attack—an experience in which vision and intelligibility seem to become divorced and in which an agency radically different from the one at work in human action appears to assert itself, the force of matter itself. In this encounter with a world suddenly stripped of the usual frame of reference, an unsettling sense of things, appearing in their pure phenomenality, and the senseless violence of matter override any effort to comprehend what is happening.

Pictorial representation and the visual arts figure in, and shape, Claude Simon's writing, both metaphorically and literally. There is a rich and sophisticated scholarship on how the remarkable proliferation of verbal images contributes to the "image-effect" of the Simonian text. Drawing on this research, my discussion focuses on the ways in which pictorial representation itself figures metaphorically, that is to say, how, very frequently, the events related are cast as though they were pictures or spectacles. In connection with the war this type of metaphorical *mise en image* often involves the appeal to a certain mythoheroic iconography that serves as a foil for the actual experience. The apparent absence of any discernible rationale for what is happening is temporarily countered and suspended by the intimation of a hidden necessity, the tokens of a higher, mythic order.

Finally, the visual arts also have a literal presence in the texts. On a number of occasions characters find themselves before actual artworks: paintings of warriors and battles that may bring to life the turmoil of the past and that the characters avidly scan for clues in their interminable search for the hidden sense of their experiences.

Perceptual Vertigo and the "Stupid and Stupefying Fury of Things"

At the core of Claude Simon's writing is a singular experience. In the early phase of World War II he is deployed as part of the French cavalry and witnesses the near-total annihilation of his squadron in an ambush in May 1940. He survives, miraculously, and is later captured, but he eventually manages to escape the German prisoner-of-war camp in which he was held. Over a period of more than fifty years and in an oeuvre comprising more than twenty books,[14] Simon has revisited and recounted the various episodes of his engagement in World War II with remarkable persistence: the mobilization of the troops, their transportation to the front in Belgium, the cavalry's winter quarters, military drills and maneuvers, riding through the war-torn landscape, the ambush, running for his life under machine-gun fire, and many others.

The most emblematic of these scenes occurs in the aftermath of the ambush. The protagonist-narrator has joined three other survivors of the attack, two officers and their orderly, all three of them still on horseback. He is assigned a horse and follows them as they ride through the battered landscape. The two officers seem utterly oblivious to what just happened but also to the threat of imminent death. As a sniper starts firing at them, one of the officers draws his saber before he is struck down. This "instinctual" and highly charged gesture imprints itself on the narrator's memory. It will resurface time and again in his attempts to recollect and put into order his war memories as something like the epitome of folly, of a modern war experienced on horseback.

Claude Simon's multiple versions of this *drôle de guerre* depart from conventional accounts of war in many respects. *Battle* and *combat* hardly seem appropriate terms for describing this experience. The enemy remains largely hidden from view. The higher-ranking officers appear ludicrously inept in dealing with the situation. The strategy of the deployment seems devoid of all sense, and soon the blatant discrepancy between the French and German resources becomes obvious in the deadly confrontation. The impulse of Simon's writing has its origin in these discrepancies, more specifically in the exposure to an unimagined kind of violence, unleashed against a subject utterly unprepared, both mentally and materially, for what was ahead. More specifically still, this writing is launched by the need not only to bear witness to a violence that is in excess of the imagination but also to account for the miracle, and enigma, of having survived. But Simon's writing has a second source that is no less important for understanding some of its most characteristic features. This other source of Simon's unending *roman fleuve*[15] lies in a polemical stance against the shortcomings of a certain notion of realism. It is a polemic against the notion of literature as a mode of representation that effaces itself before the reality it purports to render and against the related assumption that reality is a given that remains unchanged in the process of mediation.

One encounters this polemic in the fiction itself, but it is also on prominent display in the author's poetological pronouncements, such as the

Nobel lecture, as well as in numerous interviews. It is not only directed against a certain image (a caricature even) of the nineteenth-century novel but also expresses the author's reservations about any attempt (his own included) to "render the confusing, manifold and simultaneous perception of the world,"[16] any attempt that is oblivious to the inevitable modifications brought about by the transposition of experience into language. There are many instances in his books in which the narrator or a character (or often simply a voice that only gradually assumes an identity) corrects, reworks, or even revokes the account of events provided by someone else (another voice), drawing attention to the omissions, conjectures, and distortions employed for the sake of narrative unity and coherence. The most prominent instance of this are certainly Georges and Blum, the two protagonists of *La route des Flandres,* who become increasingly entangled in the stories they reconstruct (or imagine) about the tragic death of their former superior, Reixach, the officer brandishing his sword as the sniper's bullet hits him.

The polemic is on full display in Simon's rewriting of George Orwell's *Homage to Catalonia* in the fourth part of *Les Géorgiques.* Orwell's book is itself a kind of reckoning with his engagement in the Spanish civil war and with the factionalism that foiled Republican efforts, so it is somewhat odd that Simon should target it. Already in his first novel about the Spanish civil war, *Le palace,* Simon had seemed to want to outdo his predecessor in the debunking of the youthful idealism that made both of them join the Republican forces. In the texts dealing with his own involvement in Spain, which provide another set of recurring themes and motifs of the oeuvre, Simon is at great pains to demystify his "Spanish adventure." In the fourth part of *Les Géorgiques* it is Orwell's narrative of disillusionment that is systematically demolished. It appears as though the British writer's recognition of his mistakes and errors in judgment is not going far enough in Simon's view. In fact, the mere attempt to account for the intellectual and existential threat Orwell experienced in Spain in narrative terms seems to prove that he has yet to fully appreciate the inevitable and unbridgeable gap between experience and its retrospective narrative organization: his hope "that in writing his adventure he will enable some coherent meaning to emerge from it" proves illusory. "Indeed, as he writes his confusion will only get worse."[17] Simon's revision very much aims at undoing Orwell's "construct" and at getting to the amorphous "magma" of raw experience at the core of his failed engagement: the reality of danger and the terror of imminent death.[18]

In some way a similar kind of undoing is at work in Claude Simon's own texts, not only on the intertextual (Orwell) and intradiegetic level—as in Blum's carnivalistic and parodistic versions of Georges' more "romantic" accounts of Reixach's death[19]—but also in their own broader makeup. As any reader will quickly notice, Simon's texts are multilayered and dynamic. That is to say, there is a continual and at times confusing transition between different narrative layers, some of which are quickly identifiable and assume a certain consistency and some of which remain oblique. Some strands of the novels form part of the recognizable narratives that each book seems to recycle (besides the experience of the Spanish civil war and World War II, it is especially the family history that comes increasingly to the fore, above all in the later works). Others often don't seem to bear any relation to the rest. This is particularly true for many of the long descriptive passages that constitute in some sense the signature of Simon's writing. At times the different layers of a narrative are neatly separated; at times they are entwined and fused to the point of indistinction. The experience of reading Claude Simon thus takes on a rhythm that mimics the oscillation between understanding and confusion, between a certain degree of recognition and a feeling of being utterly lost. The sense of disorderliness and disorientation, the ever-changing and shifting tectonic layers that generate the texts' remarkable dynamic, is not only due to the attempt of recreating "the confusing and manifold perception of the world" but also a consequence of the inescapable interference of memories and the imagination in that very attempt. Indeed, the work of recovery and reconstruction is inevitably beset by such intrusion, continually diverting the writing from its course.

Defending himself against the charge of incoherence, of discontinuity and disregard for the conventions of plot and character, Claude Simon has often invoked a different kind of coherence and "credibility," namely the one found in the visual arts. At first, this appeal to the visual arts might seem strange, especially in view of the author's programmatic opposition to realism and mimetic writing. The appeal to a "different kind of verisimilitude"[20] and the reference to "pictorial credibility" doesn't point to a greater veracity but has to do with the fact that the internal organization of visual artworks is typically not accounted for in narrative terms but rather in terms of spatial configuration, of composition, proportions, shape, color, light, and so on. In various instances Simon has, indeed, tried to describe the structure of some of his books in highly abstract often geometrical terms, presenting his work as both a meditation on, and an exercise in, the "permutation" of certain forms or movements.[21] As formalist and, indeed, purist as such commitments may appear—Simon would later distance himself from some of these claims—the appeal to the visual arts appears to be sustained by a desire to get to the basic forms organizing human perception, a desire shared with two of the predominant intellectual and artistic trends of the writer's youth, phenomenology and cubism.[22] A similar tendency, though less preoccupied with basic forms than with base matter, is characteristic of some of the writer's artist friends and acquaintances—such as Jean Dubuffet, Joan Miró, and Gastone Novelli —whose works constitute an important point of reference and with whom he has collaborated in various ways.

It would be a mistake, however, to regard the search for the primordial, as Lucien Dällenbach has called it, merely as a transposition of painterly experiments in abstraction to the art of prose.[23] And it would be equally misleading to view this exploration of form and matter in purely polemical terms, that is to say, as a response to the reputed moralism of the existentialist novel, as Claude Simon himself has often suggested.[24] Once more, it is the experience of war that is at the origin of the peculiar preoccupation with forms and base matter.

Throughout Simon's texts one comes across descriptions of phenomena whose common denominator may not be evident: flocks of soaring birds swiftly shifting directions, drifting cloud formations, dust columns rising and then slowly settling on the ground, smoke hovering above the audience in a movie theater, the play of colors and shapes that form under closed eyelids, the ripples closing over a pebble tossed into a pond, eddies and swirls, the turbulences of particles in the air, the commotion of murky waters, and many others.[25] Again, the place and function of these recurrent motifs, often described in some detail, in the economy of the text is not immediately obvious. What arrests and unsettles the gaze drawn to these sights is the continual metamorphosis, the steady dissolution and reconstitution of volumes and forms in a self-generated dynamic that seems governed by a kind of inscrutable lawfulness—chaotic, continually changing, and organized at the same time. The shifting and swirling mass, simultaneously light and dense, voluminous and ephemeral, troubles the operations of perceptual synthesis. Instead of allowing the identification of a stable entity or object of some kind, the gaze is confronted with ever-evolving and receding forms. It is a similar kind of perceptual disorientation and incoherence that is one of the immediate effects on the mind stunned by the bomber attacks, perceiving the world in shapes and color configurations before the consciousness slowly regains a sense of its surroundings: "then suddenly nothing more (not even feeling the shock, no pain, not even the awareness of stumbling, of falling, nothing): darkness, no noise now (or perhaps a deafening uproar canceling itself out?), deaf blind, nothing, until slowly, emerging gradually like bubbles rising to the surface of murky water, appear indeterminate spots that blur, fade out, then reappear, then grow clear: triangles, polygons, pebbles, tiny blades of grass, the stones of the road where he is now on all fours like a dog" (A, 63–64; Ac, 90).[26] The war has a peculiar effect on the perception, impairing and exalting it at the same time. Fatigue, exhaustion, and a sense of futility mark the vision. In many instances a strange gap opens up between seeing and understanding, dissociating sensory perception and conceptual grasp, destabilizing the order of cause and effect. Sight and sense seem to be drifting apart. Many of the phenomena registered by the tired brigadiers assume an uncanny presence, absorbing and confounding their incredulous gaze. Seemingly emerging out of nowhere, these sights lock in the gaze but often remain thoroughly unintelligible nonetheless. The things the troopers see seem strangely out of place, stranded objects—often, quite literally, the litter and debris strewn across the devastated landscape by civilians fleeing the Germans—remnants of a domestic world from which the soldiers feel cut off and that appears increasingly unreal to them. The abandoned human artifices, objects and instruments of everyday life, assume a menacing aspect. Theirs is a strange kind of presence, an effect of the sudden displacement and disappearance of the world in which they had their place, inducing a sense of wonder and estrangement in the young recruits who have given up "that posture of the mind which consists of seeking a cause or logical explanation of what you see or what happens to you" (FR, 24; RF, 25).[27]

Confronted with spectacles that seem as elusive as they do ominously real, the perception, strained and on high alert at the same time, comes to realize the precariousness of its own operations. The work of synthesis it performs is suspended. The world appears not in its usual complexion, made up of objects that can be identified by concepts, but is fragmented and reduced to more elementary and at the same time more abstract units: basic geometrical figures (polygons, spheres, cylinders), shapes, and colors, the "stuff" out of which the mind, at least in a simple picture of its activity, constitutes the world's familiar face. The perceptual disorder, however, stems not only from an inability to find the right terms for what the gaze takes in. It is worsened by the disturbing sense that what is seen is actually not there, that the world around us is losing its solidity, its logical and its material consistency, "as if not an army but the world itself the whole world and not only in its physical reality but even in the representation the mind can make of it . . . was actually falling apart collapsing breaking into pieces dissolving into water into nothing" (*FR, 16; RF, 16*).[28]

The other dimension unveiled by the violent experience of war is that of matter. It is an encounter that takes place in the exposure both to destruction and to the elements of nature. Throughout their *errance* back and forth across the small stretch of territory that has seen armies come and go since time immemorial,[29] the troops are battered by the elements. They experience extreme hardship under rain and snow. In one of the central episodes, a never-ending ride through the night, they are drenched by incessant rainfall, and their nerves and senses are stretched to the breaking point. In the winter quarters an "apocalyptic cold" descends on them.[30] Later, in May, in the aftermath of the ambush the dazzling, glorious sunlight seems to mock their devastating defeat. But the one element with which they become most intimately familiar is the earth. The war tears into the ground, hurling up the soil, spreading layers of dust and dirt over the world. The soldiers are soon covered with it—their uniforms soaked in mud, thin layers of sweat and dirt on their faces, dust in their mouths, their eyes burning. The war seems to be revoking the creation, setting off a process of disintegration in which the earth reclaims what once issued from it. The ultimate goal of the soldiers' progress seems to be a return to the soil, the "matrix" from which they emerged. Nowhere is this regression staged more dramatically and to greater effect than in *La route des Flandres*, the story, as Simon explained in an interview, of Georges' symbolic death.[31] The protagonist is haunted by visions of his own death superimposed and fused with the sight of a dead horse, which he passes several times.

Violence itself is repeatedly presented as an effect of material processes —a force inhabiting matter, unleashed, or rather unleashing itself, for no immediately obvious reason. The deafening sound of explosions is the manifestation of something that has nothing whatsoever to do with human agency. It is rather a phenomenon unto itself, profoundly indifferent and unrelated to the affairs of human beings:

> that din (and more than din: the air, the earth shaken and ripped
> apart) which, even if one has experienced it already, strikes whomever
> it deafens with something far stronger than fear: horror, amazement,
> shock, the sudden revelation that it is no longer something which man
> has any part in but matter only, unleashed, wild, furious, indecent (the
> mix, the combination of a few inert dusts, of ores, of things extracted
> from the earth and spontaneously catching fire, as it were, with the
> usual extreme violence of natural elements, bursting, breaking free as
> if to settle a score or get even with man, in blind, insane vengeance),
> and he, flat on his face, crushed in this kind of cataclysm, of apoca-
> lypse. (G, 195; Gé, 289)[32]

It is an indifference that is asserted almost gleefully at times, noting, not without some degree of satisfaction, the futility of the mind's effort to seek any meaning in the face of "that irrefutable coherence proper to the elements and to natural laws" (A, 222; Ac, 294). Any attempt at making sense of the confrontation "with that savage and innocent violence of matter" (G, 234; Gé, 347), "the stupid and stupefying fury of things that have no need of reasons to strike" (FR, 69; RF, 84), any attempt, like Orwell's (or Georges' for that matter), to transpose a narrative order on what is an overwhelming and incommensurable experience runs aground on the senseless materiality of the world. Simon's rewriting of Orwell's account insists repeatedly on the uselessness of any of the practical knowledge that the foreign volunteer brought to his experience but also, and especially, on the irrelevance of the philosophical or ideological categories at his disposal. The contact with "taciturn, blind violence" (G, 240; Gé, 355) wipes out the system of references by which the world was organized to give way to the rule of elementary instinct, touching the "degree zero of thought" (G, 233; Gé, 346) and entering a realm of secret symbiosis with the "stupid" materiality of the world.[33]

But the emphasis on such "art brut,"[34] directed at the recovery of some kind of raw, supposedly preconceptual, experience, featuring a subject reduced to its primal urges, paralyzed and spellbound by the sudden revelation of elementary forces, is somewhat misleading. Simon's debts to the visual arts are multiple. To be sure, modernist painting serves as an important paradigm in accounting for the texts' formalist experiments reflecting both the perceptual disorientation, the stupor experienced in the aftermath of the ambush, and the disorder of memory, the halting and precarious reconstruction of the past. But the simultaneous displacement and intensification of perception and the exposure to the brute force of matter are not the only effects of the war experience, generating the never-ending recapitulations that make for the particular rhythm and halting progression of Simon's prose. In spite of what at times looks like a "primitivist" poetics, ostensibly seeking to return us to the basics of matter and form, in open defiance of any desire for meaning, the most salient feature of Simon's texts is without a doubt the appeal to images.

Pictorial Metaphors and the Iconic Archives of War

Simon's investment in images could hardly be overstated. They inform his texts on a number of levels and in multiple guises.[35] Before attempting to delineate the various dimensions of the image, a notoriously generic term, and before taking a closer look at the work on and of images in Claude Simon's fiction, I would like to touch on some of the most obvious reasons for this remarkable affinity. Apart from the well-known biographical circumstances[36] and apart from the author's routine invocation of the visual arts as a model of his poetics, the strongest appeal of the image undoubtedly resides in its putative opposition to narrative. The deployment of images challenges the narrative "flow," introducing a different kind of dynamic for which one of the most prominent metaphors, presented apropos of *La route des Flandres,* is that of the artesian well, more specifically the image of the different layers through which the groundwater circulates.[37] A dynamic of displacement, from layer to layer, and circulation supersedes the developmental model of narrative progression toward some kind of goal and resolution. The order, or rather disorder, of the image also introduces a different regime of temporality. "All the elements of the text," as Simon explained in "Fiction Word by Word," "are always *present.* Even if they are not in the foreground, they are still there, lying behind or just beneath the surface of the text as first read, and the very components of the latter are all the time recalling the others to the reader's memory" (42). The succession of the dramatic plot, the alternation of action and reaction, the pattern of intrigue and denouement are all replaced by a logic of simultaneity and supersession, of recapitulation and repetition. The texts' movement consists in continually releasing images that give rise to other images giving rise to further images and so on. Privileging the image as a counterpoint to the order of narrative may thus have some plausibility on a structural level. The appeal to the image is a way of emphasizing presence, simultaneity, and repetition over against the sequentiality of narrative. But ever since Lessing, who, of course, introduced this distinction, the image is also the very paradigm of representation that Simon's texts seek to dismantle: a representation thought to open onto the world like a window, a representation that effaces itself as medium so as to bring about the semblance of presence and immediacy. How can one reconcile the writer's insistence on the unavoidable alterations experience undergoes in the process of recollection and writing, and the appeal to a paradigm that seems oblivious to this very difficulty? As noted before, Simon's prose is simultaneously ekphrastic and iconoclastic, its image-effects, its investment in visual and pictorial representation, countered by a perpetual *démontage*. But before getting to the constitutive ambivalence that is responsible for the fascination with and the devotion to the image, its force and its fallacy, let me distinguish between the different types of images actually at work in the text.

In a very useful breakdown of the "family of images," the picture theorist W. J. T. Mitchell has provided us with the following subdivision: graphic (pictures, statues, designs); optical (mirrors, projections); perceptual (sense data, "species," appearances); mental (dreams, memories, ideas, fantasmata); and verbal (metaphors, descriptions).[38] The world of Simon's novels comprises all of these; however, their boundaries are consistently blurred. As we have seen, the images of the perception tend to be curiously unstable. Frequently, the sense of sight is extremely acute, yet the appearances are marked by uncertainty. A similar tension can be found in the mental images, as well as those of memory. Typically, past events rise before the inner eye with remarkable clarity. But the images of memory are quickly unsettled by doubt, making room for other views, both in the literal sense of giving way to other images and in the figurative sense of prompting other interpretations of recollections that become increasingly uncertain. As I noted earlier, often times the perception—and the same is true for the perceptual images recalled by visual memory ("mémoire qui voit," as it is called in *La Bataille de Pharsale* [*BPh*, 87])—is supplanted by the imagination, by the images pertaining to the vast reservoir of the individual and collective imaginary. In an essay dealing with the question of description in Proust, Simon has drawn attention to the overdetermination of perception and memory by a multitude of cultural "codes," ranging from religious and mythological iconographies to mathematical formulas and the "scripts" of drama and film.[39] Perhaps the most conspicuous and the most abundant of these archives, on which the Simonian imaginary draws so consistently, is that of graphic images, to follow Mitchell's classification: paintings, prints, drawings, and photographs; the imagery of advertisement; graffiti; the pictures on stamps, bills, coins; but also statues, monuments, ornamented façades; as well as the staged spectacles of the opera and theater, of the bullfight arena and the race track, the movies, and many more.

No less abundant, if perhaps slightly less conspicuous, is the last of group of Mitchell's taxonomy, verbal images. In his comments at the first colloquium on the New Novel, comments that have been quoted very frequently ever since then in the critical literature on Claude Simon, the author himself has explained the constitutive role of metaphor for the movement that is so characteristic of his writing. Building on the ideas and observations of Roman Jakobson, Jacques Lacan, and the poet and essayist Michel Deguy, Simon has drawn attention to the semantic ambiguity of words, to their multiple and varied meanings that allow for the sudden shifts and imperceptible transitions between different diegetic levels. The author insisted that meaning was not an unequivocal property of words. Quoting Lacan, he suggested to think about words as "nœuds de significations," nodes of meaning or semantic clusters that could point a text in unexpected directions, hence their halting and often sinuous advance.[40]

While certain terms indeed function as pivots, the far more prominent tropes are without a doubt similes and comparisons, perhaps the most conventional type of verbal images. Unlike metaphor, which typically omits the link between *comparé* and *comparant* and sometimes even the comparé itself, comparison marks the speech act by which something is assimilated to something else, asserting that x is *like* y. Metaphor does not only leave it to the ingenuity of the reader to find the *tertium comparationis* that allows the conjunction of two terms whose relation is not evident, both challenging and pleasing our wit, as the ancient theorists of rhetoric noted; it also drops the particle that signals the approximation. By contrast, the comparison never conceals the assimilation it performs. In the world of Simon's fictions, such assimilation of one thing to another is ongoing, marked by the ubiquitous *comme*, as well as a number of other connectors, including *comme si, semblable à, tel que, ainsi que, ressembler à, à la façon de,* and so on. The act of comparison, the operation of assimilating something to something else, is thus stressed throughout as part of the mind's continual efforts to organize and render its uncertain perceptions of the world. All other types of images, perceptual, mental, and graphic, are worked, formed, and transformed by the similes. The work of description, clearly the prevalent mode of this writing (incidentally also Mitchell's other example of the verbal image), submits the world whose strange appearance it tries to convey to a constant transformation even as it, itself, is changed. "The description (construction) may be continued (or completed) more or less indefinitely depending on the exhaustiveness of the treatment, the elaboration of further metaphors, the addition of other objects, whether seen in their entirety or fragmented by wear, time, a blow (or whether only partly visible within the framework of the picture), not counting the various hypotheses to which the spectacle might lend support."[41]

In a series of microscopic readings, based in part on computer-generated statistical analysis, Pascal Mougin has provided us with a broad yet elaborate account of Simon's ever-proliferating comparisons.[42] Among the chief characteristics Mougin has identified is their accumulative and at the same time digressive nature. Many times, the sight of something strange prompts not only one comparison but entire series of similes as though the mind was anxiously trying to come upon the right one to render the specificity of the troubling appearance at hand. Typically, the *comparant,* that is to say, the part of the comparison that serves as the predicate to something the aspect of which none of the available expressions seems to capture, is much longer and more elaborate than the *comparé,* the term it is meant to complement and illustrate. The effect of this is that frequently, in the course of the elaboration of (and on) the *comparant,* the *comparé* is eclipsed, slipping from view, as it were. At the same time, the terms used in the process of working out the comparant give rise, in turn, to other comparants, and so on. Here is an example, a cluster of similes describing the clashing and confusion of two armies (on Brueghel's *Battle against the Philistines on the Gilboa*), part of an episode to which we will return in the next section:

> . . . the forest of lances with which the mass of combatants bristles shuddering with eddies, waves, undulating like a wheat field under gusts of wind which makes the spears alternately bend and rise again, the movement spreading down the line (like those executed in the stages of music halls by those battalions of show girls raising and lowering their legs one after the other so that long ripples seem to run along the row of naked thighs, frozen smiles and coiffures), the whole of both armies in a confused melee racked with contractions, with slow and sinuous convulsions like those which tighten and dilate the intestines or those inextricable knots of intertwined reptiles in mortal combat where in the convoluted coils it is impossible to identify one or the other . . . the rolling field of helmets squeezed together (simple steel shells without crests), like domes like bubbles clustered on the surface of whirlpools of some thick black liquid circling slowly, expelling at its edges a dirty foam, a yellowish scum of rubbish and dead horses . . . (*BP*, 77–78; *BPh*, 113–14)

Another effect of this clustering technique consists in the recurring sense of fluctuation and disorientation as an ostensibly casual glance or remark can open onto an entirely different scene, the description of which may extend over several pages, leading to seemingly unrelated and yet detailed subnarratives. In some instances there is no clearly discernible *comparé* in the first place. What triggers the simile, or, as so often, a whole concatenation of similes, is not only, or not primarily, the disconcerting view of some occurrence but rather the unnameable sensation that view causes the beholder, designated vaguely as "quelque chose comme" or "something like." Again, the principal motivation for the dizzying proliferation of comparisons and similes is to close the gap between the experience at the center of the texts and the limited vocabulary at their disposal. Yet the words and images thus mobilized unleash even more associations, calling for further specifications and adjustments. Even if the attempt of coming upon *le mot juste,* of hitting on the right expression, is invariably beset by failure, the texts are thus engaged in a continual assimilation of unfamiliar and uncanny phenomena, whether seen, heard, felt, sensed, or remembered, to what is known and familiar. As Mougin has pointed out, most of Simon's comparisons are not far-fetched; the distance, as the theorists of metaphor might put it, between *comparé* and *comparant* is never very great.[43] That is to say that the *tertium comparationis* is typically not difficult to discern. In fact, the opposite is true; that is to say, for the most part the commonality between the two terms that the comparison asserts is rather evident; in fact, it is likeness in the literal sense of visual resemblance. According to Mougin, the great virtue of many of the similes consists precisely in their capacity to make us *see* the thing in question.[44]

It may come as no surprise that one of the most important archives providing the material for the texts' work of metaphor (in the sense of comparisons and similes) is that of visual representation, of the graphic images mentioned earlier. But on second thought, here as elsewhere, the appeal to the image is not a matter of course. Even the earliest readers who noted this tendency registered the peculiarity involved in this choice. In the words of Michel Deguy, Simon continuously treats "appearances as images; everything that is perceived reproduces, as it were, the typical image of the scene it represents." Françoise van Rossum-Guyon suggested that the recourse to what she called mimesis of the second degree somehow reinforced the effect of the first mimesis, confirming the old adage that claims that art is truer than life.[45] The appeal to some kind of generic image (as Deguy noted it is often the "typical" image of a given scene) facilitates its visualization, and at the same time it boosts the imaginary detailing of the scene. Here is a prominent example from *La route des Flandres* in which Georges tries to get Blum to remember the stop at the inn where Reixach bought them a beer, shortly before the fatal encounter with the German sniper:

> Listen: it was like one of those posters for some brand of English beer, you know? The courtyard of the old inn with dark-red brick walls and the light-coloured mortar, and the leaded windows, the sashes painted white, and the girl carrying the copper mugs and the stable-boy in yellow leather leggings with tongues and turned-up buckles watering the horses while the group of cavalrymen were standing in classical postures: hips arched, one boot forward, one hand holding

the crop resting on a hip while the other raises a mug of golden beer towards an upper window where you notice half glimpse behind a curtain a face that looks as if it came out of a pastel. (*FR*, 20; *RF*, 20)

But before this image can even "sink in," it is revoked—"Yes: with this difference that there was nothing of all that except the brick walls, only dirty, and the courtyard looked more like a barnyard" (ibid.)—to be replaced by another. The description that follows, presumably provided by Blum, supersedes Georges' idealization of the scene. In fact, in *La route des Flandres* as elsewhere, the narration—both the *discours*, to use Genette's term, and the numerous intradiegetic narratives (the stories Georges and Blum make up)—consists to a large extent of projecting images, which are then retouched, as in the process of photographic development or that of restoration.[46]

Graphic images figure on both sides of the comparisons, as both *comparé* and *comparant*. Many appear as actual objects within the fictional world (or on its margins as in the preamble to *Les Géorgiques*, which features an unfinished drawing à la David). Even more frequently they figure in the elaborate similes.[47] As these comparisons may very well take on a life of their own, the images they invoke become one of the principal vehicles by means of which the text seems to mingle and fuse its different realms, that of perception and memory, and that of the imagination.

The iconic representations thus circulating on all levels of the text can be further divided into generic images, on the one hand, and specific, identifiable works of art (individual artworks), on the other. Again, the distinction is not stable but such ambivalence points to the broader appeal of the image, the fascination and the anxiety it may inspire. Before looking at a number of actual artworks, the different battle paintings featured in *La Bataille de Pharsale*, and the enigmatic portrait of Georges' ancestor in *La route des Flandres*, I would like to delineate the major metaphoric and iconic archives in which the war experience is reflected: heroic war imagery, war as a natural event, and war as spectacle.

There are numerous "set pieces" of war iconography that, like many of the other generic images, are conjured up in some detail only to be revoked afterward. Some parts of *L'Acacia*, for example, recount the family's search for the lost tomb of the narrator's father, who perished at the beginning of World War I. Although their search is inconclusive, it ends with the invocation of a fairly detailed image of the dead father, shot through the forehead, his upper body leaning against a tree. As is soon revealed, however, there is nothing to confirm this vision, which has most likely been drawn "from the illustrations in history books or the paintings representing the death of more or less legendary warriors, almost always dying in a semi-recumbent position on the grass, head and torso more or less leaning against a tree trunk, surrounded by knights wearing coats of mail (or holding a plumed bicorne in one hand) and represented in attitudes of affliction, one knee in the dirt, concealing with one iron-gloved hand their face turned towards the ground" (*A*, 247; *Ac*, 326).

In his sustained attempt to piece together his father's trajectory toward his anonymous death, the narrator repeatedly invokes images pertaining to the register of heroic pathos. Earlier in the book, he had pictured his father's departure for war. Taking leave from his young wife and the baby, the figure, on horseback and in full battle gear, calls to mind a classical scene of parting for battle, Hector's final farewell from Andromache.[48] It is precisely the absence of information that fuels the son's imagination, especially since the father's fate appears to prefigure the son's war experience in all but its ending. Whereas the father died, the son survived, but he cannot help looking at his experiences as reenacting the fate of his father. Thus when he is dispatched to the front, he has just one thought: "And now he was going to die" (*A*, 120, 143; *Ac*, 163, 190).

Another episode juxtaposes the conspicuous absence not only of the father but of those who died anonymously and the iconic model that takes its place. The episode features a military ceremony commemorating the annihilation of the regiment to which the father had belonged. As no one has survived to be honored, decorations will be pinned to the flag, the only remnant of the lost unit. A light rain is falling on the assembled soldiers; the flag is too wet to fly in the wind, as one would like to picture it on such an occasion. The solemn but anticlimactic event takes place under a triumphal monument, the statue of a "bronze soldier" holding "his sword up to the heavens, impassive beneath the rain, mouth open, uttering his bronze shout, frozen, with his bicorne and his bronze coat, in an attitude of energy, enthusiasm, and immortality" (*A*, 39; *Ac*, 58). Turning into a statue like this one is one of the most persistent phantasms pervading the imagination and the memories of war.[49]

Throughout the novels revolving around the war experience, there is a noticeable split in the depiction of its protagonists. There is, on the one hand, the mythic and heroic register, associated, above all, with the higher officers and generals. They typically emerge either out of nowhere, in a deus-ex-machina fashion, or "straight out of . . . a painting by Cranach or Dürer" (A, 28; Ac, 44), emissaries from another world who remain strangely detached from the carnage and hardship they are about to witness and for which they bear partial responsibility. They vanish as quickly as they have materialized, producing an uncanny sense of optical illusion. Their splendid uniforms and armor liken them to "barbarian warlords out of the depths of History" (A, 39; Ac, 58). Often they appear as though they consist entirely of metal, mythic creatures, machinelike and sublime at the same time. Strange centaurs, they seem to belong to an altogether different ontological order, one their troops register with a mixture of perplexity, fear, envy, and rage. The spectral apparition of their superiors imbues the war experience with a sense of unrealness and gives them the feeling that the armored figures might actually not contain bodies at all, let alone any life.

The troopers themselves, on the other hand, are portrayed in varying imagistic registers. They, too, at times assume the form of archaic warriors, as the entire war experience itself seems but a continuation of a primal scene, periodically reenacted since time immemorial. The most spectacular instance is the description of the procession of the cavalry through the rainy night in *La route des Flandres*. As in a number of other episodes, their slow progression through the dark, in which a strange inversion of different sensations transpires—the night is liquefied; the rain takes on the color of black ink—ends in an image of paralysis and fragmentation:

> the black air harsh as metal against their faces, so that he seemed to feel (remembering those accounts of polar expeditions where the skin was described sticking to frozen iron) the cold solidified shadows sticking to his flesh, as if the air and time itself were only a single, solid mass of chilly steel (like those dead worlds extinct for billions of years and covered with ice) in whose density they were caught, immobilized for ever, their old walking horsemeat beneath them, their spurs, their sabres, their steel weapons: everything standing and intact, like the day when he would wake and discover them through the transparent, glaucous thickness appearing like an army on the march surprised by a cataclysm and which a slow invisibly advancing glacier would restore, would spit out a hundred or two hundred years from

now pell-mell with all the old lansquenets, reiters and cuirassiers of long ago tumbling down breaking in a faint tinkle of glass. (FR, 27; RF, 30)[50]

In the second part of Les Géorgiques the elements, in particular the extreme cold that descends onto the winter quarter, has a similar effect on the cavalrymen, transforming them into crystal-like images of themselves, congealed in a kind of "mineral apotheosis" (G, 95; Gé, 138). Frozen and transfixed, they seem to join ranks with their mythic superiors and predecessors, "projected out of History as it were" (G, 82; Gé, 119). But what appeared as a sort of apotheosis turns out to anticipate an apocalyptic shattering. The noise of such shattering is present throughout the account of that "apocalypse of the cold" (G, 85; Gé, 124) at the winter encampment. It is the noise of war, the noise of glass breaking and of deafening explosions, belying the phantasmatic images of an atemporal and indestructible realm of solidity.[51]

The more conspicuous type of metamorphosis that the troopers undergo foregrounds their vulnerability and the frailty of their bodies. They are assimilated to various animals, both quarry and decoy in a large-scale hunt, or to some kind of sacrificial offering in a celebration prepared, it seems, by nature herself. The images of mythic endurance, embodied by the Pegasus-like and apocalyptic figures of their commanders, are frequently contrasted with the opposite kind of transformation, the body's slow disintegration and degradation into the organic matter from which it arose. The image of the dead horse, in the process of decomposition, is the epitome of the alliance and secret symbiosis between war and nature to which the soldiers fall prey. We have already seen the importance of the peculiar relation between "la terre" and "la guerre," nature and history, much discussed in the critical literature.[52] The analogy between the two consists not only in the parallels continuously drawn between natural and man-made disasters but also in the cyclical recurrence of war, reminiscent of the return of seasons, the rhythms of growing and harvesting, of cultivation and consumption. What seems crucial in this apparent "naturalization" of war is less the idea of the eternal recurrence of the same than the notion of its pure facticity, rendering irrelevant any discussion of its presumed causes and objectives. In those who survived the destruction, against all odds, the perceived orderliness generates the paradoxical sense of an inscrutable purposiveness.[53] It springs from the mind's effort to come to terms with an experience that is in excess of its comprehension, struggling to conceive of the miraculousness and fortuitousness of survival as part of a higher order of intentionality.

There is another set of generic images that has a similar effect, that of the theater and of the spectacle. While the higher officers' attire seems to testify to an entirely different picture of war and warfare, fabulous and heroic, on the young recruits the uniforms and weapons have a parodistic effect. The ultimate symbol of the mockery they have to suffer is the sabers they have been given: "not only the officers but the plain troopers, as if in mockery, like those convicted prisoners who in a refinement of parodic cruelty are decked out for the scaffold with marks of ranks and grotesque crowns . . . ; they had been taught how to use them, or at least how to yield them—always doubtless in the same spirit of mockery, parody and masquerade" (G, 86; Gé, 126; see also FR, 128; RF, 161). The costumelike uniforms mark them, stigmatize them as the chosen few, singled out for a triumphant sacrificial celebration. As Françoise van Rossum-Guyon has pointed out in a seminal article, "La mise en spectacle chez Claude Simon," metaphors of theatricality and spectacle pervade the world of the novels. When it comes to the war, they crop up most frequently in two connections: in relation to movement and action, and in relation to the overall strategic schemes that seem to determine what is happening. Innumerable times movements and gestures are perceived as though they were part of a performance or as though determined by some stagecraft, strangely at odds with the laws of physics: horses and riders progressing without moving from the spot while the landscape, the world itself, seems to be slowly pivoting around them; Georges' semihallucinatory memory of a fellow soldier being lifted from his saddle, somersaulting through the air in slow motion; the "deus-ex-machina" appearances of the higher-ranking militaries. In many cases subjects seem to have been stripped of their agency, whose source has to be located in an inaccessible beyond. A similar tendency is at work on a more general level, that of the movement of the troops. Their constant displacements are compared to a game, or a play, "one of those ballets with complicated figures, which led their participants to take up in succession, and in accordance with a carefully worked out pattern, positions abandoned by the others" (G, 73–74; Gé, 106–7). Governed by rules and hence evincing a certain internal consistency, the purpose of this "incomprehensible game" remains hidden, unless it is simply, as the narrator of *Les Géorgiques* surmises, to familiarize the soldiers with the eternal sites of death, "comings and goings, or marches, or rather pacings up and down whose only imaginable purpose . . . was perhaps to acquaint them with the monotonous theatre of past and future butcheries" (ibid.). There are hardly any explicit references to the agency orchestrating these spectacles. What does come through is a sense of ridicule and parody, devised, it seems, by the same spirit of mockery and masquerade that had furnished the young soldiers with their swords. Describing the events *as though* they were plotted by some kind of higher power attests once more to the desire to see an intentionality, or some sort of purposiveness, where contingency prevails. At the same time, it is a desire that mocks itself, continually undoing its own projections— "as if this time the Creator had employed this interval to perfect his work, then, facetiously, to destroy it" (*A*, 27; *Ac*, 43).[54]

The Crack in the Picture: Gazing at "a Reality More Real Than the Real"

It is not only the recollection of the war experience that is cast in images. Often, contemplation of actual artworks gives rise, for its part, to the most vivid and painful memories. The longest such passage is a section of *La Bataille de Pharsale* titled "Battle." It consists of fairly detailed descriptions of four battle paintings—one by Piero della Francesca, one by Uccello, one by Brueghel the Elder, and one by Poussin—which are interspersed with flashbacks of the ambush. As many readers have noted, the writing seems to undergo a rare kind of crescendo, growing increasingly turbulent and incoherent.[55] The most striking feature of the passage, however, consists in the strange balance between detachment and involvement on the part of the beholder. The description itself shuttles back and forth between a minute analysis of the artworks' compositional features and their means of creating the illusion of presence, and itself succumbing to that very illusion. In a classically ekphrastic mode the text plays with the reader's disposition to take the scenes depicted for actual landscapes. In each instance special attention is given to the atmospheric circumstances, the light indicating the time of day, the movements of clouds and small birds, the changing colors of the sky and of the landscape. It is apropos of these colors that the description shifts almost imperceptibly to the language of coloration, gradually revealing that the world depicted is an artistic creation, an arrangement aiming at the production of certain effects. The spectacle of battle itself that is at the center of each of the paintings is described with studied indifference as to the violence exhibited. It is as though the narration endeavored to illustrate the "lesson" of Simon's many commentaries and explanations of his own work, namely that there is an order underlying the representation of disorder.

On the face of it the ekphrastic description is concerned, above all, with questions of perspective and of depth: proceeding from a very reduced and narrow space (in Piero della Francesca) to one of greater depth (in Uccello). A second concern is the issue of movement: arrested in a peculiar kind of paralysis in the first two paintings, somewhat less contained in Brueghel, and outright tumultuous in Poussin. As in Simon's other descriptions, the gaze scanning the paintings is drawn to odd details. In Piero it is the immobility and inexpressiveness of the painted figures, confined "in a space so reduced . . . that the movements of the participants, as on those exiguous dance floors squeezed between the diners' tables, have an abrupt, irregular and constrained character . . . not in attitudes of action or effort in order to deliver or evade a blow but, for the most part, upright, as if the throng, the press, permitted nothing but these slight and necessarily rigid gestures" (*BP*, 70–71; *BPh*, 103–4). This lack of expression and psychological depth is matched by the strangely material aspect of the painting's background, the sky "as hard as mortar, as material as the blue of the steel blades, as impenetrable as the faces of the combatants" (ibid.). In Uccello's extraordinary *Battle of Romano* (Florence, Galleria degli Uffizzi) the beholder is taken in by the work's use of light (and its presumably deliberate elimination of shadows) and the spatial arrangements, "riders and horses in static positions as those taken by the supernumeraries on a stage, directed, for lack of space, not so much to perform actions as to suggest them, the effect desired (flight, depth) being obtained by means of a skillful scenic management" (*BP*, 74; *BPh*, 108–9; translation slightly modified). As in much of Simon's elaborately descriptive prose, the attention spent on the detail and structure of visual configurations goes a long way in intensifying their effects while exposing the procedures of illusionistic representation at the same time. Shuttling back and forth between the representation and its internal organization, the descriptions unsettle the priority of content over form. Much of what he sees on the canvases reminds the beholder of his own experiences. In Brueghel's *Battle against the Philistines on the Gilboa* it is the sight of the two armies clashing and fusing, not only with one another but also with the surrounding landscape, merging with the elements, as it were, in a union reminiscent of the many visions of the army dissolving into, or being absorbed by, nature.[56] The oxymoronic impression of agitated stillness, of frozen movement produced by the paintings conjures up the memories of galloping horses and their riders, stopped dead in their tracks, immobilized by some invisible power, moving without advancing. The tension reaches a sort of climax in Poussin's *Joshua's Victory over the Amorites,* a victory made possible by bringing time to a halt, divine intervention arresting the heavenly bodies in their course (Joshua 10:12–13).

As much as the beholder is taken by the painterly effects explored in the ekphrastic series, he seems largely unaffected by the turmoil depicted in the paintings. But there is another voice, a kind of subliminal murmur, interwoven in the ostensibly detached discourse of the amateur, the fragmentary memories of his own war experiences swelling up and finally spilling over. When he gets to Poussin, his *studium,* to use Barthes' famous term, is suddenly undone. The sight of a body pierced by an arrow becomes the *punctum* that disrupts the beholder's detachment, drawing him into the melee. It conjures up a graphic episode from Caesar's *Civil Wars* that serves as a kind of leitmotif throughout the novel. (The same episode is also recounted in the book's two other classical intertexts, Lucan's *Pharsalia* and Plutarch's *Lives.*)[57] It is the image of a Roman soldier, Crastinus, who receives a sword stab (alternatively, it is an arrow or a spear) straight in the face. Confronted with the tumult on Poussin's painting, the careful consideration of the artistic organization of disorder breaks down. The different narrative strands momentarily become virtually indistinguishable, the tone of matter-of-fact contemplation and compositional analysis gives way to a sense of vertigo, remembering, reliving the panic experienced under attack, as the narrator struggled with his saddle while his fellow soldiers were being torn off their horses. Here is an example of the form this takes:

> the whirlwinds of thick air immobilized at the same time as the sun, the light, the bodies, the sweat, the stormy sky, the armor, all of the same opaque substance solidified, checked by the brush *the effect of light on the metal helmet achieved by a patch of yellowish white itself*

in the center of a less brilliant gray highlight flanked by two black
areas the outer curve of the helmet behind the head a glowing orange
and circling endlessly between the solemn glidings of the frames and I
in the center *red flank mahogany the tongue of the brass buckle tore*
my palm I didn't suffer dark hairs pasted down by sweat cheek
against the sour smell mauve highlights then gold running over the
withers dusty grayish grass over the slopes the saber guard knocked
against my helmet shattering noise in my head bell filled by the furi-
ous disorder Achilles motionless . . . the uproar frozen at the paroxys-
mal level where it destroys itself, it too immobilized in the silence *torn*
from his horse as if an invisible giant hand had seized him by the col-
lar of his tunic and pulled holding him there soaring through the air
suspended above me legs still spread riding an absent charger knees
bent arms bent stretched out in front of him hands open to receive
himself like a frog in mid-leap mouth wide in a cry but no sound fea-
tures distorted twisted by terror amazement expression stupid dazed
shifting yellow then black then again the sun yellow still motionless
halted no longer time no morning no night time stopped no yesterday
no last year ten years ago today. (*BP,* 80–81; *BPh,* 117–18; italics in
the original)[58]

The beholder has switched his position, from the outside to the center,
"and I no longer a stranger, spectator watching the elegant and barbarous
condottieri . . . but now in the very center of this maelstrom: space, air itself whirling, furious, light, darkness whirling" (*BP,* 79; *BPh,* 116). Drawn
into the paintings and into his own past, he is overwhelmed by the flurry
of sensations, which open onto a never-ending present. The attempt to
make out the order underlying the disorder does not guard against its eruptions. No amount of *studium* seems to be able to "fix" the past, in the double sense of coming to terms with the insistent and intractable experience
by capturing it in, and as, an image (as in the development or restoration
of photographs), and of keeping it at bay, relegating the terror of the past
to its proper place.

La Bataille de Pharsale tells the story of such a search via the study of
a host of other accounts and depictions, both narrative and pictorial. As
in many of the other works, most notably its immediate precursor, *Histoire,* this search fails. Sifting through the cultural archive, trying to focus
attention on attempts by others to come to terms with past defeats and

disasters does not lead to greater insight or better understanding.[59] The hidden meaning of it all does not reveal itself. Thus, "The Chronology of Events," the title of the third part of *La Bataille de Pharsale,* is never really established. What we get in lieu of an orderly narrative sequence are the same events described from different perspectives, shifting in both time and space, a model of representation epitomized by the "mobile," the kinetic sculpture, invoked at the end of the book's second part.[60] In spite of the effort to impose order—"Begin again, start over from zero"; "Start over, organize. First, second, third" (*BP,* 123, 125; *BPh,* 181, 184)—the carefully crafted configuration is made to collapse, culminating in the "maelstrom" of sensations, images, and voices that is the very disorder of Claude Simon's novels.

The paintings that actually figure in some of the novels can bring back to life the turmoil suffered in the moment of attack. But they may also enhance the sense of wonder and mystification that prevents the repeated attempts to come to terms with the war experience from ever achieving any closure. The portrait of Georges' ancestor in *La route des Flandres* is probably the best example of this. Unlike the battle paintings that figure so prominently in *La Bataille de Pharsale,* all by well-known painters, the portrait is by an unknown artist. Different, however, from the many other works of art invoked in the novel, this one is an actual painting. It is the portrait of one of the author's ancestors. The 1985 edition of the novel, published in Minuit's "Collection Double," featured the image on its cover.

La route des Flandres is so replete with references to artworks that there is hardly an episode that is not assimilated to some kind of image, most often, as we have seen, of a generic kind.[61] The portrait of the ancestor is what is commonly called a "generator" in the literature on Simon, that is to say, a work of art that gives rise to elaborate intradiegetic narratives.[62] It belongs to the images, to which the narrator, Georges, and his companion, Blum, return most obsessively in their attempts to make sense of what they have been through but also simply to entertain and distract themselves by concocting stories. As with the other salient images of the book, the contemporary Reixach's "glorious" death and the dead horse rotting away on the roadside, there is something deeply unsettling about the portrait that is also a source of fascination. As so often, the description draws attention to a certain tension in the perception of the painting. Again, two modes of viewing are juxtaposed and collide. The painting is the picture of an aristocratic gentleman, dressed for hunting, a rifle in his arm, the bare hint of a smile on his face, gazing directly at the beholder. But just like the narrator's incredulous visualization of the later Reixach, his cousin, drawing his saber "in the hereditary gesture of an equestrian statue," comes undone—the "statue" collapses, "like a lead soldier beginning to melt from the feet up and leaning slowly to one side then faster and faster" (*FR,* 13; *RF,* 12)—the semblance of composure is belied by another sort of *punctum:* the oil paint is coming off the portrait, and the red of the canvas looks like blood flowing from a wound on the ancestor's forehead, as if the artist had anticipated the ancestor's end. (Reixach is supposed to have died by his own hand.) This kind of material degradation is rather typical of a number of the iconic representations conjured up in *La route des Flandres* and in many of the other novels. It mirrors and anticipates the coming apart of the entire world—or rather of "the representation the mind can make of it" (*FR,* 16; *RF,* 16)—which the text stages with such remarkable insistence. It's an instance of the peculiar process of dematerialization or derealization to which the *mises en image* seem linked so invariably. Of course, any transformation of something into its own image entails a certain degree of dematerialization. As I noted earlier, the paradoxical effect of this operation is often a heightened sense of presence, a sense of being able to actually *see* the scene "pictured," though it may appear strangely unreal and is often undone subsequently, superseded by another vision. In many instances the semblance of presence achieved by this kind of ekphrastic detailing is sustained for a bit, but ultimately it is undercut by bringing into focus some material flaw in the object, whether actually seen or just imagined, that might very well turn out to be a flaw in its representation. The corrupted picture is also an anticipation of the later Reixach's death, a suicide in its own way, and of Georges' agony in the ditch, when he feels he is about to die of a kind of inner corruption, an episode that is itself prefigured in the vision of the dead horse and that won't cease to haunt him.[63] The ostensible consistency of iconic representation, its supposed solidity—the portrait of the ancestor, Reixach; Reixach petrified into a statue; the nocturnal procession of the cavalry frozen in a block of ice—doesn't escape the dissolution and liquefaction that appear not only as the pervasive effect but also as the ultimate end of war.

In spite of the material explanation for the blood oozing from the ancestor's forehead, the red spot continues to appear as a stigma, a mark of sacrilege and damnation. The "wound" is prefigured, as so much else, in the description of the dead horse, whose blood soaks the earth, giving rise to a biblical image of miraculous fertility, water springing from a rock: "The blood was still fresh: a large red spot, bright and clotted, shiny as varnish, spreading over or rather beyond the crust of mud and sticky hair as though it were gushing not from an animal, a mere murdered beast, but from some inexpiable sacrilegious wound made by men (the way, in legends, water or wine springs out of the rock or gushes from a mountain struck with a rod) in the clayey flank of the earth" (FR, 24–25; RF, 26–27). Much later, as Georges is pressing himself against the clayey bottom of the ditch, he will perceive the "hard and purple flesh of this earth" (FR, 182; RF, 232). War transforms the soldiers into earth and the earth into an open wound.

The punctum of the portrait's punctured forehead is not the only aspect of the painting that arrests and troubles the beholder. There is, as it were, a second "point" or "puncture" that confounds his attention: the ancestor's gaze. The strangeness of this gaze stems in part from the fact that the man in the portrait seems so utterly oblivious to the "wound" and the blood that is dripping over the face. "With that paradoxical impassivity characteristic of martyrs in old paintings, the motionless face went on looking straight ahead with that slightly stupid, surprised, incredulous, and gentle expression people have when they suffer a violent death, as if at the last minute something had been revealed to them about which it had never occurred to them to think, in other words undoubtedly something absolutely contrary to what thought could teach them, something so astonishing, so . . ." (FR, 59; RF, 70). The painting gives a glimpse, then, of something it never reveals, something that cannot really be seen at all. And yet, in many ways, the secret knowledge of violent death, which the picture seems at once to offer and to withhold, constitutes something like the vanishing point of all the frantic efforts to "see," that "avidité de voir" (RF, 142; FR, 114) that the novel stages so dramatically, superimposing and telescoping memories, imagined scenes, paintings, and photographs onto, and into, one another. All these images are refractions of a real that can only be gazed at indirectly, glimpsed in the cracks and fissures of representation, shining forth in its breakdown while never fully materializing. On the contrary, as we have seen, all visions are deceptive, elusive appearances: *trompe l'œil*. The "eagerness to see" is driven by the urge to grasp this incommensurable reality, by a desire to "know," which grows increasingly urgent, the more it gets frustrated. For all the acuteness of his visions, Georges' perception is, as I said earlier, strangely impaired, blurred by a veil of fatigue, sweat, and dirt. But the desire to know persists, stubbornly. Like an endless echo the phrase "comment savoir, comment savoir?" reverberates on the last pages of the novel. Reixach's gaze, innocent and ominous at the same time, does not only fuel the young men's speculations; it is not only obliquely present in the hyperprecise visualizations their descriptions produce; it is also mirrored and contrasted by the gaze of the dead and the dying Georges sees in the war. There is the empty and inexpressive look on the face of one of his comrades, torn from the saddle and hurled through the air before Georges' eyes. As he is emerging from a brief spell of unconsciousness, the narrator is looking into the same face, its features frozen, open-mouthed, and with the "stupid" look of those surprised by death.[64] And then there is the "sad" eye of another horse dying, surrounded and watched by a group of cavalrymen:

> The huge velvety eye still reflecting the circle of soldiers but as if it were unaware of them now, as if it were looking through them at something they couldn't see, their reduced silhouettes outlined on the moist sphere as on the surface of those bronze balls that seem to seize, to suck up in a dizzying perspective engulfing the whole of the visible world, as if the horse had already ceased to be there, as if it had abandoned, renounced the spectacle of this world to turn its gaze inward, concentrating on an interior vision more restful than the incessant agitation of life, a reality more real than the real, and Blum said then that except for the certainty of dying what is more real? (*FR,* 99; *RF,* 123; cf. also *FR,* 53; *RF,* 63)

The soldiers thus see themselves seeing in an eye that doesn't perceive the beholders but is turned inward, contemplating "une réalité plus réelle que le réel." The relations dramatized in this scene reflect the hermeneutic desire and frustration at work in the novel's many episodes of intent gazing. It is a gaze that is scrutinizing the mute representations with which it is confronted for clues that would allow it to see the "reality," to see what is hidden beneath the surface of things, of violence and death. The pictured scenes and spectacles often seem to contain a promise, hinting at some kind of revelation. But it is a promise that is never redeemed. As much as the images commanding the characters' attention seem to provide a glimpse of an exorbitant reality, of experiences that can't be assimilated by any conventional frame of reference, they also consistently turn away the probing gaze. As in the portrait of the ancestor, often it is precisely the apparent closure of pictorial representation, its stillness and imperturbable permanence, that sets the imagination on its restless search. Thus, the enigmatic sights the mind seeks to penetrate and decipher trigger endless flights of the imagination. In the vortex of memories, the past that Simon's narrative tries to recover keeps resurfacing and disappearing. Images are continually invoked as they vanish. Time and again the imagination succumbs to the peculiar semblance of presence that pictorial representation is able to achieve. Like in *trompe l'œil* the mind is taken in by the oxymoronic coupling of reality effect and the nimbus of unreality, absorbed and puzzled by a sense of déjà vu, and suspicious of the deceptive, inauthentic character of its visions.

The first and the last of the novels' images is that of Reixach drawing his sword as he takes the sniper's bullet.[65] It encapsulates and exemplifies the double-sidedness of the narratives' *mises en image,* freezing the figure into a monument (as happens with so many of the higher-ranking officers) and submitting it to a slow disintegration, collapsing, crumbling, melting away, like a lead soldier. In spite of the struggle to invest the spectacle of chaos and destruction with some kind of meaning, such disaggregation is the overriding mark of the war experience. Like no other, the image of Reixach brandishing his weapon also epitomizes the certainty of the narrator's own imminent death, the greatest of all certainties, as Blum puts it. For all their unruly dynamism, in one way or another, the images are all about a death that seemed all but inevitable, logical even—"And now he was going to die" (*A,* 120; *Ac,* 163)—but that never occurred. In this sense, as much as these images and scenes are about the "reality" or "truth" of violent death, they are also about the enigma of that fortuitous survival. It is this experience that drives the narrator's interminable recapitulations of the same scenes and sites/sights of the disaster he survived.

CHAPTER THREE

The Resistance to Pathos and the Pathos of Resistance

Peter Weiss

Laokoon und seine Söhne, von Schlangen umwunden, verharren in den Dehnungen und Krümmungen ihres Gefangenseins. Unaufhörlich bleibt Laokoons Bauch eingezogen, unaufhörlich sind seine Muskeln gespannt, in der Erwartung des tödlichen Bisses. Der Kopf der Schlange stößt sich in seine linke Hüfte, während er mit dem hochgestreckten rechten Arm, dessen Adern vorquellen, ihren Leib von sich abstemmt. Sein Mund, und der Mund des jüngsten Sohns, ist halb geöffnet, nicht in einem Schrei, sondern in der letzten Anstrengung vor dem Ermatten.
—PETER WEISS, "LAOKOON ODER ÜBER DIE GRENZEN DER SPRACHE"

Dein Schmerz ist eitel. Du bist die Erschütterung, die Dich überkommt, nicht wert.
—PETER WEISS, *FLUCHTPUNKT*

La mort de Marat

In one of its final scenes the play that bears the baroque title *The Persecution and Assassination of Jean-Paul Marat as Performed by the Inmates of the Asylum of Charenton under the Direction of Monsieur de Sade* reenacts in a living picture Jacques-Louis David's famous painting of Marat's death: "All surround the bathtub in a heroic tableau, its composition as follows: Marat's right arm hangs over the side of the bathtub as in David's classic painting. In his right hand he holds the pen, his left hand holds papers. Corday still holds the dagger. The Four Singers hold her from behind and pull back her arms with such force that her neck cloth opens and her breasts are revealed. Simonne is leaning over the bathtub in horror. Duperret lies on his knees. Roux stands behind the bathtub erect on a bench."[1] But even without this explicit reference to one of the emblematic images of the French Revolution, the picture of Marat expiring in his bathtub is inevitably there, present throughout the play, conjured before the spectator's or reader's inner eye, as it were. David's *La mort de Marat*, sometimes called *Marat à son dernier soupir*, is a work that mounts a complex play of references and allusions.[2] The dying man's posture invokes two prominent motifs of Western art: the *pietà*, the image of the dead Christ in his mother's arms, and the hero's funeral of antiquity. The painting associates Marat with the figure of Christ not only by the depiction and positioning of his right arm and of his head, slightly inclined to his shoulder—think of Michelangelo's pietà in St. Peter's Basilica—but also by the very noticeable incision a little below his collar bone, which recalls the wound in Christ's side. The two letters that can be seen on the painting are testimonies of the revolutionary's benevolence. Marat received his murderess, whose letter to him had appealed precisely to his "bienveillance," with the utmost kindness, seeing her the very moment he had signed a remittance of bread to a mother of five, as the second letter reveals. The last act of the expiring Marat was thus to give bread to the poor, and he received his killer, as the posture in which David portrayed him suggests, with open arms, the gesture of compassion and mercy.

At the time of his murder Marat was a figure of great controversy. The painting undertakes a reevaluation and revision of this reputation. While Marat's adversaries liked to portray him as a "buveur de sang," David shows the revolutionary lying in his own blood, the blood-stained knife that killed him at his side. By contrast, the quill in his right hand shows the "weapon" with which he, "l'Ami du peuple," another one of Marat's epithets, had engaged himself until the very end and on behalf of the people—an engagement for which, as the picture suggests, he was to pay with his life. The close proximity of the quill to the murder weapon also functions as a reminder, whether intentional or not, of the lethal effects of the littérateur's and political agitator's pen.[3] The bathtub and the white linen from which the body protrudes, unprotected and vulnerable, brings to mind Agamemnon's inglorious end and Stoic suicides like that of Seneca, who slit his wrists in a bath. These props frame a scene of death: the bathtub resembles a sarcophagus, and the white sheets recall representations of the dead Christ shrouded in linen. There is a wooden case that has David's dedication, "A Marat," the artist's signature and the date of the Revolutionary calendar on it, and that obviously figures as a kind tombstone. The conspicuous brushwork of the otherwise undefined background forms a remarkable contrast to the detail and the painterly effort that has gone into the depiction of the image's lower half. Everything has been worked with a great deal of attention: the texture of the wooden case, the bloodied papers, and Marat's immaculate and youthful body that seems free of all tension, relaxed, almost relieved. In the play of dark and light (a chiaroscuro technique reminiscent of Caravaggio), the body emerges from the uneven obscurity of the background, turning toward the beholder as if to address him or her. The small piece of paper poised on the edge of the wood case appears to protrude into the space of the beholder as well. Whether the result of the distribution of light and darkness or just an effect of the different traditions combined in the picture, the long muscular arms, the torso, and the face tilted sideways appear sculpted and waxen at the same time, and one has the peculiar impression that Marat's pale body is somehow illuminated. Indeed, the picture as a whole has a remarkable luminosity about it. (This is true even for the background, where it is particularly difficult to determine the source of light.) For all the apparent nuance and plasticity of the body, a closer look reveals that it is nonetheless left strangely diffuse. One of the most striking features of the image is, finally, the expression on Marat's face: he appears to be smiling. The hint of a smile, the relaxed posture, and the sense of relief it conveys, the largely preserved integrity of the immaculate body, all of this turns the dying Marat—it is difficult to decide, by the way, whether the painting shows Marat dying, *à son dernier soupir,* or dead—into a martyr and a figure of redemption. It reconciles the beholder with his violent end, and his smile appears to absolve even his killer, Charlotte Corday, the absent presence on David's painting.[4]

Although the configuration of David's image appears only briefly on Weiss's stage, the play as a whole consists to a large degree of tableaux, arranged for the viewer, and often supplemented with captions by a figure called herald, only to be dissolved quickly thereafter. *Marat/Sade* is made of such "stills," the attendant commentary, and the dialogue between the two main antagonists, but frequently these episodes and exchanges are interrupted and give way to frantic action, a kind of commotion and turbulence usurping the stage. There is something of a kaleidoscopic effect in this dynamic of scenic arrangements made and unmade. Weiss's play takes its cues not only from the modern theater—Brecht, Beckett, and Artaud—and its distant precursor Georg Büchner but also from the *commedia dell'arte* and related popular genres.[5] From Brecht he takes the antithetical dialectics without, however, allowing for any synthesis or sublation of the exposed antagonisms; from Beckett the sense of the absurd (history like nature appears as a spectacle profoundly indifferent to human affairs); from Artaud the notion of a theater that transgresses its own boundaries, a "theater of cruelty" that doesn't shy away from the production of violence and pain. (Originally, Weiss's play was supposed to end with an attack on the audience.) Weiss draws on lesser dramatic forms, as well—pantomime, acrobatics, litanies, ballads, even slapstick—and at times the stage resembles the arena of a circus or a fair. Like the painting that inspired it, the play is multilayered. But unlike David's *Death of Marat,* its layers do not converge in a coherent or unified image. On the contrary, the play has an overtly self-reflexive dimension—as play within a play—and provides its own metacommentary, albeit erratic. The Marquis de Sade, for instance, is supposed to be the director of the performance within the play, but he is also a character in the story. He, in fact, never appears to be directing the character of Marat, but instead he engages the revolutionary directly, as his equal and adversary. His speeches occur in the same space as Marat's and cannot lay claim to any greater authority than his. There is, at any rate, a continual mixing of the different levels of action, of time, and of reflection, a "perspectival complexity," as Martin Rector has called it, that thwarts any clear-cut conclusions or "lessons" one could attribute to the play.[6] Although the painting undoubtedly forms the backdrop to the spectacle of Weiss's *Marat/Sade,* the drama is, in fact, very much at odds with the main thrust of David's picture, its attempt to make the slain murderer Marat transcend his own violent death and reaffirm the cause of the Revolution. The pathos of David's *Marat* is undercut in a number of ways by Weiss's play. The first consists in transplanting the French Revolution to an asylum, stressing the affinity between revolution and madness. There is not much grandeur about the two main protagonists, and one finds very little of the sublime oratory of the Revolution, which Büchner, for instance, used to such great effect in *Danton's Death.* The play's Marat is for the most part a *pathetic* figure, whiny and given to grandiose pronouncements—"I a m t h e r e v o l u t i o n," he proclaims at one point—and commonplaces about the social question. The Divine Marquis, by contrast, is less hysterical and generally a bit more cool, but he is portrayed above all as *apathetic* and resigned. Once driven to his notoriously cruel fantasies by the desire to challenge and overcome the indifference of nature, at this point he has abandoned his erstwhile ambitions. Conquering nature has no more appeal for him. A radical nihilist, Sade has lost his interest in the mysteries of pain. He has chosen the role of a dispassionate observer, as he explains while being whipped mercilessly, though upon his own request, refusing compassion for the victims as much as allegiance to the cause of the Revolution or any cause whatsoever. Urged to explain the point of the spectacle he has staged with the inmates of the asylum, he refuses to provide an answer. Marat, for his part, defends the importance of taking sides— "I don't watch unmoved I intervene"—and the need for violence:

> And what's a bath full of blood
> compared to the bloodbaths still to come
> Once we thought a few hundred corpses would be enough
> then we saw thousands were still too few
> and today we can't even count all the dead
> Everywhere you look
> everywhere.[7]

Two passages stand out. Corday's vision of an execution by guillotine (perhaps her own) and Sade's description of the gruesome execution of Damiens.[8] (The latter is well known to readers of Foucault's *Discipline and Punish,* which opens with this very episode, quoting it as an example of the festival and "splendor" of early modern public executions, supplanted in the late eighteenth century by a new set of penal technologies and new rationales of punishment.) These are unapologetic depictions of violence, conjured up for no other reason, it seems, than to expose the viewer to the harrowing sight of torture and violent death, unmitigated by any kind of higher purpose.

If David's painting tried to capture a dramatic turning point in the history of the French Revolution and to condense but also attenuate some of its inherent tensions in his image, *Marat/Sade* can be viewed as a redramatization of the picture. Staging the Revolution's conflicting forces, it continually defers what is announced in its title: the death of Marat. The pattern of repetition, interruption and deferral effects a desublimation, robbing the iconic image of its pathos. It is drowned out, so to speak, by the noise and turbulence of the play's very last tableau, which, incidentally, "quotes" yet another emblematic picture of the Revolution: David's *Tennis Court Oath*.

Images of the last moment, of agony and dying, such as David's *Death of Marat*, are a signature feature of Peter Weiss's writing, from *Marat/Sade* to *The Aesthetics of Resistance*, the author's late novelistic trilogy, which owed its success in no small degree to the remarkable ekphrastic descriptions of the Pergamon frieze in Berlin, Géricault's *Raft of the Medusa*, Picasso's *Guernica*, and many other works of art featuring violent subjects. Yet from the beginning there is, on the author's part, a peculiar ambivalence about the iconic representations of suffering and death that have such a pervasive presence in his work. Clearly, the pathos they depict has a powerful appeal, but at the same time it elicits resistance. Such opposition is not only explicit in some of Weiss's own commentaries on the poetics of his texts; it is also evinced in the works themselves, where it is typically not subject to the kind of carnivalesque deflation practiced in *Marat/Sade* but often gives rise to a more austere treatment. The question is how the author balances the preoccupation with violence and suffering so much in evidence throughout his oeuvre with the programmatic distance vis-à-vis traditional models and forms of figuring violence, in particular the iconographic ones that hold such a prominent place in his texts. I begin by recalling two instances of such programmatic distancing: a brief episode in the author's second novel and the poetics elaborated in his Laocoon address. The major focus of this chapter is, then, on the two best-known works besides the *Marat/Sade*: first, the play about the Frankfurt Auschwitz trial, *The Investigation*, and second, *The Aesthetics of Resistance*. The poetological premise of the former is that the scale of the genocide disallows any form of mimetic representation. The play, therefore, programmatically abstains from illustrating or "picturing" the horrors of the Holocaust. But this dramatic proscription of the image and of the semblance of presence, of recreating the experience of the camps on the stage, is continually thwarted by the vivid and graphic testimonies by the survivors whose affective intensity is excruciating. The lengthy engagements with works of art depicting scenes of violence constitute one of the most prominent features of Weiss's last work, *The Aesthetics of Resistance*. The very pathos placed under suspicion in the Laocoon address, and that the antimimetic poetics of the Auschwitz play sought to eschew, thus returns center stage in the novel. The trilogy relates the story of the resistance group Rote Kapelle, or Red Orchestra, and more broadly the fate, that is, the defeat, of the clandestine antifascist struggle in Germany. Its objectives are twofold. On the one hand, it tries to reconstruct this story in painstaking detail and with documentary accuracy. This search for facticity is combined with the attempt to recapitulate the ideological reflections and analyses of those involved in this fateful endeavor. On the other hand, the novel seeks to reinvoke the pathos of this struggle, its grandeur and its failure, but also the determination and vigor that sustained it, a vigor shaped and informed by the encounter with visions of agony and pain, in short, with the real of the tormented and suffering body. The work's ambition is thus to recall the intellectual and ideological aspirations and the promise of a movement that, in Weiss's view, has received short shrift in the historiographical accounts of the period, but also to reclaim the inspiration of its doomed engagements: the confrontation with the real, obstinate and harrowing.

"Your Suffering Is in Vain"

In Weiss's second autobiographical novel, *Fluchtpunkt (Vanishing Point)*, the narrator recounts his first confrontation with pictures of the concentration camps, in the spring of 1945. The effect of looking at these pictures is devastating. They wipe out the budding artist's faith in the arts and culture. Everything comes apart; nothing remains the same "in the face of these ultimate pictures."[9] Any attempt at artistic creation is called into question; nothing in the cultural imaginary matches the horror of these photographs. The text does not show this horror; it says very little about what is actually in the pictures. Instead, the brief passage focuses on the affective and bodily impact the pictures have on the narrator. But even the description of his reaction is cut short abruptly and rigorously. "Your suffering is in vain, you are not worth the horror that overcomes you."[10] The horror is so exorbitant it denies the beholder the pain that overcomes him. It exceeds the imagination and overrides the quasi-instinctual reaction of sympathy and pity. Obviously, there is more than a hint of guilt that speaks in this categorical prohibition of affective response. The shock of the pictures is followed by a second "strike": the rebuke reduces the beholder to silence and to shame. At the same time, the verdictlike sentence has its own kind of pathos, indicating the magnitude of the horror by silencing its expression and suppressing any emotional response. It is the pathos of antipathos, the pathos of a pathos muting itself, the equivalent perhaps of Timanthes' painting of the sacrifice of Iphigenia, cited in Lessing's *Laocoon,* in which the painter has chosen to present the highest degree of pain precisely by not showing it, veiling the father's grief-stricken features under a cloth the artist has put over Agamemnon's head.[11]

In his speech delivered apropos of the reception of the city of Hamburg's Lessing prize, "Laokoon oder Über die Grenzen der Sprache," Weiss himself has reflected on the paragon of pathos, the Laocoon sculpture, if in a more cursory fashion than the title of his speech suggests. The speech is for the most part an account of Weiss's transition from being a visual artist to becoming a writer. The story of his commitment to "words" as opposed to images is embedded in a recapitulation of the child's initial acquisition of language; the subsequent loss of that language as the family is forced to leave Germany; and the turn to images, both of the imagination and of painting, as a response to the situation of exile. The speech then proceeds to recount the relationship first to the foreign language, in Swedish exile, and concludes with the recovery of his native tongue, uneasy at first but decisive and on a rather affirmative note in the end. Although these developments are presented in a strangely impersonal tone and in a language suggesting less of an individual experience than a universal condition, the autobiographical circumstances that have shaped the story do come through very strongly throughout the speech. As a number of readers have noted, the emphatic commitment to language with which the speech ends was not only at odds with Weiss's ongoing, if lesser known, work as a visual artist and filmmaker but also with the continuous importance of visual artworks for his own writing.[12] The apparent demotion of "images" in favor of writing is not entirely consistent with the story presented in the speech itself either. For according to the speech, images as much as words, depending on the circumstances, can very well prove to be the appropriate means of expression, just as much as both can fail in this endeavor. The pronouncement in favor of the image very obviously coincides with another development more alluded to than spelled out in the speech:

the author's politicization. In a somewhat apodictic tone, Weiss concludes his exploration of the alternation between language and images: "Images resign themselves to the pain; words want to know about the origin of the pain."[13] In this vein, as Julia Hell has pointed out, the author contrasts the figures of which the Laocoon group is composed, identifying two positions vis-à-vis the spectacle of violence and pain.[14] Weiss regards the priest and his youngest son as paralyzed in the snake's constriction. They have lost the struggle; their pain has completely muted them. For them there is no hope of liberation. The older son, however, is in a different position. He is wresting himself from the deadly embrace of the python, breaking out of the immobilized configuration to call for help and to speak of the horror suffered. His task is "to bear witness in front of those who might come to his rescue" (180–81). The opposition to the image is thus an opposition to being spellbound by the spectacle of pathos. Instead, the speech opts for undoing this spell by probing its circumstances and conditions. The distinctions proposed here are overtly schematic: language is the vehicle of analysis and critique; images are inherently affirmative, incapable of calling into question the status quo. Evidently, the author's commitment to the newly proclaimed political charge of his writing is not without its own kind of pathos.

Resistance to Pathos: *The Investigation*

The resistance to pathos as articulated both in the Laocoon speech and apropos of the first confrontation with the pictures of genocide is also in evidence in *The Investigation*, if in a paradoxical manner, for it is precisely through the play's dramaturgical means of creating distance that it produces a peculiar kind of affective intensity. The author has gone to some lengths to be as matter-of-fact and as dispassionate as possible in his reworking of the Auschwitz trial. In keeping with this emphasis, the documentary character of the play has for the longest time dominated its critical reception. In many respects *The Investigation* appears to follow the views advanced in the Laocoon speech. Unlike Weiss's other great dramatic success, the visual and musical spectacle of *Marat/Sade*, the play programmatically avoids any kind of *mise en scène* or, as I would like to put it in view of the reflections on the image in the Laocoon speech, *mise en image*. Instead, it seeks to expose the structures the author held to be responsible for the establishment of the death camps. Many critics of the play have followed Weiss's "lead," if only to criticize the partisan character of his work. But they have often neglected the dimension that is no less prominent than the drama's ostensible political analysis and commentary: the detailed depictions of killing and torture that make even just reading the play a nearly intolerable experience.

In the well-known dramaturgical preface to his piece Weiss described the rationale for the antimimetic poetics of his work: "In the presentation of the play, no attempt should be made to reconstruct the courtroom before which the proceedings of the camp trial took place. Any such reconstruction would, in the opinion of the author, be as impossible as trying to present the camp itself on the stage."[15] At first, this caveat simply appears to reassert the topos of the impossibility of representing the genocide. Yet the first part of the statement actually includes the Auschwitz trial itself as something that cannot be recreated onstage. It may have been purely practical considerations that led the author to this view. The duration and scale of the trial made finding ways of compressing the material inevitable. The author has called the result of his work "a condensation" of facts (I, 118; E, 9) in which the stories of particular individuals have been largely absorbed. Above all, he defended his decision to leave the majority of characters, especially those representing the witnesses of the prosecution, anonymous, a crucial feature of the play's approach to its subject.

For many readers Weiss's choice to write a play about the trial rather than recreate the reality of the camp was not just a consequence of technical dramaturgical constraints. According to these readers, what is on trial in the play is not only Auschwitz but the form of the trial itself. In this view The Investigation charts the limits of juridical procedures, critically reflecting on the attempt to deal with the crimes under investigation in judicial terms.[16]

Many aspects of the play support such a reading. The disputed subject matter seems to exceed any form of judicial treatment. The Investigation starts in medias res and ends abruptly, suggesting an ongoing and interminable process that will continue even after the play has ended. Just as many of the witnesses stress the persistence of the camp in their memories, the lack of an ending and the sense of a beginning that precedes the start of the play suggest that the trial fails to bring about any closure. For all the dynamic in the exchanges between judge, witnesses, defendants, attorneys, and prosecutors, the insistent questioning and the hesitant answers, at times elusive, at times defiant, there is something monotonous and serial about the procedure. The trial does not culminate in any verdict; the gathering of evidence does not seem to lead to any conclusions. The witnesses for the prosecution, former camp inmates, often interrupt their statements and fall into silence. On several occasions they stress how much everything is still before them: "I would like to forget / but I keep seeing it" (*I*, 194; *E*, 89). But at the same time, they are incapable of speaking about their experience—"I couldn't speak about it" (*I*, 169; *E*, 63)—falling silent as they are pressured by the defense attorneys who question their credibility and charge them with self-contradictions. "Counsel of the Defense: Then it was possible / to survive it after all" (*I*, 173; *E*, 67). By contrast, the defendants eloquently claim their innocence, insisting on having been restricted to their narrow field of operations and of not having noticed anything of what was going on outside their area of responsibility. The motives of their actions are rarely investigated, nor are they asked to explain themselves. There is even less room for the few moments in which the witnesses succeed in overcoming their silence to talk about what was done to them. As in one of the devices used for torture, the "Redemaschine," the bureaucratic rules of the trial always redirect the focus to the issues and facts under dispute. The witnesses get their chance to testify, but the judicial procedure is itself a mechanism that does not bother with the pain that the memories of the camps resuscitate. In the continual alternation between statements and counterstatements everything seems to disappear as quickly as it has surfaced. The testimonies are absorbed in the unceasing flow of voices.

Reading the play as a critique of judicial procedure and discourse may seem persuasive enough. As I have already suggested, however, such a reading does not account for one of the most striking features of the work: its graphic precision, both in the way it charts the space of the camp and in the excruciating descriptions of the atrocities that were committed there. It is a feature that is strangely at odds both with the antimimetic poetics of the preface and with the critical implications of Weiss's approach to Auschwitz. Before turning to the remarkable insistence on precision—graphic, visual, and spatial—I want to touch briefly on two important strategies of the play: the anonymity of the dramatic cast and the indeterminateness of the event. To many critics the abstraction that results, to a large extent, from these strategies is an indication of the author's political bias.[17]

If the voices seem continually to vanish in a large chorus, it is no coincidence. Weiss deliberately stripped the characters, especially the witnesses, of their identity, just as he stripped the event described of its historical specificity. In neglecting the historical and political circumstances of the genocide, the playwright transposes the event to an unspecified time and place, suggesting that it could occur anytime and anywhere. As a result it often seems as though the play is less preoccupied with one particular historical event than with its persistence, that is, with the continuous possibility of its recurrence. The event conditioned and produced by a set of concrete circumstances becomes an ominous condition of modernity itself. "I came out of the camp yes / but the camp is still there" (I, 193; E, 88), explains one of the witnesses of the persecution. Shortly before, another witness had invoked the possibility of a repetition that would exceed its antecedent:

> We
> who still live with these images
> know that millions could stand again
> waiting to be destroyed
> and that the new destruction
> will be far more efficient. (I, 192; E, 86)

This shift from the singularity of the Holocaust to an abiding and all-encompassing condition is based on an economic explanation of the genocide. Throughout the play there is the implicit suggestion that the concentration camps were profitable extensions of Germany's capitalist industries. It is this "Kontinuitätsthese" that prompted an outcry among critics when the play was first performed.[18] With fascism as a consequence of "late capitalism," the identity of the victims becomes a matter of secondary importance. In a few instances even the distinction between victims and perpetrators is blurred. A witness explains:

> Many of those who were destined
> to play the part of prisoners
> had grown up with the same ideas

as those

who found themselves acting as guards. (*I,* 190–91; *E,* 85)

And one of the defendants argues, "We were nothing but numbers / just like the prisoners" (*I,* 244; *E,* 143).

Curiously, the play's ostensible abstraction from the identity of the victims, and from historical circumstance, is outweighed by the opposite tendency, the urge for a remarkable degree of concreteness, which has not always been sufficiently taken into account in the critical literature. In spite of the programmatic opposition to recreating the realities of the camp (or the courtroom), there is an almost obsessive concern with facts, numbers, and details, a concern, above all, with the topography of the camp, the organization of this space, its structures, facilities, and procedures. Time and again, the witnesses are pressed to be more precise in their descriptions, to specify and to elaborate. Often they are asked to provide figures, the exact measurements of a space, for example, and the number of people in it. The witnesses are repeatedly asked for estimates of how many people were killed in a given location. It is obviously part of any court's task to establish the facts, but there is something obsessive in the play's focus on statistics and on the topographical organization of the camp.

In a text written a few years earlier the author provided some clues about what might be at issue in this obsessive concern with the locality. "Meine Ortschaft" was written for an anthology that invited contributors to describe a place that had played an important role in their lives. Weiss chose a place for which, as he put it, he was "destined" but had never reached.[19] The description of his first visit to Auschwitz is, above all, an account of his inability to picture the events that had taken place there. He wanders through the ruins of the camps, but his visit is marked by a disconnect between his prior knowledge about the place and its emptiness, which no effort of the imagination is able to fill. "I had seen it as I heard about it and as I was reading about it. Now I don't see it," he writes.[20] The visitor soon limits himself to simply registering and enumerating what is before him, mechanically asserting the existence of the camp's various facilities. But the feeling persists that he is incapable of imagining the horrors that actually took place here. The only way of knowing what it was like would be to have been there, he muses at the end of his visit.

In view of the experience described in "Meine Ortschaft," it is hard not to conceive of *The Investigation* as an attempt to counter and overcome this inability to imagine what happened in the camp. For all the resistance to mimetic reconstruction, to "picturing" the camp onstage, the charting of its topography often achieves an extraordinary sense of presentness, of being there and of "seeing" what is being described. It is precisely the meticulousness of some of the depictions that forces the described scenes on the imagination, often in ways that are extremely difficult to bear.

The remarkable attention devoted to the spatial organization of the camp is matched only by the closely related focus on the countless ways of killing and torturing that took place in the different sites of the camp charted by the investigation. The number of atrocities that come up in the different "cantos" seems virtually endless. It is not just the detail but also the serial character that creates an effect that is alternately nauseating and numbing. If the narrator of "Meine Ortschaft" appeared to feel guilty for not feeling anything as he visited Auschwitz, it very much appears as though in *The Investigation* Weiss had sought to find a way of bringing about the sense of shock and of pain so conspicuously absent during his visit. It is true, the nearly intolerable catalogue of suffering and death, which took place on an unheard-of scale, stands in sharp contrast to the court's preoccupation with the camp operations. But the court's continual demand to learn more about the technical side of how the camp was run is less an indictment of the judiciary's disregard for the "human factor" than a means of intensifying the horror, precisely because it is treated with such ostensible detachment. There is a second "counterpoint" to the endless list of atrocities that makes up this play: it is the continual laughter and chuckling of the defendants, an effective contrast to the sense of disbelief and shock the horrors depicted cause us.

As I remarked at the beginning of this section, *The Investigation* exhibits a similar ambivalence vis-à-vis the representation of suffering and pain as the Laocoon speech or *Vanishing Point*. Although the author clearly marks his distance from any rendering of the camps that would suggest a kind of immediate access, the ban on images that is issued in the prefatory note to the play is effectively undercut by the very form of the trial. For what we get in the testimonies that make up the play are the most vivid and indeed shockingly graphic accounts of suffering and violence. The power of these descriptions is increased by two factors. On the one hand, there are the accumulative tendencies of the testimonies: the depictions confront us with a seemingly endless series of atrocities. On the other hand, owing to the protocols of judicial testimony, the depictions are largely stripped of any affect or expressiveness. As a consequence, it becomes exceedingly difficult to respond with pity or empathy to the gruesome spectacles placed before us. The most likely reaction these spectacles elicit is a mix of unresolvable horror and shame. In this case, then, resistance to pathos is the resistance to any form of attenuation. Put differently, *The Investigation* forces the gaze on the spectacle of suffering without allowing it to rise above it or to transform it into anything else. It is certainly possible to read the play as a critique of the trial form or as a denunciation of the unacknowledged complicity of the military-industrial complex in the construction of the camps and, by extension, of the supposed continuity between "late capitalism" and the totalitarian system of Nazi Germany. But the way in which the play gives center stage to the cruelties and terrors of the camp makes it difficult to view the pain and the violence, presented with such a disturbing degree of detachment and detail, merely as an accessory feature.

The Pathos of Resistance in *The Aesthetics of Resistance*

In many respects, and in spite of the obvious generic differences, *The Aesthetics of Resistance* follows in the tracks of *The Investigation*. Depictions of suffering and pain, often fairly elaborate, constitute one of the central elements of the novel. Time and again, an almost compulsive attraction draws the protagonists to the spectacles of violence and terror, whether real or artistic. In ways similar to the dramaturgy of *The Investigation*, the novel stages a series of confrontations that appear to test the characters' ability to sustain the sight of suffering. But different from the previous experiments with the urge to recoil before the utmost horror, the book's lengthy engagements with scenes of death and destruction—all figurations of pathos of one kind or another—are no less about recreating the sense of pain and paralysis in the face of radical crisis than about transforming the shock of the image into a force, the experience of pain into passion: enlisting pathos in the service both of resistance and of commemoration. I want to begin with an episode in the novel that echoes the poetics of *The Investigation* like no other. But let me anticipate that the similarities should not make us overlook the difference. The Plötzensee episode of *The Aesthetics of Resistance* does not only point back to the play about the Auschwitz trial but also refers us to the novel's countless representations of violence and suffering that appear to exalt the *pathos of resistance*.

PLÖTZENSEE

The disturbing combination of detail and detachment by which *The Investigation* achieved its most excruciating effects is also one of the overriding characteristics of the famous Plötzensee episode, which recounts the execution of the members of Rote Kapelle, the resistance group at the center of Weiss's trilogy.[21] The violent deaths of Hans Coppi, Libertas and Harro Schulze-Boysen, Arvid Harnack, Horst Heilmann, and a number of others are rendered in painstaking detail. As in *The Investigation* a great deal of attention is given to the locale and to the procedure of the execution. For a moment one could think the focus on the factual circumstances was a way of distracting from the horror that is about to take place. But the tone of the description does not change as it depicts the execution proper and the metamorphosis to which it submits the bodies of the condemned men and women. Rather than veiling their agony, instead of hiding the instant of death itself, their suffering is brought into full view, exposed in the glaring light of the execution chamber, in which the unflinching gaze seems to zero in on every detail of their mangled bodies: "In the bright light [one could see] every wrinkle, every tear, every bruise on the faces, and the abrasions, the deep, round burn marks, the scabbing and festering wounds."[22] A few moments later, we are made to see the same bodies twisting in their final convulsions. It appears almost as though it was precisely through its absorption in the spectacle of suffering that the gaze is able to become oblivious to the agony before it.

On the face of it the execution is rendered in a remarkably unemotional key. It is treated as a process rather than as a tragic event. The description appears concerned primarily with the technical aspects of this process: its "mechanics" but also its physiological side, more specifically the physiognomic transformation to which it submits its victims. The focus on the precise circumstances and on the visual aspects of the event is grounded undoubtedly in the ideal of documentary accurateness, which has done away with any hierarchy of significance. Everything is of similar importance. As is well known, part of Weiss's aspiration for his novel was to reconstruct the story of the resistance with the greatest possible precision, which meant, above all, not to omit anything. Yet in this instance the accuracy and the detail seem strangely excessive, not least in view of the fact that the episode of the deaths at Plötzensee concludes the story the book has been telling, at least in some sense. Given that this is the end, then, what is conspicuously absent from the episode is any kind of epitaph or any sense of closure. Instead, the last thing mentioned is the soiled bodies and the odors of blood and excrement that quickly start to fill the room. It is true that these deaths will be remembered in the subsequent and final sections, in Lotte Bischoff's reflections on the future commemoration of the resistance movement, of which she herself is the sole survivor. But there is a studied restraint at work in the rendering of these deaths, and the silence that follows is palpable, as though the only adequate stance vis-à-vis this end was the meticulous and matter-of-fact recording of what happened. Like the glaring light that illuminates the scene, the episode speaks of these deaths in crude material terms, making a point of noting the blood and squalor that come with the physical destruction of the human body but also of resisting the temptation to mystify these deaths. In many ways such resistance seems to be the main objective of the troubling focus on detail and the ostensible detachment that characterize the episode.

But the sense of detachment is deceptive. A closer look at some of the specifics reveals a subtle inflection through which the Plötzensee episode is brought into alignment with some of the other episodes of extreme suffering and violent death depicted throughout the novel. For all the apparent reticence on the part of the narrator and the insistence on the prosaic character of these deaths, one can nonetheless discern a counter-tendency elevating the sentenced men and women above the sordid circumstances of their execution. Underlying the realism and literalness of the description is a network of motifs that counteracts, at least to some degree, the irreducible facticity of these deaths. On the one hand, we get a set of oblique biblical references, which liken the last moments of the condemned men and women to the end of Christ. The text notes the cross-shaped building complex (3:212); the wall around the prison structure is crowned with barbed wire; the executioner tears open the curtain concealing the guillotine (3:215; cf. Matt. 27:51); the site of the execution is referred to as "Hinrichtungs*stätte*" (3:217), as though it was another Golgatha. As Libertas is taken into the execution chamber, the contours of her figure are said to dissolve in the dazzling light; she appears to be undergoing a kind of transfiguration in the "blinding brightness" (3:215) that is emerging from the room.[23] The language of the episode is often strikingly archaic, especially in the way it describes those administering the execution: the terms *Scharfrichter* (henchman) and his *Gesellen* (assistants) or *Burschen* (lads) invoke figures stepping out of a medieval or early modern canvas. The veiled motifs borrowed from the Passion story are supplemented by references to medieval representations of martyrdom; in fact, some masters of the genre are mentioned explicitly.[24] But these allusions to Christ's death and to a certain Christian iconography are in a sense too oblique to countervail against the apparent futility of these deaths and of the struggle they embodied. It is basically two additional perspectives—one that is very much present in the episode itself and another that is more indirect—which transform these deaths, whose baseness is so much emphasized, into something dignified and meaningful. Unlike much of the rest of the book the executions at Plötzensee are not told from the point of view of the nameless first-person narrator nor any other member of the resistance itself but rather, at least to a large extent, from the perspective of the prison priest, Harald Poelchau.[25] The clergyman is torn by feelings of solidarity and compassion and an overwhelming sense of his own powerlessness. He performs his task as best he can, but he is clearly at a loss and helpless in view of what he is about to witness. His attempts to offer some comfort are either rejected or met with a sense of calm and serenity that seems to have risen above the circumstances whose horror the witness feels so keenly. In some way the priest himself, the survivor, which is how he thinks of himself, seems to be more in need of comfort and consolation than those condemned to death. Their persistence and "Unbeugsamkeit" (3:211) in the face of the end makes a profound impression on the distraught Poelchau, and it is almost as though the men he is accompanying to the execution chamber were silently comforting him rather than the other way around. As a last favor, one of them, Harnack, asks Poelchau to read him Plato's *Apology*—the paragon of a death accepted without regret or lamentation, a death without pathos.

That there is nonetheless something profoundly moving in the serene detachment with which some of the members of Rote Kapelle meet their death is also evident in the second eyewitness account. It is by one of the prison supervisors named Schwarz.[26] Although unlike Poelchau, he is not particularly sympathetic to the condemned men and is concerned above all with the proper procedure, he cannot help being affected by the men standing before him in the dark. Schwarz reassures himself that he bears no responsibility for their fate. Reading out their names, he even feels vindicated because he is asserting their lives one last time. But as with Poelchau, an odd reversal occurs: the passage creates the impression that the living need to justify themselves before these men and women who are about to die and that, in fact, it is the latter who absolve the former from their guilt and commit them to their example. For all the insistence on the absence of any signs of transcendence or redemption and for all the stylistic matter-of-factness of the episode, the description nonetheless pays homage to these dead who seem to confer a sense of obligation on those they leave behind.

The Plötzensee episode quite evidently inherits the poetics of *The Investigation*: its graphic precision and the tacit ban on commentary or any attempt to aestheticize the violence and the suffering. What is paramount is the acknowledgment and recognition of these deaths, without allowing for empathy or identification with the victims nor for any sort of cathartic relief. Yet the ostensibly "anaesthetic" aesthetics of the execution scene needs to be viewed not only through the episode's internal focalization (Poelchau and Schwarz) but also in conjunction with the long series of other representations of violence and suffering that have contributed so considerably to the book's reputation. The ban on the image issued in *Vanishing Point* apropos of the first pictures from Auschwitz, the turn from painting to writing advocated in the Laocoon address, and finally, the antimimetic dramaturgy of *The Investigation*—all this seems to be reversed in the often elaborate ekphrastic passages of *The Aesthetics of Resistance*.

The resistance to pathos that I have traced thus far is the resistance to representations that allow, and invite, the beholder to transcend or sublate the spectacle of suffering and pain to which they expose him or her. The disturbing appeal of *The Investigation* consisted in forestalling such a solution. It is quite evident that throughout *The Aesthetics of Resistance* the author revisits and experiments with the same configuration, albeit in a modified way. In a discussion about Dante's *Inferno* in the first volume, one of the characters, Heilmann, invokes the concept of anaesthesia, which has often been regarded as one of the keys for understanding the novel's preoccupation with violence and suffering and their representation.[27] Taking another look at the novel's ekphrastic descriptions, I want to suggest that the *antipathos* of the earlier work is superseded by the return of, and to, pathos, not only literally by recalling the pain and suffering but also in its attempt to recuperate the passion of those who committed themselves to the resistance. It is this passion that the book both mourns and exalts.

EKPHRASIS

Famous as the ekphrastic descriptions of *The Aesthetics of Resistance* are, they remain somewhat of an oddity in the book. Although there are more artworks mentioned than one is likely to recall, at least after a first reading, and although the ones that stand out—the Pergamon frieze, Géricault's *Raft of the Medusa,* Picasso's *Guernica,* several paintings by Brueghel, and Delacroix's *Liberty Guiding the People*—have invariably preoccupied the critical literature, the ekphrastic is not the novel's predominant "key."[28] To be sure, in a general sense the descriptive, not only descriptions of artworks but also of places and settings, is an important register of Weiss's narrative, but the book's more prominent registers are those of discourse and dialogue, for to a large extent the narrative is made up of discussions and debates among an ever-changing set of characters convened in different locales all over Europe: Berlin, various places in Spain, Paris, Stockholm. The text is thus woven by a chorus of voices pitted against one another in an attempt to secure common ideological ground in the midst of the historical turmoil of their times. The topics touched on in these conversations are wide-ranging, relating for the most part to the political situation of the mid-1930s to the early 1940s in Europe: Germany's failed revolution of 1918, the contentious relationship between Communists and Social Democrats during the years of the Weimar Republic, the possible reasons for the Republican defeat in the Spanish civil war, the Moscow trials, questions of self-censorship, party loyalty and dissent, and so forth. Though limited to the point of view of a few key protagonists, many of which are historical figures, the book's account of communist resistance, first in the Spanish civil war and later against the Nazis, is both refracted and amplified in this echo chamber of voices, extended and further elaborated in countless historical flashbacks and digressions. As a result, what we get is less of a narrative in the conventional sense—in fact, character psychology and plot are conspicuously absent from the work[29]—than an intellectual and discursive space in which the resistance movement is struggling, both with the external circumstances it is facing and with itself, with its own doubts, the conflicts and differences that are threatening its unity from within.[30]

In one sense the remarkable preoccupation with works of art is part and parcel of the debates over the necessary commitments and positions in the political struggle. The manifest reason for the characters' unlikely engagement with questions of art and art history (unlikely in view of the exigencies of their time-consuming political activism) is the desire to gain access to a cultural heritage from which they have been barred. As in many of the other discussions that occur in the book, the primary impulse in the face of art is to wonder how the works they contemplate might be enlisted for their struggle. As a consequence, their approach quite often tends to be schematic and deliberately anachronistic. Thus they invariably seek for clues that would enable them to relate the work of art to their own situation. Occasionally, there is some exploration of historical and cultural context, as for example apropos of their discussion of the Pergamon frieze. But in many instances the artworks are brought to bear more or less directly on the present. It makes little difference whether they date from the second century BC (Pergamon), the twelfth (Angkor Wat), or the nineteenth and twentieth century (Géricault, Delacroix, Picasso). Most often the works are co-opted without much ado for the interpretation of contemporary events.[31] One of the preferred interpretive strategies in doing so is to decipher the conflicts and antagonisms depicted as allegorical representations of what is going on in the present. However, the search for the antithetical forces that the protagonists presume to be at stake in some of the masterpieces studied does not always converge in a persuasive account of the works. It is mostly in the instances in which the somewhat forced readings cease to make any headway that the irreducible interpretive openness of art is emphasized. Against their own forced allegorical readings the discussants suddenly insist that the artworks need to be situated not only in their time (that is, most often in the politics of their time) but in the artistic and generic traditions from which they hail. The discussion of Picasso's *Guernica* may provide one of the best examples of the shifting positions the characters take in the course of their engagements with artworks. But as in many of the political discussions that conclude in vaguely reconciliatory terms, the concessions made and the compromises on which they seemed to settle are invariably eclipsed by the need to assert political unity over the internal conflicts that the characters seek to resolve.[32]

From this angle, then, the works of art do not seem to differ all that much from many of the other topics covered in the ceaseless exchange of arguments that makes up the bulk of the novel. At the same time, however, the ekphrastic descriptions introduce a dimension to the text that is very much the obverse to the spirit of analysis and inquiry that drives the novel's lengthy discussions. If the murmur of different voices, chronicled and orchestrated by the narrator, is like a slow and steady stream, seamlessly moving from one issue to the next, the ekphrastic passages open up like a vortex, absorbing the characters and undercutting their efforts of arriving at a clear picture of things. The descriptions can effect a kind of perceptual vertigo, a disturbing sense of disorientation and crisis. In a number of instances, perhaps nowhere as prominently as on the very first pages, the depiction of the Pergamon frieze, which both opens and concludes the trilogy, the spectators are placed in the midst of tumultuous action. Suddenly, they are confronted with a view of violence and agony, close-up. "All around us the bodies rose out of the stone, crowded into groups, intertwined, or shattered into fragments, hinting at their shapes with a torso, a propped-up arm, a burst hip, a scabbed shard, always in warlike gestures, dodging, rebounding, attacking, shielding themselves . . . a gigantic wrestling, emerging from the grey wall, recalling a perfection, sinking back into formlessness" (AR, 3; cf. AW, 1:7). In contradistinction to the multiple layers of discourse and commentary covering, but also effecting a certain distance to, the events and the experiences that preoccupy the protagonists, many of the ekphrastic moments are marked by a sense of immediacy and exposure, suggesting an imminent threat. The artworks thus become the site of an excess otherwise absent from much of the rest of the book. The consistent attempts to identify the clashing forces, to distinguish, often in unapologetically schematic fashion, between the oppressors and the oppressed, are repeatedly troubled by the works' power to seize and disturb the beholders, by the arrested energy that is contained in them and the curious tension between agitation and paralysis it produces. "With mask-like countenances, clutching one another, clambering over one another, sliding from horses, entangled in the reins, utterly vulnerable in nakedness . . . grimacing in pain and despair, thus they clashed with one another . . . dreaming, motionless in insane vehemence, mute in inaudible roaring, all of them woven into a metamorphosis of pain, shuddering, persisting, waiting for an awakening, in perpetual endurance and perpetual rebellion, in outrageous impact, and in an extreme exertion to subdue the threat, to provoke the decision" (*AR*, 4; *AW*, 1:8). Although in many instances the characters' lengthy engagements with the visual arts are legitimated, retrospectively, by the fact that they confirm their Marxist views of history, what accounts for the force and appeal of these encounters is above all the confrontation with this kind of commotion and stillness. Returning, time and again, to the representations of violent death and destruction is to immerse themselves in, and to experience, if only vicariously, some of the anxiety, shock, panic, rush, and turmoil captured on the relief and, later, on the canvases they study.

The silent contemplation of suffering, the sense of numbness and the extreme discomfort that marked the poetics of *The Investigation* and, to a lesser extent, the description of the execution at Plötzensee, gives way to a much more dramatic scene, a scene that engages the spectator in a powerful yet often paradoxical manner. As though they were alternately assuming the positions of Laocoon's younger and his older son, the beholders both succumb to the violence of the spectacle and seek to come to terms with it. This is possible in part because the sense of radical crisis, triggered by some of the most celebrated representations of suffering in Western tradition, is continually offset by an alternative perspective contained in them. As much as these artworks feature moments of turmoil and despair, the beholders frequently detect signs that suggest a possible reversal of the situation. "We turned back toward the relief, which throughout its bands demonstrated the instant when tremendous change was about to take place, the moment when the concentrated strength portends the ineluctable consequence. By seeing the lance immediately before its throw, the club before its whizzing plunge, the run before the jump, the hauling-back before the clash, our eyes were driven from figure to figure, from one situation to the next, and the stone began to quiver all around us" (*AR*, 7; *AW*, 1:11). In this perspective even the vision of imminent defeat bears the marks of its opposite: the pictures seem to annunciate a different turn of events, intimating an alternative course of history. Whether it is on the Pergamon frieze, Delacroix's *La liberté mène le peuple*, or Goya's *El tres de Mayo 1808*, which features a group of Spanish peasants before a firing squad, the gaze is invariably drawn to the peculiar temporality of these representations, oscillating between a heightened sense of presence, of a "now" about to open itself up to something else, and unending permanence. "The suspense of waiting for the salvo was unbearable because the tension would never end" (*AR*, 304; *AW*, 1:346). The pictures feature moments of suspended time, which produces a sense of doom *and* urgency, but also the strange feeling that the imminent catastrophe might be averted, that things might be turned around. Thus the beholders inevitably search for "die völlige Umstellung" (the radical shift) (*AW*, 2:22). The utterly dystopian experience to which the artworks give rise is shot through with utopian traces. This sense of a heightened temporality is nowhere as palpable as in the lengthy description of Géricault's *Raft of the Medusa*.

After coming across a reproduction of the painting at the end of the first book, the narrator sets out at the beginning of the second volume to look at the original in the Louvre. But before actually facing Géricault's masterpiece, he immerses himself in a contemporary account of the catastrophic event on which the picture is based, and he imagines Géricault's painstaking labor on his painting. The narrator's interest in the artwork is ostensibly motivated by the experience of the Republican defeat in the Spanish civil war, from which he has just returned to Paris. But his attempt at a political reading is superseded by the fascination with the unimaginable conditions on the raft, especially the cannibalism of the survivors. Yet, what really captures the narrator's attention as he finally stands before the painting itself is a tension in its organization. Like many of the other artworks featured in the novel, Géricault's composition mounts a complex interplay between movement and stillness, defeat and salvation. In the lower left foreground the painting shows an old man holding the naked, immaculate body of a young boy, presumably his son. This configuration recalls that of the pietà; the old man's posture is reminiscent of allegorical representations of melancholy; but the figure also brings to mind Ugolino, the father who presumably ate his sons, or an ogre cowering over his quarry.[33] Entirely oblivious to the tumult around him, the man's empty gaze seems absorbed by an unfathomable inner vision. The figure's inwardness and the stillness that seems to envelop him form a sharp contrast to the commotion around him. Géricault's painting is, above all, a picture of bodies rushing forward, pulled upward, as though by an invisible force, toward a point on the far horizon, the rescue vessel *Argus* that was indeed to save them but, appearing as hardly more than a dot, is very difficult to make out on the canvas. Rising from the beautiful corpses around them, the group, thrusting itself forward in one unified movement, appears to be seized by an experience midway between resurrection and revelation. It is surely no coincidence that the sculpted bodies of the ship-wrecked have reminded critics of the figures on Michelangelo's *Last Judgement*.[34] What strikes the narrator, above all, is this suspense between de-struction and rescue, the possibility of sudden reversal, or rather the intense anticipation of such a reversal. It is in the experience of this intensity, and tension, that the painting appears to assume life, to become real, and it is as if its energy became available for the present, precisely in this "second of contradictory hopes" (*AR*, 302; *AW*, 1:343). Time and again, the be-holders seek to seize this moment in which the forces captured on the art-works come to life and allow a glimpse of a different turn of things, the "radical shift" mentioned earlier.

If any kind of pathos was studiously avoided in the play about the Auschwitz trial, clearly it is very much at the center of the novel's ekphras-tic descriptions—not only thematically, in that these descriptions revolve around scenes of suffering and violence, but also in the responses they elicit from the novel's protagonists. Far from the emotional restraint exercised in the earlier work, in a number of cases the protagonists become deeply engrossed by what they see, and they imagine themselves as being part of the world depicted, often assuming the role of victim. As the example of Géricault illustrates, this identification with the victims, which seemed so problematic to the author of *The Investigation* and of the Laocoon essay, is not without risk.[35] But the immersion in the suffering of others serves as a kind of initiation into the very "aesthetic of resistance" that is an-nounced in the title of the novel. Understanding its investment in the scenes of pathos is therefore tantamount to understanding the pathos sustaining the book itself.

On the diegetic level what takes place in the immersion of some of the characters in the countless representations of oppression and defeat is a kind of foreshadowing. The detailed accounts of violent death anticipate the defeat the resistance is going to suffer.[36] In this perspective the executions at Plötzensee recapitulate and complete the long series of defeats captured in the artworks. In their continual return to the images of pain, the protagonists familiarize themselves with the sight of suffering. And the reader gradually comes to realize that looking at the works of art, the characters are contemplating their own death. The novel's obsession with the representation of violence is a way of commemorating, proleptically, the fate of the resistance.

But the sustained engagement with the spectacle of suffering is not only in the service of expressing and thereby commemorating the horrors of those years. It is not just to endow the resistance with a lineage that would dignify it. The confrontation, staged in the text with such insistence, is also to recognize the ubiquity and persistence of violence and terror so as to learn how to withstand their impact and enlist their force. As Heilmann explains apropos of a discussion of Dante's *Inferno*, the exposure is about transforming the paralysis with which the spectacle of suffering strikes those who witness it into aggression.[37] If the beholders of the images were looking for the tokens of a reversal, the sudden shift that would turn around the imminent defeat, the continual confrontation with the visions of agony seeks to bring about a transformation in their attitude toward violence and its victims, including their own sacrifice. As much as it appears to leave the subjects disoriented and distraught, forcing their gaze to dwell on the sight of suffering and pain is not to instill guilt or shame but rather to commit them to the struggle in full awareness of the enormous toll in human life it is exacting. The recognition of the violence suffered and inflicted is no less about acknowledging its victims than about overcoming the urge to recoil before the horror of these innumerable deaths. As Bischoff puts it in her reflections apropos of the countless members of the resistance, arrested, tortured, and executed in Nazi camps and prisons, a movement like theirs cannot overly concern itself with individual deaths; it even requires a certain contempt for one's own death.[38]

One will find little evidence of such "contempt" in *The Aesthetics of Resistance*, at least not after a cursory survey. On the contrary, there is, as we have seen, a great deal of concern over the question of how to do justice to the countless dead of those years—after all, the story of resistance is the story of its failure and of its dead. The description of the executions at Plötzensee can be viewed as the paradigmatic attempt to wrest a few of those deaths from anonymity and to place them before our eyes.

But in its tacit proximity to the book's numerous other representations of suffering and dying, this portrayal of individual death is also a portrayal of a collective experience. To be sure, whether individual or collective, it is an experience that the book laments. At the same time, insofar as these deaths exemplify a collective experience, they take on a different valence. Set against the foil of centuries of oppression and slaughter, which can be glimpsed in the works of art, individual death and suffering are inevitably put into perspective. "Has the history of mankind not been a history of murder?" asks Hodann, one of the protagonists. "Haven't men been enslaved and slaughtered by the hundreds of thousands, by the millions, from time immemorial?" (AW, 3:47).[39] Time and again, telescopic flashbacks open up world-historical panoramas, dramatic tableaux featuring history as an unending succession of carnage that dwarfs the sacrifices of the moment.[40] Perhaps the most explicit recognition of the necessity to accept and even affirm certain sacrifices is made in connection with the Moscow trials. During their last days in Spain some of the characters discuss reports about the exchanges between Bukharin and the Soviet prosecutor. They do seem concerned about the legitimacy of the trials, but the latest news from Moscow is juxtaposed and contrasted with news of Germany's annexation of Austria, the advance of Franco's troops, and the Western states' tacit approval of these developments—all of which eclipses the concerns both about the trials and the fateful divisions among the Republican forces: they are, as it were, the lesser evil.[41]

The two voices that conclude the book are those of the narrator and of Lotte Bischoff. They assume the charge of giving testimony, delivering from oblivion some of those who gave their life for the resistance. Like Dante's pilgrim, Bischoff and the nameless narrator return from a *katabasis* to speak of, and for, the dead they have encountered during their years with the resistance. Conversing with the dead, lending them a voice, is part lamentation and part exaltation. On the last pages of the novel, what was prefigured in the works of art proves to be the universal fate of the resistance. But remembering the dead and shouldering the burden is not to be bowed down in grief but, paradoxically, to be driven on and sustained by their commitment. Bischoff is said to have "absorbed" the dead, whose long procession passes before her inner eye (AW, 3:232). She carries their deaths within herself and can't think of it other than as a collective experience. Curiously enough, the thought relieves and encourages her. The same seems to be true for the narrator. In one of his final reflections he joins together grief and hope, feelings of loss and endurance: "Grief would overcome me whenever I would think about them, they would accompany me day and night, and with every step I would ask myself where they found the energy for their courage and stamina, and the only possible explanation would be that trembling, tenacious and daring hope, the hope that is found, to this day, in all dungeons" (*AW*, 3:266).[42]

The "pathos" of resistance is not just the suffering of the resistance but also its "passionate" perseverance, its persistence. It is a persistence not only in the face of the tremendous amount of suffering it has incurred in its course but one that appears to draw its strength precisely from this strange capital. This is the ambiguity of the pathos of resistance and hence of the pathos that sustains and animates the novel itself. It is, I believe, at the root of the very different reactions the work has generated: the sense of wonder and estrangement, on the one hand, and the enthusiastic and impassioned reception, on the other. Although *The Aesthetics of Resistance* is very much at pains to tell the story of the communist resistance from a contemporary perspective, from the beginning the movement's efforts and struggles are inevitably overshadowed by its end, that is, its failure. In this respect the story told is a tragic story, a story of noble aspirations and their defeat. But the novel is not only mobilizing the pathos of compassion, of sympathy with a noble but lost cause. Its project is not merely that of commemoration and lament, even though that is the predominant theme, especially of its last pages. There is also the desire to recover and to reappropriate some of the perseverance that sustained the resistance. It is the pathos of dedication and resolve, against all odds, as it were, which, in turn, set *The Aesthetics of Resistance* against its own time.

CHAPTER FOUR

Medeamachine

The "Fallout" of Violence in Heiner Müller

Der lebenslange Sehzwang, das Bombardement der Bilder (Baum Haus Frau), die Augenlider weggesprengt.

—HEINER MÜLLER, *TRAKTOR*

Description of an Image

In one of the most erratic texts of Heiner Müller's later so-called post-dramatic works, *Bildbeschreibung,* translated into English as *Explosion of a Memory,* we are summoned before an ever-changing nightmarish scenario. The elements of the image are generic: a barren, desertlike landscape under the glaring sun, some mountains in the background, a few clouds above, a house, a couple of trees, a bird in one of them, a man, a woman, a table, a chair, a glass, and so on. The gaze scans the composition or "experimental arrangement" for clues as to its meaning.[1] It imagines different sequences of action, and the domestic scene becomes increasingly apocalyptic: from the intimation of some kind of sacrifice, to violent intercourse, to graphic murder, culminating in the vision of the dead rising from their graves in a kind of cosmic insurrection. In the end, in a cascading series of conjectures about the picture and the I before it, the stasis of the setting gives way to a growing sense of panic; the entire configuration seems to start spinning and collapses, or rather, is blasted apart to then finally come to a halt in the image of a frozen storm. The unraveling that takes place in the description is accompanied by oracular dicta, some drawn from the author's own works, portending doom and disaster. The image appears to be the materialization of an inescapable and inscrutable curse: the cyclical recurrence of violent death and resurrection, captured in a demented, disturbing vision of copulation and catastrophe.

Roman woman has increased the possibility of inner strife and civil war. The Horatian is first celebrated, solemnly and ceremoniously, to then be put to death, again accompanied by all the relevant symbolic gestures: he is decapitated, his corpse is desecrated, dismembered, and left to the dogs.

Even more than the preceding plays of the series, *Mauser,* openly acknowledging its debt to Brecht's notorious *The Measures Taken,* a precursor it seeks to overcome and to critique at the same time, brings into sharp focus the disastrous "fallout" of the unconditional and unflinching commitment to violence. The play is based on an episode from Mikhail Sholokhov's novel *And Quiet Flows the Don,* about the Red Terror in the Soviet Union.[17] "A" is in charge of organizing the elimination of peasants and other people suspected of counterrevolutionary activities. As if to foreshadow his own fate, the first man on A's list is his predecessor, who, in a moment of pity, released some of the suspects who were to be executed. After a period of doing his "work," A asks to be relieved of his duty. The request is denied. Seized by madness, he doesn't merely execute the suspects; in a kind of ritualistic killing frenzy he desecrates their bodies. This transgression cannot be tolerated, and A himself is put before the firing squad. The violence exercised in the name of the revolution is indiscriminate and unrelenting. It finally claims the executioner himself, who, at the close of the play, is shown consenting to his own death, pronouncing the very slogan that he used to speak to the firing squad: "Death to the enemies of the revolution!" Violence has become the order of the day; another kind of "work," a form of production even, it cannot be held at bay; it overwhelms and consumes even those who "dispense" it (to use one of the play's own terms).

Given these summaries, one could view *Versuchsreihe* as a critique of violence run amok. But indignation over the unforeseen consequences of the use of violence is not really the point of the series, and such a reading doesn't account for what is so unsettling about these plays: the aporetic deadlock exhibited in all of them. In a number of comments, as in the essays and notes appended to the book edition of *Versuchsreihe,* but also in various interviews, including his autobiography, the author has stressed his commitment to the very positions that the plays seem to call into question. But even if we weren't aware of Heiner Müller's signature cynicism and his flirtatious, and by no means ironic, relationship to apocalyptic thinking,[18] the point of *Versuchsreihe* is precisely to chastise the stance that purports to occupy the moral high ground, the position that seems to presuppose one could renounce or forgo the use of violence in a struggle for political survival. At the same time, however, the works do not propose an uncritically affirmative attitude toward violence but rather one that maintains, and exhibits, a clear awareness of its dilemmas and risks. Notwithstanding the author's dismissal of the learning play, the Brechtian "Lehrstück" and its pedagogical mission, *Versuchsreihe* is itself driven by an underlying moral agenda, but it is difficult, if not impossible, to square its "morality" with our received notions of what is morally acceptable. What is targeted in the three plays is a certain moral "doxa," a morality derived from the ideals of humanism, which, to the extent that we find the plays' solutions hard to stomach, is still ours. One of the ways of striking at this "doxa" is by systematically countering the emotional response that the dramatic events are most likely to elicit in the spectator: a sense of compassion and pity for the victims. The "experiment" staged in *Versuchsreihe* is about dismantling these notions, or rather, reassigning them.

PHILOCTETES

... Und vieles
Wie auf den Schultern eine
Last von Scheitern ist
Zu behalten
—FRIEDRICH HÖLDERLIN, *MNEMOSYNE*

In Müller's *Philoctetes* the centrality of pity is evident in the choice of the material itself. Ever since Lessing's *Laocoon* the figure of Philoctetes has served as the paradigmatic case of the representation of suffering. According to Lessing's own premise, excessive suffering is not suitable for the stage because the spectacle of sheer physical pain can never achieve "the sole aim of the tragic stage," namely, to arouse our pity, for "we are generally unable to respond with the same degree of sympathy to physical pain as to other suffering."[19] The sight and sound of perpetual physical torment, let alone of an open festering wound, would be too repulsive to be the subject of imitation since "feelings of disgust are . . . always real and never imitation."[20] Their impact is too immediate, on a quasi-visceral level, and they undercut the distance necessary for aesthetic appreciation and the sentiment of sympathy. According to Lessing, Sophocles' *Philoctetes* avoids these pitfalls by a number of different means, all of which serve to attenuate the expression of pain, chief among them the hero's "steadfastness" and "moral greatness."[21] Only these virtues allow the spectator to react with empathy and identification. The suffering hero is shown not simply succumbing to his physical pain but rather as standing by his principles. The spectacle of physical pain and the hero's endurance in the throes of such pain elicit admiration and appeal to the spectator's humanity.

Not surprisingly, Heiner Müller's *Philoctetes* reverses these priorities and revokes the enlightened desire for reconciliation and unity under the auspices of a common humanity. In his adaptation of the Sophoclean model the urge toward compassion is systematically thwarted and derided.[22] Driven to the verge of madness by his infected wound, stigma, and continual reminder of the injustice done to him, his Philoctetes rages and rants, wallowing in disgust over his own rotting body and reveling in fantasies of slowly putting to death his archenemy, Odysseus. The notion of the human, along with that of the Greek, prompt his scorn and anger; he is driven by a hatred of a universal scope, but at the same time it is a private, personal affect that has become the decisive feature of his identity. Philoctetes is forever unwilling to compromise, to be co-opted, again for any venture that doesn't have to do with himself and the satisfaction of his vengefulness. Cast out, he has assumed a position of radical self-interest, a position that is grounded in the constant and all-consuming pain and resentment over the treatment he has suffered. This is a position that cannot be mediated with the exigencies of the community, represented by Odysseus. For the latter, ending the war has absolute priority, and he keeps reminding his two antagonists of what losing the struggle would entail: the devastation of their own hometowns: "if Troy stays intact, our cities are doomed." Of the three, Odysseus is the pragmatist, the representative of the *raison d'état*: victory over Troy trumps all other concerns. And time is pressing. It is in a situation of imminent crisis and urgency that these irreconcilable positions and claims clash with one another.

The figure that tries to mediate between the two positions is Neoptolemos—but to no avail. In fact, the young idealist fails in the most devastating manner. He tries to side both with Philoctetes and with the cause of the Greeks. He sees in Philoctetes one of the legendary warriors to whose rank he aspires. Moreover, like Philoctetes, he bears a grudge against Odysseus, who has tricked him out of his slain father's armory. At the same time, Neoptolemos is obliged to the Greek cause, in whose service his father has met his death. Despite his lofty ideals, Neoptolemos submits to Odysseus's machinations to win back Philoctetes. When he tries to undo his lies, he sets off a series of events at the end of which he runs his sword into Philoctetes' back to save Odysseus's life. It is precisely Neoptolemos's youthful investment in the ideal of heroism, his compassion for the agonizing Philoctetes, tormented by his wound, that brings about the least desirable outcome. Odysseus had even anticipated this turn of events, admonishing his indocile pupil: "Get rid of your compassion it tastes like blood / no room for virtue now nor time."[23] In the words of the author: "Because he didn't want to lie, he has to kill."[24] It is only through Odysseus's proverbial ingenuity that the predicament Neoptolemos has caused is solved.

The author's own account of his play has varied over the years. In an attempt to counter the charge of pessimism (raised by East German censorship), he claimed that the story was set in "prehistory" (in the Marxist sense of the term) and had nothing to do with the realities of the socialist German state. As Werner Mittenzwei had suggested, *Philoctetes* was an antiwar drama, a play about the barbarity of times past. Müller later conceded that the subtext of his drama was in fact Stalinism, pointing out that, at the time, such issues could not be addressed openly. Despite the mythological guise, it would have been quite clear to the contemporary audience that the play was actually about the impossible rehabilitation of political renegades, about the difficult reintegration of the victims of political persecutions. In other comments Müller has suggested to view the work as a kind of parable of the dialectics of enlightenment. Reminiscent of Horkheimer's and Adorno's famous speculation about the origins of modernity and modern totalitarianism, the play formulates a critique of "instrumental reason" and the ruthless domination of nature (both inner and outer) by humans, with Odysseus as its chief proponent (very much as in the philosophers' account of things).[25] But in what is perhaps the most prominent explication of his play, a letter to the Bulgarian director Mitko Gotscheff, the author has undertaken a rather puzzling reappraisal of the figure of Odysseus, departing from his earlier view, according to which the three positions were equally untenable.[26] In his programmatic letter to Gotscheff he clearly privileges Odysseus over the other two characters. A true "political animal,"[27] he is the opposite of Hegel's plastic

Greek ("die Gegenfigur zum Plastischen Griechen Hegels"), whose representative, Neoptolemos, fails so terrifically, but also to the tragic hero's "stolze Dummheit," his proud stupidity or stubborness.[28] At the same time, Odysseus is said to have a tragic dimension himself. He, too, had to renounce home and family before joining "Operation Helena," as the letter calls it. And as he tells his "pupil" Neoptolemos, "You are not the first in this affair to do what you don't like."[29] In a series of suggestively vague characterizations, the letter describes him as both a liminal and a transgressive figure.[30] The harbinger of the transition from clan to statehood, Odysseus himself is said to be traversed (and torn apart) by the boundary, by the dividing line he is the first to pass. The first to undo the work of fate, "producer and destroyer of tragedy,"[31] he overcomes the world of mythic doom entering the era of rational domination and manipulation, the world of politics. His near-total identification with the given assignment foreshadows the fervor of the later executioners, especially of *Mauser,* where the identification with the mission is symbolized in the merging of the executioner with his weapon. The letter speaks of Odysseus as "the tool."[32] The reading of the play as a critique of instrumental reason (apparently shared by the author himself, at least for a while) is thus replaced by one that champions the sly Greek, precisely because of his unscrupulous "instrumentalization" of Philoctetes' dead body, his breathtakingly quick adaptation to the new situation, and his utter disregard for principles or moral considerations. As for *Philoctetes,* the author has pointed out that the success of the play depended on preventing any kind of identification or sympathy with the tormented hero. "The play can only be performed if the audience is kept from empathizing with Philoctetes, at the latest, when his hatred of Greeks turns into a universal hatred of mankind because he can't see any alternative."[33]

THE HORATIAN

... zwischen Lorbeer und Beil ...
—HEINER MÜLLER, *DER HORATIER*[34]

As in *Philoctetes,* the title character of *The Horatian* is a hero and an outcast, distinguished through the highest merit, for having secured the unity of the alliance, and stigmatized for the killing of his sister, a fellow citizen, putting at risk the very unity he has achieved. The skillfully patterned play can be read as reiterating the same gesture, that of mercy denied. Killing his opponent, the Horatian is impervious to the latter's plea for mercy; he then kills his sister, whose outcry at the sight of her slain husband seems to be as much pain over her loss as it is indignation over her brother's gratuitous cruelty; the Horatian's father's plea for his son's life is overruled by the city; finally, the city's own hesitations about adding another victim to the chain of death are outweighed by its own sense of justice.

Compared to the first mention of the episode in Livy and to the later adaptation by Corneille, the absence of a merciful solution in Müller's version of the story becomes even more striking. In Corneille it is the ruler who pardons the Horatian. In Livy the people absolve the Horatian, "more in view of his bravery than out of legal considerations" (*History of Rome*, bk 1, 26). In both of the earlier renderings of the story, the episode served precisely to illustrate how a rift is overcome, how an irreconcilable contradiction is resolved, "aufgehoben," so to speak.[35] By contrast, Müller's paradoxical solution to the predicament—honoring the victor *and* punishing the murderer—is remarkable in its refusal of any dialectical sublation of the contradiction.

As in *Philoctetes,* where the murdered hero is taken away on the shoulders of his henchmen, the most gruesome image of *The Horatian* is that of the dismembered body that has been stitched together in order to honor the dead fighter. The image of a body whose integrity has been restored but whose mutilation remains visible epitomizes the impossible solution. The antithesis of merit and guilt (Verdienst/Schuld), of the murderer/victor (Mörder/Sieger or Sieger/Mörder) structures the tribunal's deliberations, which at times seem closer to declamation, or even incantation, than to the actual weighing of different arguments. The negotiation pits sentence against sentence, judgment against judgment. Nearly every act and every utterance is repeated but with the opposite sense, creating a peculiar sense of symmetry and balance; yet it is a balance that seems slightly odd, skewed, as it were. The text's repetitions, alternations, and slight variations result in a rare rhythmic quality but also give it an oddly mechanical character; its paratactical constructions effect a certain monotony and liturgy-like insistence.[36] Repetition governs the text not only on the sentence level but also in its larger segments, as in the depiction of the two subsequent rituals—the tribute paid to the hero and his punishment. The curious doubling is repeated even after the sentence has been executed: the dead man is first honored and then given over to the scavengers (all this is rendered with a certain loving attention to the bloody details of these acts). Notwithstanding the liturgical and quasi-mechanical character of the discourse that describes and accompanies the execution of the tribunal's paradoxical decision, there is a demonstrative insistence on distinguishing and keeping separate the two deeds and their consequences, "their fallout." The ideal invoked at the end of the play—an ideal that seems to be the outcome of their solution, as well as the underlying guiding principle—is that of "reinliche Scheidung."[37] The tribunal's insistence on such "neat separation," or "clear distinction," combines the idea of distinctness, in a cognitive sense—"Deadly to humans is what they can't understand"[38]—with that of purity in a moral and linguistic sense: "the words must be kept pure."[39] The antithetical parts of the sentence are not allowed to eclipse each other to then reappear in a synthesis on a higher level. Instead, they need to be kept separate, and, no less important, the contradiction must be kept in mind; its memory needs to be kept alive: "not hiding the rest / That wasn't resolved in the unceasing change of things."[40]

MAUSER

Eine Arbeit wie jede andere / . . . / Eine Arbeit wie keine andere
—HEINER MÜLLER, *MAUSER*[41]

Like *The Horatian, Mauser* is about coming to terms with the contradictions of violence deployed to battle violence; the necessity of killing to end all killing. Like the tribunal in *The Horatian,* the chorus in *Mauser* is at pains to uphold the distinction between authorized and unauthorized killing, legitimate and illegitimate slaughter. As in *Philoctetes* (but in reverse order), the main character of the play, A, was once useful to the revolution but ends up being a liability ("used up by his work"). Once instrumental in the revolution's plan, he has become detrimental to the cause and needs to be eliminated himself: "Then we knew that his work had used him up / And his time had passed and we led him away."[42]

At first glance *Mauser* is a chilling experiment in the exercise of indiscriminate and unquestioned violence. It is difficult to tell whether the revolutionary violence that is on the stand, as it were, is affirmed as necessary and inevitable or whether the ruthless and antihumanistic logic that seeks to justify it is denounced. In a famous dramaturgical endnote the author has endorsed the very part that appears most scandalous: the killing in the name of the revolution, which is presented as a kind of work and a necessary precondition for the advent of "man" that the revolution seeks to bring about. In the sentence that concludes the endnote, the author has indicated his belief that this is an ongoing process and the lesson of the play therefore still pertinent. "The city of Vitebsk is representative of all places in which a revolution was is will be forced to kill its enemies."[43] If the premise is that revolutions, wherever they may take place, have to kill, systematically and with a clear understanding that innocents will be among those killed, as in the story, then the play appears to "test" and demonstrate how to come to terms with this task and legacy. It imagines a case in which somebody, the nameless "A," is placed in an extreme situation. Importantly, some of A's speeches are taken over by the character's apparent antagonist, the chorus representing the voice of the party. This role change serves to destabilize the different subject positions. The antagonism featured on the stage is, in fact, that of the party with itself: "Who are you, different from us / Or special, who insists on his weakness."[44] The questions and the doubts that A represents are not brought to the process from the outside but rather from within. A represents the struggle that the revolution—"The revolution itself / Isn't one with itself"—is fighting with itself.[45] In his endnote the author has also suggested to involve the audience in the production by letting different groups read different parts in a rotating fashion so as not to identify too quickly and too exclusively with one of the different positions. Facetiously or not, the author had envisioned the party seminary as the ideal venue for staging his play.

Mauser disqualifies two attitudes vis-à-vis the indiscriminate killing: doubt and compassion, on the one hand, and the perverse identification with the slaughter on the other. The first is undoubtedly the more prominent one, and its prominence can easily overshadow the significance of the second. It is virtually impossible for the executioner not to be affected by his "work" of killing. In this respect the story seems indeed very much construed to expose and overcome the kind of compassion that is inevitably going to affect A as much as anybody else. The latter's appeal to our common humanity—the alleged traitors facing the barrels become human, "before my revolver a man"[46]—is countered unequivocally with the axiomatic pronouncement that "man" has yet to appear and that the work of killing and destruction is, in fact, a form of production precisely in that it makes room for this appearance. In the dramaturgical endnote, the author had provided another formula for this axiom, "SO THAT SOMETHING CAN ARRIVE SOMETHING HAS TO GO THE FIRST SHAPE OF HOPE IS FEAR THE FIRST APPEARANCE OF THE NEW IS TERROR."[47]

Throughout, killing as work and production is associated with giving life, perhaps nowhere as explicitly as in the phrase that functions as a kind of leitmotif of the whole:

> The daily bread of the Revolution
> Is the death of its enemies, knowing, even the grass
> We must tear up so it will stay green.[48]

The henchman "dispenses" death like a sacrament. The sacrifice made is not that of the life of his enemies but rather of his own humanity, the urge for compassion that he has to suspend. As A demands to know whether the killing will stop once the revolution has triumphed, he is given a sibylline answer:

> You know what we know, we know what you know
> The Revolution will triumph or Man will not be
> But disappear in the increasing mass of mankind.[49]

The only adequate response to doubt as to whether the "work"—a work "like any other work," as he was told, and "like no other work," as he soon realizes—will bear the promised fruit is to continue. This is obviously a maddening logic, endlessly deferring the reward and, as a consequence, driving A into his killing frenzy. It is difficult to decide whether the audience is meant to settle for this logic in which nothing guarantees the outcome. But there are a number of reasons that suggest as much. One is that there is a similar tendency of rewarding unscrupulousness and punishing compassion in the other two plays of the series. Yet it is important to remember that it is not only his human weakness, the identification with the enemy as fellow human being and neighbor, that is being punished. He is executed himself because he has stripped the dead of their dignity, treating them as quarry, "Beute," desecrating their bodies in a sudden bout of atavistic frenzy. The chorus by contrast insists that the dead are not quarry but rather the burden or yoke that the revolutionary needs to shoulder. It is the price to be paid, and it is a debt that can only be redeemed by being kept alive in memory, carrying the dead along into the future, which will yield the fruits of this "production." In short, the experiment of *Versuchsreihe* insists on the unavoidability of violence and the necessity of acknowledging the price paid in the process. Once dead, the enemies are to be treated as humans. If the "work" of indiscriminate slaughter threatens to dehumanize and delegitimize those acting on behalf of the revolution, then paying respect to the dead and bearing in mind their sacrifice vindicates, in a perverse way, the revolutionaries' actions.

Horst Domdey has suggested that Heiner Müller's *Mauser* attempts to reconcile the position of Kreon and that of Antigone,[50] but the same is true for the other two plays. On the one hand, executing one's own people/relatives, as presumed traitors, is defended in the name of "Staatsraison"—throughout, the situation is portrayed as one of acute danger, of a state of emergency in which the "cause," that is, the revolution, trumps everything else, including, and especially, doubt as to its righteousness. At the same time, Kreon's position, if it can be called that, is counterbalanced by Antigone's concern with the dead. We must kill our brothers, the enemy within ourselves, the nagging doubt as to the righteousness of our cause. In a sense the killing, the sacrifice, is no less a matter of expediency than a proof of the strength of our faith, our belief in the given cause. But this is legitimated, ultimately, by treating the dead as human—treating our brothers, and by implication ourselves, as enemies and treating the dead as brothers and neighbors (in the biblical sense). Therein lies the harrowing task of the revolution. The play suggests that we must not do one without the other.

As we have seen, the other two plays of *Versuchsreihe* "experiment" with similar problems. They deal with the relation between means and ends, world revolution and the violence required to bring it about—necessary and authorized violence, on the one hand, and spontaneous, impulsive, and potentially perverted violence, on the other. The question seems to be, What kind of posture could prevent the violence exercised from contaminating or corrupting the cause for which it is deployed? The three plays give slightly different answers to this predicament, but they all perform a curious role reversal between victims and executioners. The compassion for the victims of violence is replaced by a sublime feeling of moral sacrifice on the part of the perpetrators. Their crimes come to resemble sacrificial acts and acquire an almost sacred aura. He who takes it on himself to sacrifice his own humanity by "dispensing death" to others is the one who claims our admiration and awe. Compassion for the actual victims of his violence is replaced by a form of piety, a violent act, both cursed and sacred, performed for the sake of overcoming all violence. The idea of catharsis is replaced by the "Schauer der Entfremdung," the frisson or shudder of alienation, as the author put it in one of his commentaries on the series (apropos of the figure of Odysseus).[51] Again, the crux of these plays is to determine whether we are seriously asked to endorse the logic of sacrifice that continually inverts the positions of executioner and victim, of the perpetrators of violence and those suffering and dying from it (the difference is erased in the most literal fashion imaginable in *Mauser*), or whether A's creaturely protest is stronger, unassimilable, impossible to integrate, "as the rest that wasn't resolved," the recalcitrant remainder. As troubling as it might be, the two positions are advanced as not mutually exclusive. Not losing consciousness of the "fallout" of violence is the only tenable position in "the increasing noise of the battle" that forms the backdrop to *Mauser* and is the condition of (and reason for) the urgency of the depicted actions.

As the author himself has put it, however, "the eschatological horizon of Brecht's *The Measures Taken* is gone."[52] The expectation of imminent upheaval has passed, and the extreme measures advocated and the pathos of that advocacy seem exceedingly strange. If the plays of *Versuchsreihe* were meant as an experiment and a sort of training for those committed to the socialist utopia, an opportunity to "work through," to embrace, and to brace themselves against, the inevitable fallout of violence, today they seem more like an atonement that doesn't afford itself absolution.

"The Pictures of Those Flogged to Death": Postdramatic Necromancy

Und immer geht der Tote meinen Schritt
Ich atme esse trinke schlafe nachts
In meinem Kopf der Krieg hört nicht mehr auf
Die eine Salve und die andre Salve
Gehn zwischen meinen Schläfen hin und her
Und die Medaillen glühn auf meiner Brust
Wenn er zu mir spricht mit geschlossnen Lippen
Und hebt zum Gruß seine zerschossene Hand
—HEINER MÜLLER, *WOLOKOLAMSKER CHAUSSEE*

The image of the paradoxical union of victims and perpetrators remains in place in the postdramatic work; it is even taken to another extreme as we are confronted with characters given to acts of extreme self-destruction, not merely in an indirect manner, by inflicting violence on those close to them, their allies or kin, but on themselves. Yet the characteristic ambiguity is also displaced in favor of a rather unconditional affirmation of the redemptive and emancipative potential of violence. The exclusive focus seems to be on redeeming the dead; indeed, the emancipatory project seems to have no other objective than such redemption. It is not the future of the collective that prevails over death ("Death means nothing," as the chorus in *Mauser* had proclaimed). Instead, it is the dead themselves (or rather the undead) who have the last word. The later texts are increasingly about giving them a voice. Unlike the attempt in *Versuchsreihe* to find ways of integrating the "fallout" into the process that produced it, the postdramatic texts like *Bildbeschreibung,* but also the two I want to examine now, *Hamletmaschine* and *Verkommenes Ufer Medeamaterial Landschaft mit Argonauten,* speak in the name of "those flogged to death"[53] without seeking to defend the cause for which they were sacrificed or to condemn it. In a way it is the radically antagonistic and agonistic position of Philoctetes that seems to prevail in them. Instead of mourning the failed commitments of the past, the figures revel in their hatred, celebrating it in their hymns to destruction and death, in the hope, one feels, of releasing the pent-up energies of revenge.

In the dramaturgical note appended to one of his last works, *Woloko-lamsker Chaussee,* translated as *Volokolamsk Highway,* the author has put forth a disturbing image that is supposed to encapsulate what he calls the "proletarian tragedy in the age of the counterrevolution," of which the cycle of five short plays is the last example (the other two are *Germania Tod in Berlin* and *Zement*). The image features "a wounded man who in slow-motion rips off his bandages, who in quick motion is swathed again with bandages, etc., in perpetuum."[54] It remains unclear whether the man's attempt to rid himself of his bandages, or fetters, is premature because he is not yet healed and whether the unending effort at emancipation calls for our sympathy.[55] It is similar images of gagged emancipation, of stifled resistance, that pervade the postdramatic work—images of a paralysis brought about by violence and whose only solution seems to be more violence.

Plays such as *Hamletmaschine, Verkommenes Ufer Medeamaterial Landschaft mit Argonauten,* or *Leben Gundlings Friedrich von Preußen Lessings Schlaf Traum Schrei* are made up of tableaulike episodes whose connection often remains enigmatic.[56] Indeed, they mostly consist of "material" that is arranged into series (as is obvious from some of the titles) without being integrated in any kind of plotlike structures; it is material that remains largely untreated, so to speak. Its organization is highly associative and ostensibly random. It is generally difficult, if not impossible, to attribute the different voices at work in the plays to individual characters. The semantic registers mobilized are extremely heterogeneous, ranging from the sublime pathos of classical tragedy (as in Medea's monologue in the middle part of *Verkommenes Ufer Medeamaterial Landschaft mit Argonauten*) to the language of commercials, from poetry (Hölderlin, T. S. Eliot, Shakespeare) and sententious folk wisdom to obscene graffiti. In a telling commentary Heiner Müller has pointed out that these late works were meant, above all, to attack, and stimulate, the audience's imagination.[57] Conceding that it was more or less impossible to perform these texts onstage, he nonetheless insisted that they were written for the theater. But in his own productions, which would typically combine several works, he would often have the texts simply read or recited rather than actually performed.[58] While he had envisioned, a bit naively to be sure, *Mauser* to be performed at the Party school as part of the training of future functionaries, a dramaturgical note to *Verkommenes Ufer Medeamaterial Landschaft mit Argonauten* ironically suggests that the triptych be staged in a stripper's club, in the bathing facility of a nerve clinic, or, ideally, on a dead planet. The deliberate randomness and the challenge to performability, characteristic of many of the late works, seems less directed against the audience, whose bafflement and disaffection seem rather side-effects than the texts' principal objective, but is a revocation of the earlier works' formal perfection, their great degree of cohesion and their austere elegance.

The first part of *Verkommenes Ufer Medeamaterial Landschaft mit Argonauten* begins with the depiction of a shore littered with waste, a place of random sexual encounters and the site of an impending ecological disaster. Like the eye of a camera, a disembodied gaze travels over a cityscape, reminiscent of the infamous "Plattenbau" architecture of East Berlin, taking in the desolation of urban life marked by alcoholism, violent sexuality, and the cycles of giving birth and dying. The passage contains a few allusions to the myth of Jason and the Argonauts, as well as a number of oblique references to T. S. Eliot's *The Wasteland*.[59] The first tableau of the triptych ends on a stark contrast: two images of the dead, drawn from very different cultural-historical archives and yet highly characteristic of the playwright's pictorial repertoire. The first is a recurrent scene in Heiner Müller:

> EINGE HINGEN AN LICHTMASTEN ZUNGE HERAUS
> VOR DEM BAUCH DAS SCHILD ICH BIN EIN FEIGLING
> [SOME WERE DANGLING FROM THE LAMP POSTS TONGUES
>   HANGING OUT THEIR MOUTHS
> IN FRONT OF THEIR BELLIES THE CARDBOARD SIGNS I'M A
>   COWARD][60]

Uncommented, the lines recall a well-known image, one that most readers are likely to have seen in one version or another. The image appears more than once in Müller's own work: at the beginning of the play *Traktor,* as the subject of a short poem, and in the final episode of *Die Schlacht*.[61] It is an image of the display of violent death; the public humiliation and exhibition of extreme atrocity, the particular cruelty of these deaths, "tongues protruding" (in Carl Weber's translation). It is a testimony to German brutality, especially during the last weeks of the war, when many soldiers, who were ready to surrender to the advancing Allied troops, were summarily hanged (probably a familiar sight for someone lost in the countryside at the end of World War II, like Heiner Müller himself, then fifteen years old). They are also particularly senseless deaths, deaths yet to be redeemed.

The last image of the first part is as follows:

> Auf dem Grund aber
> Medea den zerstückten
> Bruder im Arm die Kennerin
> Der Gifte
> [On the bottom of the sea though
> Medea her carved-up
> Brother in her arms Expert
> In poisons][62]

As numerous readers have pointed out, Medea's gesture evokes several other images. It recalls the dismembered body of the Horatian in *The Ho-*

ratian, stitched back together so as to be honored as victor. It also recalls a well-known moment in Brecht's *The Measures Taken.* As the young comrade, whose incaution and misguided compassion has jeopardized the work of the communist agitators, is about to be executed, he is asked to embrace his fellow revolutionaries: "Lean your head against our arm / Close your eyes."[63] Consenting to his own death, he reaffirms the collective bond in a gesture of love and brotherhood. Finally, the configuration "quotes" both the motif of the pietà and, as Slavoj Žižek has noted, Antigone's recovery and burial of her brother's remains.[64] Yet, unlike Antigone's determined commitment to her familial obligation over and against the exigencies of the state, Medea "rescues" the victim of her own violence: it is she who has killed and dismembered Apsyrtus, her brother. If Antigone is the defender and guardian of the bonds of blood, Medea is the figure who transgresses and undoes them. As Horst Domdey notes, Medea in fact instrumentalizes the bonds of kinship: she stops her father, who is pursuing her, in his tracks by throwing the limbs of her dead brother at him.[65] Respect for the dead obliges the father to collect and bury the limbs of his murdered son, allowing Medea and Jason to escape. As in *Versuchsreihe,* we are confronted with an image of murderer and victim brought together in a moment of peculiar intimacy and kinship. Reuniting with her dismembered victim in a loving embrace, it is an image of forgiveness and reconciliation.

A similar image of the paradoxical split and identity of perpetrator and victim is at the center of an episode of *Hamletmaschine,* a dramatic collage about the Marxist intellectual's stance vis-à-vis the rotten heritage of the socialist utopia and arguably the text that has contributed to Heiner Müller's international reputation like no other.[66] The "ruins" of Europe at his back, Hamlet, whose doubts and inability, or unwillingness, to take action have become something of a commonplace, speaks against the waves, rejecting the heritage bequeathed unto him. (He also renounces the literary legacy that he has inherited, declaring numerous times that he refuses to play his part.) Despite the rather cryptic character of the work, a number of fairly direct references to Stalin and to the Budapest uprising in 1956 and its subsequent oppression point to the political subtext of the drama. In one of the play's episodes the characteristic coupling of irreconcilable positions reoccurs. In a filmlike sequence, with quick shots and countershots, images of the insurrection appear. It starts after the statue of "a man who has made history" is brought down. "The petrification of hope," the monument epitomizes the aborted utopian promises, but it also preserves them.[67] The actor playing Hamlet has given up his role and insists that the drama is over. "I am not Hamlet. . . . My drama does not take place any more." If it were to take place, he explains, it would be "at the time of the uprising."[68]

> I am standing in the sweat stench of the crowd hurling stones at police soldiers tanks bullet-proof glass. Looking through the double doors of bullet-proof glass on to the crowd pushing forwards and I smell the sweat of my fear. Seized by a sudden urge to throw up, I shake my fist at myself who is standing behind the bullet-proof glass. Shaken by fear and contempt, I see myself within the crowd pushing forwards, foaming at my mouth, shaking my fist at myself. . . . I am the soldier inside the tank turret, my head is empty inside my helmet, the throttled scream underneath the tracks. . . . I tie the noose when the ringleaders are hung up, pull the stool from under their feet, break my neck. The parts I play are spit and sputum cup knife and wound tooth and throat neck and noose. . . . Bleeding within the crowd. Catching my breath behind the double doors.[69]

But this time, the uneasy position "between the fronts" gives way to an overwhelming sense of repulsion and resentment against the ambivalent position of the intellectual and his characteristic wavering between involvement and detachment. Disgust and repulsion are indeed the pervasive sentiments in much of *Hamletmaschine:* disgust prompted by the world of capitalist commodity culture and its lures but also by the special privileges enjoyed by the author. Indeed, repulsion itself has become a dubious privilege.[70] Resignation and retreat mark the mood of the text and generate its morbid atmosphere, culminating in images of regression and self-destruction. As a picture of the author is burnt on the stage, a voice, presumably male, declares the desire to disappear, to get rid of his nagging conscience and to revert to a purely bodily existence or even to become a machine.

A similar spirit of refusal and negation animates the second and the last "tableaux" of the series. They feature two female characters, Ophelia and Electra (in fact, in the second instance, it is Ophelia who declares to be Electra). Different from the Hamlet character's passivity and indecision, the humiliation and violence suffered by these two, depicted in remarkable detail, endows them with a resoluteness that is largely absent from the male figure's elusive meditations. The first of the two scenes shows the figure of Ophelia recalling her suicides: "I am Ophelia. The one the river didn't keep. The woman dangling from the rope. The woman with her arteries slit open. The woman with the overdose."[71] The self-annihilation invoked, however, is not an act of resignation but of defiance. The extreme ruthlessness of what appears to be a potentially infinite multiplication of the woman's self-destructive acts is a form of revolt. Ophelia's disregard and contempt for death give her the power to declare war on the world, endowing her with an unimagined force. Anticipating the image of the fettered figure evoked in the dramaturgical endnote to *Wolokolamsker Chaussee,* the final scene of *Hamletmaschine* features Electra/Ophelia swathed to a wheelchair with bandages. Set in the deep sea ("Tiefsee"), like the image of Medea and her carved-up brother on the bottom of the ocean, the play's last "tableau" becomes something like the epitome of paralysis. And yet, again, it is this strange figure, humiliated and nearly muted, who emits a speech replete with hatred and apocalyptic visions of disaster. A kind of universal curse, articulated "in the name of the victims," her speech is a hymn to destruction, a global revocation of creation and procreativity. "Long live hatred, contempt, uprising, death."[72]

This spirit of revocation and revolt is echoed in Medea's long monologue in *Medeamaterial,* the middle piece of *Verkommenes Ufer Medeamaterial Landschaft mit Argonauten.* This stirring speech in the tradition of *genus grande,* or the grand style, culminates in the evocation of the murder of her children. Jason's "treason," his plan to marry Kreon's daughter, has made Medea realize the full scale of her own betrayal, of Colchis, of her city, and of her family. Faced with Jason's ostentatious disregard for her sacrifice and haunted by "the screams of massacre" and the "pictures of those flogged to death," she is overtaken by a boundless desire for retribution. The scheme she conjures up is not only to match her own past crime, the murder of Apsyrtus, but to surpass it. Medea's infanticide is both an act of self-destruction and an assault on the order of things, on social conventions and the bonds of motherhood. Her vengefulness trumps her maternal instincts, overriding all inhibitions and releasing an unrealized destructive potential. Like the figures in

Mauser, The Horatian, and *Philoctetes,* or even in *Russian Opening,* the first play in the *Volokolamsk Highway* cycle, Medea has sacrificed what was dearest to her. But we meet her when she comes to realize that her sacrifice did not bring about what it was meant to yield. *Medeamaterial* focuses on the moment in which the character recognizes the full scale of her (self-)deception. This realization and its consequences seem to be all that matters.

In the earlier plays the overarching purpose of the sacrifice advocated is generally left in vague terms. Although the ultimate cause for which the protagonists kill remains rather abstract, most often the threat of an imminent attack provides the immediate pretext for and lends urgency to the measures taken.[73] What *Versuchsreihe* actually sought to accomplish was to confront an ongoing project with its own contradictions. The plays suggest that only such a confrontation could consolidate the project, protect it against its own doubts, and render it legitimate. They are about acknowledging the sacrifices made, about shouldering the burden of the dead, required by the ongoing revolutionary efforts. The lines from Hölderlin's famous *Mnemosyne* poem, quoted earlier, encapsulate this agenda:

> And much
> As on the shoulders a
> Burden of failure must be
> Retained.[74]

In contrast, *Medeamaterial,* and this is true of many of the other postdramatic texts as well, is about the claims of the dead as it becomes clear that these efforts have failed. Instead of achieving the "project" so as to finally redeem the sacrifices made in its name, redeeming the dead is the only project left. It is a redemption that does not seek reconciliation. Recalling and restaging "the pictures of those flogged to death" is not about coming to terms with the past. It aims at unsettling and disturbing the prevailing inertia; its goal is to break the spell of resignation and paralysis. The characters' self-destructive acts, repeating and replicating but also outdoing the violence visited upon them, constitute a kind of self-empowerment, brazenly suspending the taboos and inhibitions in the way of their radical engagements.[75] In view of the measure or balance sought in *Versuchsreihe,* between "guilt" and "merit," necessary and unnecessary killing,

in view of the series' insistence that the excess caused needs to be reinte-
grated, the postdramatic works exhibit this excess itself, the "remainder /
That wasn't resolved in the unceasing change of things." Staging this excess is supposed to set free the lethal energies of revolt and destruction. It
is often hard to distinguish between the element of pathos and that of
hysteria in these experiments, the "explosion of a memory in an extinct
dramatic structure."[76]

Epilogue

Between *hubris* and *humilitas*

The real is a remarkably fluid notion. An abstract term that suggests concreteness, it has an air not only of drama and definitiveness about it but also of mere triviality.[1] It could be everything or nothing. For Badiou's account of the twentieth century it is, in a sense, everything—nothing less than the pivotal dimension when it comes to understanding the century's aspirations and failures. Badiou, of course, mobilizes the concept of the real well aware of the connotations it has taken on in Lacanian psychoanalysis, but he extends and revises the term so as to adapt it to his political ontology. It thus moves from being a topological category in a tripartite model (Real/Imaginary/Symbolic), developed to account for the impasses and struggles within our libidinal economy, to a category of action, agency, and *kairos*. The real refers to the moment in which the given order suddenly gives way to something else, to a possibility unthinkable within the framework of the existing regime of things. It is both the blind spot and the point of intervention that allows us to overturn a situation that, viewed from within and on its own terms, appears unassailable.[2] In this sense the real is, above all, a cipher for the hidden emancipatory potential of a given symbolic field, and the "passion of the real" is the readiness to seize this potential and opportunity, if need be by violent means. In fact, very often it appears as though it is nothing other than the name for the resolve to resort to extreme measures. Hence the sense of urgency, decisionism, and violence the term evokes, signaling both the unexpected opening, or crack, in the order of reality and the alertness and determination required to make the leap into the unknown.

But the real is not only the dimension in which the Badiouian subject's passionate effort to recast the space of the political "realizes" itself; it is also a force, or event, that transcends and transforms this subject. In other words, the real is both a moment to be seized and the seizure of those involved in a process that exceeds them. It conflates the voluntarist commitment to radical change and the impersonal claim of an utterly unpredictable and inscrutable event.[3] Badiou's "passion of the real" solicits the subject's embrace *and* its surrender, empowering the subject *and* enlisting it for its militant cause. The "passion of the real" is the unfailing commitment to this cause, as well as the ruthlessness employed in its name. But often it also appears as the name of this cause itself: it is the dimension that manifests itself in the split or impasse in the order of things summoning us to a new beginning. The passion it is supposed to arouse implies a form of subjection, of being overpowered by its appeal, and a form of empowerment, of being elevated with a new, if diffuse, sense of purpose.

In many respects the different encounters with forms of violent excess that stand at the center of this book exhibit some striking similarities to Badiou's "passion of the real." The most prominent one is undoubtedly the idea, present, in one way or the other, in all the texts considered here, that the advent of violence, more specifically its sight, somehow shatters reality itself, splitting it open and providing access to a different dimension of being. Moreover, there is a sense that this opening, for all the horror and fear it causes, has the potential to transform those willing to expose themselves to it. One might call this the mysticism of the real, that is to say the expectation of some revelation, the nature of which is unknown. Speaking in the broadest terms, the texts discussed here could also be regarded as being about the experience of a break with the present, the irresistible and yet disturbing appeal issuing from this event, and, finally, the prospect of some kind of transfiguration or conversion, a sort of realignment of the given order. But even though the works we looked at exhibit some elements of the script, if I may put it this way, in which Badiou casts his "passion of the real," clearly their scenarios cannot be fitted neatly into the dramaturgy of *The Century*. Nor is it very obvious what actually motivates and sustains these engagements with the experience of excess, rupture, and violence. The purpose of the philosopher's deliberately dramatic look back on the twentieth century was, as we saw, to recover the drive and enthusiasm, which, at least in his view, are so patently and regrettably absent from the political landscape of the present. In a sense, harking back to the real is a defense of twentieth-century radical emancipatory politics against its denunciation as protototalitarian. Though he tries to take his distance from the allegedly corrupted forms of the "passion of the real" in Nazism and Stalinism, the revision he undertakes includes a defense of violence precisely as index or evidence of the very kind of change the prevailing liberal doxa is not prepared to contemplate. Though typically, when he invokes events like the October Revolution, for example, Badiou tends to emphasize their unforeseeable and radically innovative character rather than dwell on the terror that followed in their wake. He is simply much less interested, it seems, in the messy aftermath of such events or in the fallout of their violent eruption. What counts is their advent and the commitment it entails, even though Badiou concedes that there are various ways in which one can fail in this commitment, in the fidelity to the event, as he calls it, various ways of missing the real.

In contrast to this largely unequivocal and emphatic reclamation of the passion of the real, the engagements with the real, with the spectacles of violence and suffering staged in the different works considered in this book, are much more ambivalent and conflicted, far less unified and certainly less programmatic than in Badiou. These engagements with the real are operative on three levels. First of all, and in a very literal sense, there is the encounter with the reality of irreducible physical pain, the facticity of destruction and mindless violence, exposing the subject to an excess that it can't get a handle on. It is the real of creaturely corporeality but also the real of things assuming a menacing agency, of a hidden force, erupting and shattering the familiar face of the world. As we have seen, these encounters prompt mixed reactions: fear and terror, to be sure, but also an irresistible fascination and the peculiar urge to discern in this event the signs of some kind of higher purpose or to find the break in the intolerable spectacle that would either mitigate or sublate its horror. This is the real in its most concrete and perhaps most familiar guise: the repulsive and fascinating view of the agonizing and wounded body, causing the beholders a feeling of paralysis and turmoil at the same time. In a second sense, broader and more abstract, the real figures as the name for the incommensurable and ineffable horrors of the twentieth century. Not unlike Badiou's *The Century*, coming to terms with, or at least finding ways of situating oneself vis-à-vis, the century's record of violent excess—real not only because it took place and cannot be undone but also because its scale dwarfs all lesser events, defying and bewildering the imagination—

is the challenge the works take on, whether explicitly or in more oblique ways. Their *solutions*, if that is the right term, to this are contradictory and aporetic. The real is a recalcitrant remainder, stubbornly persisting and resisting sublation. In one way or another the attempts to convert, or salvage, this excess and to undo the paralysis it causes fails. And that failure is what in part constitutes the muted kind of pathos they so often exhibit. The third sense in which the texts can be said to be preoccupied with the real has to be located on a slightly different level. On the one hand, it concerns their ambition to bring about a kind of *effet de réel* (though not in the Barthesian sense), to break through the virtuality of representation by the force of their affective impact—hence the appeal to pathos and its quasi-contagious spread. But it is also related to their emphasis on the visual and on visualization. In a classically ekphrastic key, oftentimes the texts seek to produce a semblance of presence by inviting readers to imagine a picture, or a scene that looks like a picture. The appeal to pictorial representation aims at reproducing, in the reader's imagination, the vividness of the image: the real as a kind of simulacrum, present but ontologically ambivalent. No less frequently the sense of illusion thus achieved is subsequently undone, often by means of a violent disruption: the real as inherently iconoclastic. As we have seen, the texts conjure up a great number of images or imagelike scenes, which, in many instances, serve as the occasion for staging a kind of heightened and troubled sense of seeing, strangely exalted and at the same time radically unsettling visions. What is at stake here is the way in which pictorial representation summons the viewer's attention, how pictures captivate and astonish their beholders, striking and startling us. Indeed, the turn to artworks often appears to be motivated by the shock they deal the beholder, their power to disturb and to distress, to lock in the gaze in a spectacle from which it is all but impossible to wrest the eyes.

Against the somewhat lopsided exaltation of the real proposed in *The Century,* I have enlisted a notion that encompasses and goes beyond the passion of the real, which Badiou is so eager to recover. My contention has been that "pathos" allows for a more nuanced account of the claims on, and of, the real. On the most obvious level, *pathos* refers to the quasi-contagious, intolerable, and yet also inescapable appeal exerted by the spectacle of suffering. Furthermore, it implies a sense of grandeur and momentousness *as well as* of failure and futility. And last but not least, it carries with it suspicions of inauthenticity, feigned emotions, and theatricality. The *pathos of the real* spans a set of contradictory tendencies: a sense of awe in the face of horror; the drama and exaltation—but also the delusion—brought on by a decisive encounter or emphatic engagement; and, finally, the sense of resignation in light of its failure. In a strange coincidence of opposites, the pathos of the real indicates both *hubris* and *humilitas:* the notion of taking on what is impossible to take on, to endure and resist in the face of overpowering opposition, thereby rising above it, and that of sorrow and compassion vis-à-vis a pain that cannot be mitigated.

The readings gathered under the title of the pathos of the real have taken very different trajectories. In keeping with the antagonistic tendencies implied in this title, they have all revolved around certain tensions: the similarity and difference between Bataille's aesthetics of transgression and Kafka's parodistic poetics of pathos and transfiguration; the opposition between the ekphrastic appeal to visual representation and the iconoclasm of Claude Simon's efforts to come to terms with his traumatic war experiences; the programmatic injunction against pathos, on the one hand, and the persistent return to some of the most iconic representations of agony and death, on the other, in the works of Peter Weiss; and, finally, the surgical coolness of Heiner Müller's dramatic parables about the unintended consequences or "fallout" of revolutionary terror, set against the grotesque excess staged in his postdramatic tableaux. At some level all these works militate against pathos as the codified representation of violence and pain, and thus against a certain notion of the image. They do so in the name of the real, that is, in the name of a violence and suffering that resists and disrupts representation. Their reservation vis-à-vis the idea of pathos is a reservation vis-à-vis the idea of aesthetic reconciliation or transfiguration. Their investment in the real is an investment in that which defies this desire. At the same time, as we have seen, there is a strong affinity between the concept of pathos, qua overwhelming hardship, pain, and sorrow, and the violence of the incommensurable real. And ironically, one way of bringing this real into view, of getting at it precisely in its incommensurability and recalcitrance, is by isolating the visions of pain and suffering in the image, stripping them of any context or meaning, fixating and intensifying the sight of agony in muted stillness. The texts marshal the image not because of any presumed verisimilitude but for its "evidentiary punch," as Susan Sontag has called it, or, in the words of Roland Barthes, its *punctum*.[4] One could call this the pathos of the image, its capacity to strike and to injure, to break through the protective shields of the symbolic order. Hence as much as the real is pitted against pathos, there is, in fact, a profound complicity between the concepts. If the real is what always returns to its place, as Lacan says, what returns with it is pathos, both in the sense of the exaltation experienced before an imminent revelation and of the sorrow and disappointment before its nonmaterialization.

Francis Bacon

Each of the preceding chapters has begun with the description of an image: the horrific photographs of *ling'chi,* the panorama of Waterloo, David's *Death of Marat,* and the anonymous drawing of an apocalyptic scene. I want to conclude with a set of images of a similar kind and turn to a work that exemplifies, if in a different medium, the conflicting aspirations and impulses we have tracked throughout this book. The art of Francis Bacon instantiates what I have called the pathos of the real like few other oeuvres in the twentieth century, both in terms of its aesthetic ambitions and its agonistic outlook.

As we have seen, the literary attempts to grasp and to "enlist" the real have very often taken the form of experiments on the boundaries between text and image, in which the image figures as the ideal, foil, and negative limit to the textual ambition to move beyond representation. Turning to Francis Bacon is to look at how this same ambition is fleshed out in the field of visual representation itself. For Bacon's painting, too, is centrally concerned with a certain excess and with probing and transgressing the limits and protocols of pictorial representation, modernist as well as classical, in terms of form as well as in terms of content. Against the modernist predilections for abstraction, Bacon returns to art as incarnation: the human body, or rather flesh, forms his predominant subject. Against expectations raised by this return to the tradition and some of its well-known formulas and formats, such as the triptych, the artist places his subjects in laboratory-like spaces, subordinating notions of passion and compassion, associated with the suffering body and the flesh, to the abstract and material beauty of the paint.

The appeal to the real—or, in the artist's language, to "the brutality of fact"—is a recurrent motif in the numerous interviews in which Bacon has tried to articulate the premises and goals of his work, though the term is certainly not used in the sense it has assumed in the wake of Lacanian psychoanalysis. Time and again Bacon has claimed that his paintings seek to capture and convey the violence of reality, and the aesthetic program that is outlined in the conversations with David Sylvester continually invokes a dimension beyond or, to be exact, on this side of the symbolic. By contrast, he has never spoken about his work in terms of pathos, and it is certainly not a prominent term in the considerable amount of critical literature written about him. This absence is actually rather surprising, for there are a number of ways in which questions of pathos seem to bear on his art. First and foremost, there is the painter's preferred subject matter of violence, pain, and suffering, even though he used to dispute that he had any particular interest in what his paintings are so ostensibly about on the level of content. The issue of pathos is present, second, by virtue of the iconographic and mythological themes and motifs Bacon's paintings borrow from the tradition (another instance, surely not coincidental, in which the artist adamantly refused to accord any significance to his rather remarkable choices). Among the precursors of Bacon's art are some of the most prominent iconic representations of pathos in the history of Western painting. On a more conceptual level the painter's own account of what he hoped his paintings would achieve could also easily be translated into the language of pathos. As a matter of fact, Bacon's ideal is very much that of a "pathic" or somatic art, as we will see momentarily. The artist's account of the rationale behind his work, though presented with characteristic wryness, is itself often tinged with a certain pathos: the idea of disclosing a dimension this side of the symbolic, to confront viewers not just with any kind of violence—the extreme violence of the twentieth century, for example, as his interlocutors insist—but a more pervasive and yet strangely unfathomable and elusive force: the violence of reality.

In ways quite similar to the literary examples discussed in the previous chapters, the pathos of the real very much encapsulates the programmatic thrust of Bacon's painting, but it is also that which exceeds and displaces the avowed project. It is the name of an ambition and its inherent ambiguities. After briefly reviewing some of the distinctive features of Bacon's painting, I will touch on a number of crucial issues, reading them in light of Bacon's own programmatic claims but also against the grain of the aesthetic positions the painter has defended so vocally. They include the interrelated questions of expressivity, violence, the flesh, compassion, and theatricality.

BACON'S SINGULARITY

Soon after first entering the scene in the early 1950s, the British painter quickly claimed his preeminent position in postwar European art. Indeed, few artists seem to have assumed, and maintained, such an iconic status in the second half of the century. (The two other names that come to mind are Andy Warhol and Gerhard Richter.) Bacon's distinct manner seemed to represent a force and phenomenon unto itself, incommensurable with most contemporary trends, though there are some conspicuous family resemblances, say, to his colleagues and friends in Great Britain, Graham Sutherland, Frank Auerbach, and Lucian Freud, as well as some obvious affiliations with other, mostly older, contemporaries such as Picasso and Giacometti, for instance.[5] At the beginning of his career Bacon was famously labeled insufficiently surrealist to participate in an exhibition devoted to British surrealist art, and his work has largely remained outside the usual categories and classifications of painting in the twentieth century. The iconicity this work has achieved has to do with a number of signature features: its favorite subject matter, of course, the tormented, agonizing body, violence, and sexuality, but also its apparent capacity to span the divide between figurative and abstract, even though Bacon himself has frequently dismissed abstract art as "decorative." Furthermore, there is the remarkable coexistence of, or tension between, a virtuoso craftsmanship, if I may put it this way, and the artist's readiness to undo his own achievement so as to allow something else, something altogether unplanned, to come to the fore. There is also the keen awareness of being part of a great tradition, ranging from Egyptian art to Michelangelo, Velázquez, Rembrandt, Soutine, and so forth.[6] The appeal to this tradition is eclectic, to be sure, but even the untrained eye will not fail to register its influence. Besides many references, at times overt, at times more oblique, to traditional iconographic and mythological motifs (Oedipus and the Sphinx, the crucifixion, the Erinyes), Bacon's sources include a number of other pictorial archives as well, most prominently the motion photography of Eadweard Muybridge but also popular image culture as evidenced by the random newspaper and magazine clippings that littered the floor of his studio.[7] What I call Bacon's iconicity, by which I mean not only his unmistakable style but also his unique and irrefutable place in the modernist or late modernist canon, is promoted, finally, by the fact that the artist continually repeated and enhanced his own pictorial formulas. To be sure, there are different periods in his oeuvre. But at the same time a distinct set of conventions, a kind of *dispositif,* is asserted and remains in place throughout his work of the 1960s, 1970s, and 1980s (while a number of subjects present in the works of the 1950s disappear). A nondescript, often monochromatic, background is divided and organized by a few lines that suggest a domestic interior that is furnished with very few objects. This space is further defined by the introduction of platform structures—a pedestal, cubicle, cage, rostrum, or glass box—staging devices that are supposed to isolate and bring into focus the human figures whose organic carnality, voluptuous and tormented at the same time, forms a sharp contrast to the nondescript setting. The emergence of this template does not mean that there is no space for variation and innovation. But the persistence of a number of motifs and of a more or less fixed set of elements organizing the picture space is an important factor when it comes to understanding the instant recognizability of a Bacon painting. Another aspect contributing to the distinctiveness of Bacon's art is that he often worked in series, resuming and amplifying earlier work; think, for instance, of his popes after Velázquez, but also, more and more, after himself, as it were, for Bacon did not only quote iconic moments from the history of Western painting but also, increasingly, from his own pictures.[8] Finally, the sense of familiarity is further consolidated by the fact that Bacon kept returning to the same models, his friends and lovers.

"THE BRUTALITY OF FACT"

Bacon's art forms a body of work that, to many, has proved extremely compelling and suggestive—compelling in the formal and technical mastery it exhibits, suggestive in its ominous symbolism and allusiveness. The artist, however, has consistently discouraged critics from reading too much into his paintings, with a particular averseness, it seems, to interpretations along the lines of the works' most salient thematic preoccupations: violence, pain, horror. In his interviews with David Sylvester, Bacon has pretty much obstructed all the most obvious avenues toward his art, rejecting any intimation of symbolism or deeper meaning. He claims, for instance, that what interested him about the crucifixion was primarily the way the cross exposes the human body, serving as a kind of framing device.[9] Mythological references to the *Oresteia*, a work Bacon admits to admiring very much, or to T. S. Eliot's *Sweeney Agonistes*, for example, are said to be more or less fortuitous. Bacon regularly distances himself from any attempt to identify possible clues that would disclose a work's purported "message." He chastises art that would conform to such expectations as illustrational. In fact, *illustration* and *narrative* are the negative terms most frequently invoked in these interviews to mark the distinctive character of his project. In other words, he has been at pains to defend his art as not being "about" anything in the conventional sense. It is not about, say, the "modern condition," *le mal du siècle*, or our "transcendental homelessness," to use Georg Lukács's apt phrase, nor is it about transgressive sexuality and death, or the tension between eros and thanatos.[10] Bacon has been particularly resistant to readings that have attempted to view the violence so evident in his paintings as somehow reflecting the disastrous experiences that have marked the twentieth century, though he has also remarked that the war was, in many ways, the decisive event for his generation. (Interestingly enough, the first paintings that would "count" in the eyes of the painter date from the mid-1940s: *Three Studies for Figures at the Base of a Crucifixion* [1944] and *Painting 1946* [1946], to which I will return below.) The refusal to accommodate expectations based on notions of illustration or narrative has been accompanied by the appeal to a different set of terms that shift the attention from questions of subject matter and motif to the creative process and its desired effects. In the interviews with Sylvester questions of intention and meaning are typically deflected by stressing the role of chance and instinct, and the unintended directions his works often take as a consequence. Considerations about a viewer's efforts at interpreting the images give way to notions of "poignancy," "immediacy," "energy," and "intensity." Bacon claims that what he is interested in is sensation, something that is supposed to affect the "nervous system" directly, bypassing the conceptual, or symbolic, "screens" through which we perceive the world.[11] He invariably describes the objective of his painting as that of impacting the beholder on a neuronal or visceral level, rather than speaking to her or his intelligence or imagination, and tearing away the "veils" obstructing reality. The violence so often attributed to his work is not that of war or any of the other disasters of the twentieth century but, more broadly, and more abstractly, the violence of reality or, in the terms of this book, of the real.[12] Bacon does not say much to specify the character of this violence, but from what he says, one can infer that what he has in mind is a kind of primordial force, a predatory vitality that sustains and threatens life, the fact of "one thing living off another," as he puts it in one of the interviews.[13]

The painter professes a kind of materialism, seeking to "unlock," as he likes to say in the interviews, the "brutality of fact." The strategies for doing so are twofold. The first has to do with the materiality of the medium, with the incalculable characteristics of oil paint. "People don't realize," he says, "how mysterious and fluid a medium oil-painting is."[14] In keeping with this view, long stretches of the interviews he gave are about his working techniques, especially the creative use of chance in applying the paint to the canvas. According to Bacon handling the paint freely can produce unexpected effects overriding whatever the painter may have set out to do initially. The manipulation of chance foils intentionality and is supposed to be closer to the instinct, the artist's as much as the beholder's, for the real is that which can only be encountered by accident, not intentionally. The materialism of Bacon's art thus concerns the base matter of human physicality as much as the conspicuous materiality of paint. At times giving the impression of oozing from the canvas, at times transforming it into a thick-textured, pasty surface, the paint makes for a drama all its own. About his portraits, in which the smudging, mixing, and layering of the paint is particularly striking, Bacon remarked that he hoped to achieve something that would look like the Sahara Desert.[15] It is true that frequently the frontal views of his friends' faces resemble rugged landscapes as much as human physiognomies. Typically, the portraits keep a precarious balance between achieving a certain likeness to the person portrayed and allowing the handling of the paint to exert its remarkable effects. Bacon himself described the departure from appearance as a form of detour leading back to appearance, one kind of likeness undone to make room for another. The second way of "unlocking," and exposing the viewer to, the "brutality of fact" has to be situated on the level of the imagistic repertoire on which Bacon draws so consistently. It is directed against the pictures and clichés that populate the modern lifeworld and our imagination. Bacon's art stages an assault on the images that are always already there, haunting the empty canvas, to bring out an image that would obliterate these specters, "hoping . . . to paint the one picture which will annihilate all the other ones" or, in a different formulation, "to make the image that sums up all the others"—an ideal that, as he admitted, he never achieved.[16] It is the ambition to create an absolute image that will arrest the beholders because it is unlike anything seen, deliberately at odds with the received iconic models.

As I have said, Bacon's painting is very much in dialogue with both the art-historical tradition and the contemporary archives furnished by the new media, especially film and photography. Indeed, it very manifestly derives part of its force from the fact that it draws on many familiar motifs and topoi from the history of Western painting. At the same time, however, the aesthetic sensibility at work in this endeavor continually challenges academic protocols of representation in pursuit of its own vision. In the artist's attempts to account for this vision, the matter of representation, as I have mentioned, is routinely superseded by reflections on the impact he would like his paintings to have and on the means employed to achieve this. Bacon's insistence on "immediacy," "intensity," "inevitability," and a number of similar terms appears to call for a quasi-physiological aesthetics, invoking, by turns, the visceral and the neural, and thereby effectively removing the work from critical analysis. From this perspective the paintings are indeed less about rendering a given subject than about transmitting certain feelings and sensations from the painter's "nervous system" to that of the beholder. In spite of the appeal to chance and contingency, the assumptions underlying this operation seem oddly mechanistic, leaving little room for the notion that the impact aimed for is intricately interwoven with the persistence of figurative and narrative elements and that it might not be as unequivocal as suggested in the interviews. Given the artist's tendency to describe the actual production of his works as a more or less unfathomable and incalculable process, in which the painter is basically waiting for something unforeseen to happen on the canvas, it would perhaps seem appropriate to try to account for their effectiveness in terms of the bodily or visceral reaction they elicit rather than on the level of the viewers' efforts somehow to make sense of what they see. But it is of course not obvious at all how one would gauge the degree to which a painting may impact our "nervous system," let alone how one would talk about it. Premised on a kind of stimulus-and-response pattern, this would seem a curiously reductive undertaking, deliberately disregarding the complex interplay of affect and the imaginary that is actually at work in the paintings. The observations that follow are therefore less concerned with the alleged visceral effects of the work than with the pathos staged and revoked in it, its ostentatious engagement with scenes of agony and anguish, at once fraught with suggestive meaning and resolutely "impervious to interpretation."[17]

ANGUISH, AGONY, PATHOS

The affective charge of Bacon's work is as palpable as it is difficult to define. One of the places where it seems to manifest itself in a fairly straightforward manner is in the series of screaming popes, though here as elsewhere the paintings' striking efficacy cannot be reduced to a simple formula. As is well known, capturing the scream was one of Bacon's obsessions for the longest time, inspired not so much by Edvard Munch as by Poussin's *Massacre of the Innocents* and by the famous close-up of the bloodied face of a nurse, shrieking with terror, in Eisenstein's *Battleship Potemkin*. The series of popes (not all of which are actually shown screaming) is accompanied and complemented by pictures of screaming men in dark business suits and of primates, in particular a baboon and a chimpanzee, baring their canine teeth, all of them placed in similar cagelike and claustrophobic settings. Characteristically evasive when it comes to providing a possible account for the anguish that is so much in evidence in these paintings, Bacon remarked that he did not so much intend to paint the horror as the gaping mouth emitting a cry. In fact, it is to no small extent that this very absence of any hint at the source or meaning of the panic that appears to have seized the figures makes for the troubling effect of these paintings. Their screams, though of course inaudible, seem to drown out everything; howling before an invisible terror, they appear to be consumed by their own interminable wails. There is another crucial feature, however, that adds to the peculiar poignancy of the series of figures, or rather creatures, wailing and screaming. For their creatureliness or animality, reinforced by their crouching position and their "primal" scream (if that is what it is), is counterbalanced by a peculiar sense of spectrality. It is the indistinct and vague quality of the subjects that appears to be dissolving as they emit their never-ending howls. It is actually often impossible to tell whether they scream because they are losing their contours and their consistence or whether their apparent dispersion is a consequence of their silent screaming. Yet, in spite of the blur that so often veils their features and gives them a ghostly appearance, their faces are the site of utmost expressivity. The popes and men in business suits are characters of an indeterminate order of being, conjured into existence from nowhere and on the brink of receding into the dark background, real and unreal at the same time. What is more is that in many cases it is not only the screaming men who appear threatened by dissolution but actually the space around them itself. It is precisely this array of different and partly incongruous possibilities that gives these pictures their startling, indeed their hallucinatory, power.

The affective charge of the later works is more difficult to describe. At first glance the anguish of the figures appears to have given way to agony, though the nature of the depicted affliction is far from obvious, vacillating between extreme pain and extreme pleasure, torment and ecstasy. The peculiarly transparent quality of the subjects of the early paintings, their indistinct presence and apparent immateriality, has been supplanted by an unmistakable emphasis on the corporeal. The figures at the center of these paintings are often featured as a pulsating, dense mass of flesh, contorted and twitching, with the suggestion of density and volume being as much a result of the handling of the paint as a characteristic of the bodies, which appear sculpted, in the flesh, as it were. The scream has disappeared, and the faces, as generally in Bacon's later portraiture, are sites of a veritable devastation. There remains only a faint trace of the former expressiveness, the eyes gazing out from under or behind the devastation visited on the figures. It is a gaze that is strangely oblivious with respect to the destruction unleashed against the subject. Amid this near absence of any signs of expressiveness, the muteness of the gaze forms a sharp contrast to the agitation that has seized the bodies. As in the series of screaming men from the 1950s, it is unclear where to locate the origin of the commotion that seems to be stirring the canvas.

In many instances it appears as though the depicted struggle was, above all, one in which the bodies were engaged with themselves. As Deleuze, Bacon's most inspired reader, has observed, oftentimes one gets the impression that these bodies are trying to escape from themselves, to leave their own frame and assume a form that is less fixed.[18] Think of the puddles into which some of the figures seem to empty themselves or the mysterious processes of liquefaction depicted on a number of other paintings. The bodily forms frequently appear not to coincide with themselves, strangely displaced vis-à-vis their own center. Clearly, Bacon is at pains to undo the symmetry and integrity of the classical body, not in a cubist fashion by breaking down the object into views from different angles but rather by telescoping, magnifying, and condensing a series of movements into each other, "hoping to deform people into appearance," as he put it to Sylvester.[19] It is as though Muybridge's photographs of the human body in motion had been superimposed on one another. As a result we become witness to a peculiar biomorphic mutation, midway between birth and contraction, an uncertain metamorphosis in which the human form is stretched to the limits of its recognizability.

As Deleuze also noted in connection with these monstrous metamorphoses, the becoming-animal, as he calls it, of Bacon's figures, there is something strangely impersonal about the agony the figures are undergoing. The extreme affects overpowering them do not seem to be properly theirs.[20] In fact, there is a disconnect between the forces ravaging the bodies and the attitude of the figures, their apparent absent-mindedness, their introverted gazes, coming at us from a great distance, as though from a different realm entirely, and a violence that is erupting out of nowhere, striking indiscriminately at whatever comes in its way. It is no surprise that the apparent mindlessness of the suffering and violence depicted on Bacon's canvases has led critics to accuse the artist of pessimism. Although he typically rejects suggestions of any moral intent, whether positive or negative, the painter has countered this criticism by declaring the spirit of his work as one of "exhilarated despair." And Deleuze has defended the reputed fatalism of the paintings as the sign of an "extraordinary vitality" rather than of the tragic vision so often associated with Bacon's work.[21]

The earlier works, especially the popes, are patterned after the state portrait. They evoke a sense of pathos in the grand manner, featuring dignitaries with all the official trappings of their power. But the serenity so characteristic of the genre has given way to outright panic and anguish. The equanimity and composure of the representative of power is discomposed and disrupted by an uncontrollable agitation. Bacon's paintings "infect" the sublime pathos of supreme authority with the primal fear of the cornered animal. If the mark of sovereignty is the power over life and death, here it has become subject to the very violence it used to command: Giorgio Agamben's bare life and sovereign power in one.[22] Merging the image of such sovereignty with the vision of creaturely anguish is at the heart of the powerful dissonance of many of the early portraits.

In a number of cases the configuration of terror and authority is a somewhat different one though. The animality that appears to eclipse the gravitas of representation and the presumed dignity of the human is less that of primal fear than of predatory instincts and ferocity. Think, for example, of *Head I* and *II,* in which an indefinable beast seems to emerge from within the silhouetted human form, baring a menacing set of canine teeth, or *Painting 1946,* another one of Bacon's signature pieces. This latter painting is a picture of a dark, brooding figure, with blood on its upper lip, framed by a black umbrella and the sumptuous carcass of a partitioned bull looming behind it, a construction midway between canopy and cross, announcing the equally famous, later crucifixions (*Three Studies for a Crucifixion* [1962] and *Crucifixion* [1965]). The features of the man at the center of the image are partly hidden. Receding into the dark shade of the umbrella, he conjures up the figure of the executioner, masked so as to keep his anonymity but also to enhance the aura of violence that the painting exudes.[23] The title of the work dates the image and inevitably offers it as an oblique commentary on the times, however much the painter has resisted such a possibility. Rather than signaling a departure into a new era, after the end of the war, the picture confronts the beholder with a strangely archaic and faceless vision, conflating the spheres of sacral authority and the butcher shop. We can easily discern the traces of the state portrait in the grand manner, but it is infused with an atmosphere midway between slaughterhouse and torture chamber.

If the meat had functioned as a kind of accessory in *Painting 1946,* the insignia of brute force, it starts to take center stage in the two later crucifixion paintings, which seem less about their ostensible religious subject matter than about the grained, marmoreal beauty of red meat, as Bacon himself has repeatedly emphasized. The creatures crawling down the crosslike structure are strange hybrids—half human, half animal. Rather than resembling any recognizable species, what slides down the cross calls to mind "the river of flesh" Bacon invoked in one of the interviews with Sylvester and from which many of the figures in his later paintings seem to emerge.[24] In view of its ubiquitous presence, Bacon has often been called the painter of flesh, dedicated to painting the flesh for its own sake, so to speak, as the organic, elementary substance of life, featured in its fluid plasticity and "convulsive beauty." On some level the pathos of the later work appears above all the pathos of this flesh. It seems to be the true object of Bacon's compassion and is figured in a variety of forms: flayed, wounded, worn by exhaustion, contracting in a spasm, whether from pain or in erotic entanglement, sculpted like the body of an athlete (or one of Michelangelo's marvelous slaves) but also strangely diaphanous at times, as in an X-ray image. This array of different appearances of the flesh is matched by the variation in its formal treatment. The flesh is often subject to the violence of the paint, paint thrown on the canvas, smudged and spread in broad strokes, but there are also a few instances where it is treated more gently, with a softening touch, as it were, shrouding the agitation on display in a sort of haziness. The affective charge of the paintings is reflected not only in the strangely indeterminate attitude of the figures but also in their creator's touch, alternately violent and tender.

Though Bacon insists that he is attracted above all by its material beauty and sheer immanence, clearly, the painterly fascination with flesh cannot be dissociated from its relation to sexuality and death, our desires, fears, and bodily needs, in short, with a certain kind of creatureliness that can inspire both extreme discomfort and compassion. In other words, as much as the flesh seems to figure as the paragon of mindless matter, it is also a motif that will invariably conjure up a set of familiar associations, evoking notions of lust and desire as much as vulnerability, mortality, and compassion. Needless to say, the varying degrees to which the tormented creatureliness depicted on Bacon's later paintings gives rise to any of these affects and emotions are very hard to determine. It is far from certain, for instance, whether the tormented creatureliness depicted on many of the later paintings actually gives rise to any compassion. If the mark of pathos is the sufferer's ability to maintain a reflective distance to his or her own suffering, to assert a minimal degree of freedom in the midst of turmoil, then Bacon's visions of agony seem in a strange way to conform to this definition. But as we have seen, many of the figures appear strangely numbed, as if oblivious to the violence visited on them, and this near total lack of a sense of depth or reflexivity on the part of the figures seems to foreclose the very possibility of compassion. In a paradoxical fashion there is the pathos of the flesh, soliciting our compassion for creaturely suffering, and then there is the pathos, if one can put it this way, of the impossibility of compassion, the distinct sense of being confronted with a spectacle that denies us the comfort of an unequivocal affective response.

I would like to conclude by turning to another dimension of Bacon's art that contributes to what one might call the affective indeterminacy of the paintings or the peculiar dialectics of pathos and deflation they seem to stage. It is a dimension very much at odds with the insistence on the non-figurative, nonsemantic, and so forth, and one that the criticism that has adopted Bacon's own critical terms has largely missed.[25] I am speaking of the paintings' rather obvious concern with *mise en scène*. For all the insistence, both by the artist himself and the critics writing in his wake, on instinct, intensity, energy, and the like, what I have called the affective charge and efficacy of his paintings is sustained in many of them, above all in the triptychs, by a strong intimation of *drama*.

This impression is based not just on the stagelike structures that elevate and focus what is going on but also, more generally, by the "scenic" look of many of the situations depicted in Bacon's paintings. A great number of the pictures call to mind crime scenes or evoke sites that bear the traces of some horrific, inscrutable spectacle. Mirrors, windows, shutters, doorways, and other openings underline this scenic aspect, too, catering to a voyeuristic and searching gaze. At times a spectator or witness figure is included within the picture itself, thus reinforcing the beholder's sense of becoming privy to some mysterious or illicit goings-on. Circling and magnifying certain sections of a body or face, as in radiation photography, or using little arrows, the paintings also frequently draw attention to certain details as though they want to present us with some kind of evidence, clues for a possible story, but this story itself remains elusive. We are looking at its abbreviated or condensed form, without being afforded any kind of resolution or relief. The arrangements on these paintings, of nondescript, sterile interiors, furnished with props from everyday life, human and animal figures, suggest a complicated web of relations: couples in an agonistic embrace, either wrestling or making love, sometimes framed by curious onlookers, or doubled and mirrored by figures wrenching their bodies and engaged in the most bizarre exertions. Clearly, there is a sense of tension and conflict, but the significance of these relations remains enigmatic. This is also true for the paintings that feature single figures. Placed in a void that seems alternately ominous and mundane, even banal, they appear to bear testimony to something, figurations of a silent memento, but, again, any possible revelation as to the nature of their apparent affliction, ennui or exasperation, is withheld from the beholder. Obviously, the bareness of the setting forms a contrast to (and thus reinforces) the agitation experienced by the figures. In some sense it gives rise to imaginary scenarios that would allow us to make sense of the situation, but it also thwarts our innate urge to discern the narrative presumably underlying the scene. To be sure, these tendencies are very much in conformity with the painter's opposition to storytelling and, more generally, to the banality, as he puts it, of narrative and illustration. At the same time, however, the strong sense of mise en scène inevitably enforces the notion that the display, erratic and mystifying as it is, is given with some purpose in mind; indeed, it seems to urge the beholder to make sense of the symbolic charge of the painting. The striking appeal of Bacon's pictures derives from the very tension between a sense of suspense, generating a desire for relief and resolution, and the unapologetic display of muted suffering and mindless violence.

If we take pathos to imply the attempt to endow suffering and pain with dignity and with a quasi-redemptive streak, if it designates a form of rising above or transcending the hardships suffered precisely as one is submitted to them, then Bacon's appeal to the real is very much pitted against the possibility of pathos. He effectively denies the beholders of his pictures the relief or resolution of a narrative that would allow them to discern a rationale for what is being depicted. The suffering featured on his paintings is never subject to any form of sublation or transfiguration. Nor is there any intimation of reconciliation. It is true that he "quotes" a number of what one could call "pathos formulae," both in terms of the formats and of the motifs he has chosen, the triptych, the crucifixion, the Sphinx, or the Erinyes, all of them subjects that, in one way or the other, are related to some kind of mythic doom. But the pathos associated with these subjects is strangely unsettled.

As in the other works examined in this book, Bacon's pathos of the real is double-edged. It designates the inadequacy of our reactions in the face of the spectacle of violence and excess, the inadequacy, also, of the critical readings Bacon likes to dismiss in favor of the appeal to a fundamentally "unreadable" and unrecognizable real. But it also refers to the opposite notion, namely, that the engagement with that which resists assimilation holds a momentous lesson, all the more so for being utterly undecipherable—hence the peculiar combination of heightened drama and its deflation, the simultaneity of a sense of exaltation and of perplexity, of pathos and apathy, that marks the encounter with the real staged in Bacon's art.

Throughout these pages the "pathos of the real" has designated an ambition rather than a unified program. It has also named, if perhaps less explicitly, a certain skepticism vis-à-vis this ambition. As I have said, the phrase mixes hubris and humiliation, the highest aspirations with a sense of futility, the promise of breakthrough and the disconcerting experience of lasting opacity, alterity, nonsense. On the face of it pathos is the pathos of such ambition, but it is an ambition that fails. As a consequence the pathos in question, the pathos of the real, is in equal measure the pathos of this failure. The pattern is by now familiar. The preceding readings have all been preoccupied with similar puzzles, based on a certain coincidence of opposites: the refusal of pathos as a site of transfiguration and as a means of reconciliation, *and* the pathos of this refusal; the encounter with the real as a transformative experience, portending a different economy of suffering and pain, *and* the confrontation with the facticity of violence, erratic and unsublatable. In some sense the pathos of the real appears to be both itself and its own negation, an ambition and its disappointment, a refusal and the return of that which is refused on a different level. Though marked by a certain tension, this structure, dialectical but without synthesis as one might say, hinges as much on the opposition between the two terms of the formula as on their nexus, the contradictory and complementary character of pathos and the real. As excess the latter is pitted against the former as codified affect; at the same time pathos is a certain kind of excess itself, a response to, and an instance of, violation and transgression. As the counterpart to the symbolic and the imaginary, the real is, of course, antithetical to the notion of representation *tout court,* but as we have seen throughout, it very often has an air of drama about itself, indeed, of pathos. For all its irreducible opacity, it is nonetheless presented as pregnant with meaning. This troubled dialectic is what makes for the sense of indecision and ambiguity between ambition and failure at the core of engagement with the real.

NOTES

Introduction

1. See Hobsbawm, *The Age of Extremes.*
2. Badiou, *The Century,* 32.
3. See, e.g., "On Subtraction" and "Truth: Forcing and the Unnameable," both in Badiou, *Conditions,* 113–28, 129–44.
4. For Badiou these normativities are exemplified in such proclivities as "resignation, renunciation, the lesser evil, together with moderation, the end of humanity as a spiritual force, and the critique of 'grand narratives'" (Badiou, *The Century,* 31).
5. Badiou, "Destruction, Negation, Subtraction—On Pier Paolo Pasolini," www.lacan.com/badpas.htm (accessed Aug. 5, 2008).
6. Hallward, *Badiou,* 14. See also Badiou's claim that the "notion of the real refuse[s] its early Lacanian associations with horror, brute materiality, mystery, and fixity" (*The Century,* 15).
7. Hallward, *Badiou,* 14.
8. See, e.g., in *The Century:*

If you think the world can and must change absolutely; that there is neither a nature of things to be respected nor pre-formed subjects to be maintained, you thereby admit that the individual may be sacrificable. *Meaning that the individual is not independently endowed with any intrinsic nature that would deserve our striving to perpetuate it.* (99; emphasis added)

You can observe the emergence of a link between the thesis that the subject is of the order not of what is but of what happens—of the order of the event—and *the idea that the individual can be sacrificed to a historical cause that exceeds him.* Since the being of the subject is the lack-of-being, it is only by dissolving itself into a project that exceeds him that an individual can hope to attain some subjective real. Thenceforth, the only "we" constructed in and by this project is the only thing that is truly real —subjectively real for the individual who supports it. The individual, truth be told, is nothing. The subject is the new man, emerging as the point of self-lack. *The individual is thus, in its very essence, the nothing that must be dissolved into a we-subject.* (100–101; emphasis added)

9. Badiou, "Beyond Formalization," 131.

10. The only time in *The Century* in which Badiou relates the real to the two other Lacanian "registers," he writes, "Either the twentieth century is the Real of that for which the nineteenth century was the Imaginary; or it is the Real of that for which the nineteenth was the Symbolic (i.e., what the nineteenth produced in terms of doctrine; what it thought and organized)" (19).

11. Unfortunately, there is no *locus classicus* in which Lacan would give a conclusive account of his notion of the Real. In fact, it very much evolves over time, from its initial appearance in the first two seminars to a more oblique presence in Seminar VII and further elaborations in Seminars XI and XX. For one of the most dramatic accounts see the discussion of Irma's dream in Lacan, *The Ego in Freud's Theory and in the Technique of Psychoanalysis, 1954–1955* (154–55, 164). On the idea of the Borromean knot see Lacan, *On Feminine Sexuality,* 133.

12. Lacan, *The Four Fundamental Concepts of Psychoanalysis,* 53–64.

13. "Tarrying with the negative" is a Hegelian locution that provided the title for one of Žižek's books in which he explores the links, as he does, in fact, in all his works, between German idealism and Lacanian psychoanalysis. See Žižek, *Tarrying with the Negative.*

14. "Man's desire finds its meaning in the desire of the other, not so much because the other holds the key to the object desired, as because the first object of desire is to be recognized by the other" (Lacan, *Écrits,* 58). See also *The Four Fundamental Concepts of Psychoanalysis,* 38, 115.

15. See, e.g., Lacan's assertion that "desire *is* a metonymy" (Lacan, *Écrits,* 175). In the words of Slavoj Žižek, "desire is defined by this *ce n'est pas ça*: that is, its most elementary and ultimate aim is to sustain itself as desire, in its state of non-satisfaction" (Žižek, *The Ticklish Subject,* 297).

16. See Lacan, *L'éthique de la psychanalyse,* 55–86; and Lacan, *The Ethics of Psychoanalysis,* 43–70. See also Evans, *An Introductory Dictionary of Lacanian Psychoanalysis,* 204–5.

17. On sublimation see Lacan, *The Ethics of Psychoanalysis,* 87–164. For a very good discussion see Zupančič, *Esthétique du désir, éthique de la jouissance,* 43–58; and Zupančič, *The Shortest Shadow,* 73–85.

18. Žižek, *The Ticklish Subject,* 264. In an earlier formulation Žižek described the space between two deaths thus: "Ce lieu 'entre deux morts', lieu où apparaissent aussi bien la beauté sublime que les monstres effrayants, est celui de *das Ding,* l'objet-cause du désir, du noyau réel-traumatique au cœur du symbolique" (Žižek, *Le plus sublime des hystériques,* 232).

19. Žižek, *The Abyss of Freedom,* 80 (emphasis in the original).

20. "The century's threshold of tolerance for that which, from the vantage point of our weary, pacified present, constitutes the worst, was incredibly high—

regardless of which camp one pledged allegiance to. This is obviously what leads some today to speak of the century's 'barbarity.' *Nevertheless, it is entirely unjust to isolate this dimension of the passion of the real*" (Badiou, *The Century*, 63; emphasis added).

21. See Žižek, *Le plus sublime des hystériques*, 77–79.

22. Žižek, *The Abyss of Freedom*, 22.

23. "Le réel . . . c'est ce qui se retrouve toujours à la même place" (*L'éthique de la psychanalyse*, 85; *The Ethics of Psychoanalysis*, 70).

24. This is to my mind one of the main thrusts in Santner's latest work: the question of how what he calls our "undeadness" can be undone. See Santner, *On Creaturely Life*; and Santner, "Miracles Happen."

25. See Badiou, *The Century*, 55–56 ("Nothing will have taken place but the place" [my translation]).

26. Pathos is a neglected category, at least in literary studies. The situation is a bit different in other areas of the humanities, such as theater, performance, and film studies.

27. See the entries on pathos in two recent encyclopedias: Ueding, *Historisches Wörterbuch der Rhetorik;* and Barck, Fontius, et al., *Ästhetische Grundbegriffe*. See also the fine study by Dachselt, *Pathos;* and Bohrer, "Pathos im Zivilisationsprozeß."

28. See Aristotle's *Rhetoric* 1.2.1356a.

29. See, e.g., Quintilian, *Institutiones Oratoriae* [The Orator's Education] 6.2.26–36; (Pseudo-)Longinus, *On the Sublime* 15.1–3; Cicero, *De oratore* [On the Orator] 2.189f., 3.202. See also Campe, "Affizieren und Selbstaffizieren."

30. See Zierl, *Affekte in der Tragödie*, 58–61; and Gould, *The Ancient Quarrel between Poetry and Philosophy*, 36–54.

31. See Auerbach, "Passio als Leidenschaft"; reprinted as "Gloria passionis." See also Gould, *The Ancient Quarrel between Poetry and Philosophy*, 63–69.

32. Auerbach, "Gloria passionis," 68–69 (emphasis added).

33. One of the most prominent representatives of this view in the German tradition is Friedrich Schiller: "Ein guter Geschmack . . . gestattet keine, wenn gleich noch so kraftvolle Darstellung des Affekts, die bloß physisches Leiden und physischen Widerstand ausdrückt, ohne zugleich die höhere Menschheit, die Gegenwart eines übersinnlichen Vermögens, sichtbar zu machen—und zwar . . . weil nie das Leiden an sich, nur der Widerstand gegen das Leiden pathetisch und der Darstellung würdig ist" (Schiller, "Über das Pathetische," 429). ["Good taste permits no display of passion alone, however so powerful, if it only expresses physical suffering and physical resistance without at the same time making visible the nobler side of humanity, the presence of a capacity beyond the senses. The obvious reason for this . . . is the fact that only the resistance to suffering, never the

suffering in itself, is pathetic and deserves to be portrayed" (Schiller, *On the Pathetic,* 50).]

34. As far as I have been able to determine, the first usage occurs in 1906 in Warburg's lecture "Dürer und die italienische Antike."

35. "Wo irgend Pathos zum Vorschein kam, mußte es in antiker Form geschehen" (Gombrich, *Aby Warburg,* 179n). For a more detailed discussion of the genesis and structure of Warburg's idea, see Settis, "Pathos und Ethos"; Port, "'Katharsis des Leidens'"; and Zumbusch, *Wissenschaft in Bildern.*

36. "Die Ausdrucksformen des maximalen inneren Ergriffenseins" (Warburg, *Der Bilderatlas Mnemosyne,* 3 ["Einleitung"]).

37. Gombrich, *Aby Warburg,* 296.

Chapter One: In Praise of Cruelty

1. Elkins, *The Object Stares Back,* 101–16.

2. See Brook, Bourgon, and Blue, *Death by a Thousand Cuts.*

3. Institut d'Asie Orientale, Chinese Torture; Supplices Chinois, http://turandot .ish-lyon.cnrs.fr/Essay.php?ID=40 (accessed March 25, 2010).

4. Bataille's engagement with the pictures has also given rise to a host of literary and artistic responses, notably in Latin America; see esp. Elizondo, *Farabeuf o la crónica de un instante;* the image plays a more oblique role in Cortázar's *Rayuela,* in the novels of Mario Vargas Llosa, and in the fiction of Juan García Ponce. On all of these writers see Ubilluz, *Sacred Eroticism.* The images have also been discussed in the context of religious studies, mostly in connection with Bataille; see, e.g., Connor, *Georges Bataille and the Mysticism of Sin,* 3–6, 161–62; Hollywood, *Sensible Ecstasy,* 25–110; and Agamben, *Homo Sacer,* 112–15.

5. See Elkins, "The Very Theory of Transgression."

6. See Bois and Krauss, *Formless;* originally published as *L'informe,* the catalogue was intended as a "guide" to an exhibition mounted at the Centre Georges Pompidou and curated by the two authors. Elkins's other target is the work of Didi-Huberman, notably his book on Bataille, *La ressemblance informe ou le gai savoir visuel selon Georges Bataille.*

7. Elkins, "The Very Theory of Transgression," 12.

8. Ibid.

9. Ibid., 12, 14.

10. See Barthes, *Camera Lucida.*

11. Though not, at least in my judgment, of the Bataille who is at the center of Krauss's and Bois's *Formless* or Didi-Huberman's book on Bataille.

12. See Heindl, *Meine Reise nach den Strafkolonien;* see also Heindl's "Strafrechtstheorie und Praxis"; as well as his voluminous *Der Berufsverbrecher.* The

connection to Heindl has often elicited commentary. See, e.g., Müller-Seidel, *Die Deportation des Menschen;* Neumeyer, "'Das Land der Paradoxa' (Robert Heindl)"; and Kittler, "In dubio pro reo."

13. Corngold, *Lambent Traces,* 86.

14. See Bourgon, "Chinese Executions"; and Bourgon, "Agony by Proxy." A much-expanded version of these two articles can be found in Brook, Bourgon, and Blue, *Death by a Thousand Cuts,* 152–242.

15. Bourgon, "Chinese Executions," 158.

16. Ibid., 159. The author's reference here is to Edgerton, *Pictures and Punishment,* 13. Bourgon's other major sources are Foucault's *Discipline and Punish* and Spierenburg's *The Spectacle of Suffering.* The number of studies on the cultural and legal history of executions (and torture) has grown continually since publication of Foucault's *Discipline and Punish* and was especially prolific during the last two decades of the twentieth century. See, e.g., Arasse, *La guillotine et l'imaginaire de la Terreur;* Dülmen, *Theater des Schreckens;* and Puppi, *Le splendore dei supplizi.* For the Middle Ages see Enders, *The Medieval Theater of Cruelty.*

17. Bourgon, "Chinese Executions," 168.

18. Bataille, *The Tears of Eros,* 206–7.

19. Here is a slightly earlier description of the nexus between sacrifice and some kind of revelation: "A violent death disrupts the creature's discontinuity; what remains, what the tense onlookers experience in the succeeding silence, is the continuity of all existence with which the victim is now one. Only a spectacular killing, carried out as the solemn and collective nature of religious dictates, has the power to reveal what normally escapes notice" (Bataille, *Erotism,* 22).

20. Bataille, *The Tears of Eros,* 206.

21. See the footnotes and the correspondence with the editor, J. M. Lo Duca, included in the book.

22. Bataille, "Attraction and Repulsion II," 114.

23. Bataille, *Guilty,* 35; *Œuvres complètes* 5:272; see also *Expérience intérieure,* 177–90. He did not reproduce any of the pictures, and the accounts are given in passing, so the pictures had a more covert presence back then.

24. On this mystique technique see Largier, *In Praise of the Whip,* 58–66, 184–98.

25. *Erotism* was published in 1957, *The Accursed Share* (posthumously) in 1967, and *Theory of Religion* in 1973.

26. Bataille, *The Accursed Share,* 28. The term *cosmovision* appears in Ubilluz, *Sacred Eroticism,* 27. As for the origin of Bataille's solar "mythology," everything points to Aztec culture (or the author's vision thereof), an important point of reference throughout Bataille's later writings. See Bataille, *The Accursed Share,* 45–61.

27. Bataille, *Theory of Religion*, 48–49.

28. "Thingness," the differentiation of subjects and objects, is opposed to a presumed intimacy with the world; in *Erotism* this intimacy is called "continuity." For "things" see especially Bataille, *Theory of Religion*.

29. Bataille, *Erotism*, 195.

30. Auffret, *Kojève*, 350–52. Bataille later said that Kojève's seminar left him "rompu, broyé, tué dix fois: suffoqué et cloué" (broken, shattered, killed ten times over, suffocated and paralyzed) (ibid.).

31. Bataille, *Erotism*, 38 (translation modified).

32. Caillois, "Festival," 295; see also Caillois, *Man and the Sacred*, 97–127.

33. Bataille, *Erotism*, 36.

34. Gray, "Disjunctive Signs," 218.

35. Kafka, *Briefe an Milena*, 105–6: "das Foltern ist mir äußerst wichtig, ich beschäftige mich mit nichts anderem als mit Gefoltertwerden und Foltern." Recall the famous remark in a letter to Oskar Pollak, Jan. 27, 1904: "Ein Buch muß die Axt sein für das gefrorene Meer in uns."

36. See Menninghaus, *Disgust*, 227–341.

37. See, e.g., Mladek, "'Ein eigentümlicher Apparat.'" For a useful overview of different approaches to the story see Gray, "Disjunctive Signs"; see also Kittler, "Schreibmaschinen, Sprechmaschinen"; Pan, "Kafka as a Populist"; and Treichel, "Fleischwerdung der Schrift und Schriftwerdung des Leibes." My own reading is indebted to these interpretations; however, unlike any of the interpretations of the story I know, the one attempted here will focus on the conjunction of spectacularity and specularity. The story projects a spectacle of death and transfiguration only to undo it; the "image" conjured up is displaced and refracted in the reflections and commentary it elicits.

38. See Kafka, *In der Strafkolonie*: "sollten noch kleine Unsicherheiten bestehen, so wird der Anblick der Exekution sie beseitigen" (231); and Corngold's translation in Kafka, *In the Penal Colony*: "should some small uncertainties still remain, the sight of the execution will do away with them" (51). In subsequent citations in which I have juxtaposed the original German with Corngold's English translation, I will use the abbreviations *S* and *P* respectively.

39. *P*, 49 (emphasis added). The officer continues: "It is effective even when it stands by itself in this valley." ("Im übrigen [despite some minor technical problems] arbeitet die Maschine noch und wirkt für sich. Sie wirkt für sich, auch wenn sie allein in diesem Tal steht" [*S*, 227].) In an earlier instance the officer had finished his preparations by announcing, "from now on the machine works entirely on its own" (*P*, 36); "von jetzt an aber arbeitet der Apparat ganz allein" (*S*, 204–5).

40. "Sie werden etwa sagen: 'Bei uns ist das Gerichtsverfahren ein anderes,' oder 'Bei uns wird der Angeklagte vor dem Urteil verhört,' oder 'Bei uns erfährt

der Angeklagte das Urteil,' oder 'Bei uns gibt es auch andere Strafen als Todesstra-fen,' oder 'Bei uns gab es Folterungen nur im Mittelalter.' Das alles sind Bemerkun-gen, die ebenso richtig sind, als sie Ihnen selbstverständlich erscheinen, unschuldige Bemerkungen, die mein Verfahren nicht antasten" (*S*, 229); "All these remarks are just as correct as they seem self-evident to you, innocent remarks that don't invalidate my procedure" (*P*, 50).

41. Cf. Matt. 17:1–3; Mark 9:1–3; and Luke 9:27–29.

42. Other prominent biblical motifs in the story are the illumination setting in at the sixth hour (Matt. 27:45); the twelve-hour martyrium of the condemned man; and his failure to keep watch by falling asleep (Mark 14:32). See Rohde, *Und blätterte ein wenig in der Bibel*, 76–105.

43. See *S*, 205; *P*, 37. "Completion," which is how Corngold renders the term, is quite accurate given the immediate context of the term. In view of the broader context though—in other words, of the story as a whole—the other connotations impose themselves.

44. Cf. *S*: "machen Sie mit der Wahrheit Lärm (. . .), brüllen Sie, aber ja, brüllen Sie dem Kommandanten Ihre Meinung, Ihre unerschütterliche Meinung zu" (234).

45. In reaction to the traveler's question about whether the condemned man knows his sentence, the officer "paused for a moment as if demanding from the traveler a more cogent reason for his question" (*P*, 40). After answering in the neg-ative to the traveler's follow-up question about whether the condemned man "knows that he has been condemned," the officer "smiled at the traveler, as if he now expected to have a few strange revelations from him." His response to the traveler's final question—"You mean that even now the man does not know how his defense was received?"—is given without looking at the traveler, as if to spare him the embarrassment of "telling him things that were so obvious to him" (*P*, 40).

46. Kafka, *The Penal Colony*, 204.

47. For a more complex treatment of this aspect, from a postcolonial per-spective, see Goebel, "Kafka and Postcolonial Critique"; and Müller-Seidel, *Die Deportation des Menschen*.

48. "Nun beginnt das Spiel" (*S*, 215). The semantic scope of *Spiel* is quite broad. Here it connotes "Schauspiel," that is, "performance," "show," "drama," but also "play" in the sense of the coordinated movements taking place between the "Bed" and the "Harrow." *Spiel*, of course, also means "game."

49. *Chinese* refers above all to a moment of disturbance in the perceived pat-terns of looking at and rationalizing pain in the West. For Kafka's relation to China —"Im Grunde bin ich ja Chinese"—see Hsia, *Kafka and China*, 1 (for the re-mark about his own "Chineseness"); Goebel, *Constructing China;* and Zilcosky, *Kafka's Travels*.

50. Discussing the "mediatic" character of Chinese executions, Bourgon writes,

"'readability': the execution is only the realisation of a legal message, stressing the equivalence between the 'name' of a crime and the 'punishment'" (Bourgon, "Chinese Executions," 168). A page later he adds, as though commenting on Kafka's story: "no fellow-feeling is allowed to obscure the transparent message delivered by the state to the populace: 'See justice being done, where the punishment fits the crime.'"

51. See Honold, "In der Strafkolonie."

52. Santner, *On Creaturely Life,* 40.

53. Nietzsche, *On the Genealogy of Morals,* 61 (second essay, sec. 3).

54. Think of "Report for an Academy" but also "The Metamorphosis," which is, of course, an inverted account of such humanization.

55. See, e.g., Kremer, *Kafka.*

56. Anderson, *Kafka's Clothes,* 187.

57. On the tension between life and writing in Kafka and Flaubert see Kremer, *Kafka,* 118–52.

58. See Anderson, *Kafka's Clothes,* 188. On the association of writing as a peculiar kind of death, at times ecstatic, at times prosaic, see also Corngold, *Lambent Traces,* 81–94.

Chapter Two: Fragmentary Description of a Disaster

I would like to thank Hannah V. Eldridge, who has translated the first section of this chapter.

1. Da Vinci, *Leonardo on Painting,* 229–32.

2. Sebald, *The Rings of Saturn,* 124; subsequent references are cited parenthetically in the text. The German suggests a slightly different image, especially in the way it describes the "mummers": "Eine Zeitlang schaute ich diesen, wie es mir schien, vom ewigen Umgang getriebenen Gestalten nach, die bald zwischen den Häusern verschwanden, bald an einer anderen Stelle wieder hervorkamen" (*Die Ringe des Saturn,* 158).

3. "Das also, denkt man, indem man langsam im Kreis geht, ist die Kunst der Repräsentation der Geschichte. Sie beruht auf einer Fälschung der Perspektive. Wir, die Überlebenden, sehen alles von oben herunter, sehen alles zugleich und wissen dennoch nicht, wie es war" (Sebald, *Die Ringe des Saturn,* 157–58). A bit earlier the narrator had drawn similar conclusions apropos of some paintings of the Battle of Sole Bay: "Even celebrated painters . . . fail to convey any true impression of how it must have been to be on board one of these ships" (76–77).

4. Sebald, *Austerlitz,* 69; subsequent references are cited parenthetically in the text.

5. "Wir alle, auch diejenigen, die meinen, selbst auf das Geringfügigste geachtet

zu haben, behelfen uns nur mit Versatzstücken, die von anderen schon oft genug auf der Bühne herumgeschoben worden sind. Wir versuchen, die Wirklichkeit wiederzugeben, aber je angestrengter wir es versuchen, desto mehr drängt sich uns das auf, was auf dem historischen Theater von jeher zu sehen war: der gefallene Trommler, der Infanterist, der gerade einen anderen niedersticht, das brechende Auge eines Pferdes, der unverwundbare Kaiser, umgeben von seinen Generalen, mitten in dem erstarrten Kampfgewühl. Unsere Beschäftigung mit der Geschichte, so habe Hilarys These gelautet, sei eine Beschäftigung mit immer schon vorgefertigten, in das Innere unserer Köpfe gravierten Bildern, auf die wir andauernd starrten" (*Austerlitz*, 105).

Irrespective of his doubts about the credibility of war representations, Hilary concludes his depiction with yet another picture, both vivid and blurry, which he sees, as he stresses, as though through the eyes of somebody else:

Every attempt to understand the course of events inevitably turns into that one scene where the hosts of Russian and Austrian soldiers are fleeing on foot and horseback onto the frozen Satschen ponds. I see cannonballs suspended for an eternity in the air, I see others crashing into the ice, I see the unfortunate victims flinging up their arms as they slide from the toppling floes, and I see them, strangely, not with my own eyes but with those of short-sighted Marshal Davout, who has made a forced march with his regiments from Vienna. (*Austerlitz*, 72)

[Jeder Versuch, den Ablauf des sogenannten Kampfgeschehens zu begreifen, geht unweigerlich über in diese Szene, in welcher Scharen der russischen und österreichischen Soldaten zu Fuß und Pferde auf den gefrorenen Satschener Weiher fliehen. Ich sehe die Kanonenkugeln eine Ewigkeit lang stillstehen in der Luft, sehe andere einschlagen in das Eis, sehe die Unglücklichen mit hochgerissenen Armen von den kippenden Schollen gleiten, und sehe sie, seltsamerweise, nicht mit meinen eigenen Augen, sondern mit denen des kurzsichtigen Marschalls Davout, der mit seinen Regimentern in einem Gewaltmarsch von Wien heraufgekommen ist. (106)]

6. Sebald relates Stendhal's remark in his own text about Beyle (see Sebald, *Vertigo*, 7–8).

7. See Prendergast, *Napoleon and History Painting*.

8. Badiou, *The Century*, 34 (italics in the original). The next paragraph continues, "The fundamental concepts through which the century has come to think of itself or its own creative energy have all been subordinated to the semantics of war."

9. See Sebald, *On the Natural History of Destruction*. The German title of

the book, based on a series of lectures delivered in Zurich in 1997, is *Literatur und Luftkrieg [Literature and Aerial Warfare]*.

10. Santner, *On Creaturely Life*, 57.

11. The notable exception is Sebald's own description of the bombing of Hamburg in his lectures on "Air War and Literature" (see *On the Natural History of Destruction*, 26–28). Claudia Öhlschläger has analyzed the passage and taken issue with Sebald, arguing that he is succumbing to the very kind of voyeurism and the false suggestion of "being there" for which he chastises some of the authors he discusses in his lectures. See Öhlschläger, *Beschädigtes Leben*, 193–202. For a different view of the same passage see Presner, "'What a Synoptic and Artificial View Reveals.'" For a remarkable extension and revision of Sebald's statements about the air war and the apparent failure to deal with it adequately see the accounts of the air raids by foreigners, authors and newspaper correspondents for the most part, who happened to be in Germany at the time. Their texts are anthologized in Lubrich, *Berichte aus der Abwurfzone*.

12. Badiou, *The Century*, 38, 36.

13. Sebald, *The Rings of Saturn*, 77.

14. The author himself has largely dismissed his early production (published in the 1940s and 1950s). For the sake of economy I will draw mainly on the books that feature the war experience most prominently: above all *La route des Flandres* (1960) and *Les Géorgiques* (1981), probably Simon's two best-known works, as well as *La Bataille de Pharsale* (1969) and *L'Acacia* (1989). To distinguish between the French texts and their English translations, I will be using use the following abbreviations: *The Flanders Road (FR)*, *La route des Flandres (RF)*, *The Battle of Pharsalus (BP)*, *La Bataille de Pharsale (BPh)*, *The Georgics (G)*, *Les Géorgiques (Gé)*, *The Acacia (A)*, *L'Acacia (Ac)*.

15. The term *roman fleuve* refers to the French tradition of multivolume novels, of which Proust's *À la recherche du temps perdu*, one of Simon's models and foils, is the most prominent representative in the twentieth century. Simon himself has designated many of his books as novels. In a very perceptive appreciation, the English translator of most of his work, the poet Richard Howard, has stressed the generic hybridity of Simon's text. See Howard, "Divination by Ashes." In the spirit of Howard's observation the following readings will be deliberately selective; that is to say, they are less concerned with individual works than with specific techniques and effects operative in all of them.

16. I take the expression from the aptly titled interview with Jacqueline Piatier for *Le Monde des livres*, "Rendre la perception confuse multiple et simultanée du monde," April 26, 1967, v. For Simon's polemic against the nineteenth-century realist novel and its twentieth-century heirs see his "Nobel Lecture, December 9,

1985." For the ostensible powerlessness of words (and language) see the preface to *Orion Aveugle;* as well as the programmatic "Fiction Word by Word."

17. *G,* 209–10; *Gé,* 310–11 ("au fur et à mesure qu'il écrit son désarroi ne cessera de croître").

18. Simon has often described the substratum of his own writing as a kind of "magma" of memories and sensations. See, e.g., the preface to *Orion Aveugle.*

19. See Nitsch, *Sprache und Gewalt bei Claude Simon,* 64–97.

20. See his essay "Fiction Word by Word," where he notes that "there too [in the visual arts] it is not imitative verisimilitude that matters but a different kind of verisimilitude and credibility, in other words, pictorial credibility" (38) [ce n'est pas la vraisemblance imitative qui importe mais aussi une autre espèce de vraisemblance et de crédibilité, . . . la crédibilité picturale ("La fiction mot à mot," 81)]. See also Simon, "Réponses à quelque questions écrites de Ludovic Janvier," 20; as well as Simon, "Nobel Lecture, December 9, 1985," 68–69.

21. For the use of the term *permutation* to describe the dynamic of his texts see Simon, "Fiction Word by Word," 46. The structure of *Le palace,* for instance, is said to follow the form of a spiral while *Leçon des choses,* as the writer came to realize in retrospect, turned out to be all about the idea of "chute," of falling. (See Simon, "Roman, description et action," 25; see also "The Crossing of the Image," 55.) The three parts of *Triptyque* are meticulously organized according to a set of color schemes; so is *La route des Flandres,* whose ostensible disorder conceals the novel's hidden plot symmetries. In *Les corps conducteurs* S-shaped forms and movements play a key role. In *La Bataille de Pharsale* a section titled "O" redescribes one of the book's central episodes as a "system of relations" of different visual axes and viewpoints, an experiment that culminates in the invocation of the "mobile," a kinetic sculpture that critics have identified as an image of the text itself: "we must represent the totality of the system as a moving body ceaselessly alternating around a few fixed points" (*BP,* 127) ["on doit se figurer l'ensemble du système comme un mobile se déformant sans cesse autour de quelques points fixes" (*BPh,* 186)].

22. See Merleau-Ponty, "Five Notes on Claude Simon" (1961), as well as Merleau-Ponty's letter to Claude Simon, written that same year, in Britton, *Claude Simon,* 35–40. See also Duffy, "Claude Simon, Merleau-Ponty and Perception." On the writer's training in cubism see his own ironic account in *L'Acacia* (*A,* 126–27; *Ac,* 170–71).

23. See Dällenbach, "La question primordiale." For a more detailed discussion of the role of the visual arts as a model of Simon's writing see Ferrato-Combe, *Écrire en peintre,* 9–60.

24. His debt to the materialism and sensualism of *L'étranger* or *La nausée*

seems much greater than he cared to admit. See Duncan, "Simon and Sartre"; see also Simon, "Für wen schreibt denn Sartre?"

25. Unfortunately, the passages are too numerous to quote. Two examples will have to suffice: "ils s'envolèrent brusquement, comme une nuée de plumes, l'air au-dessus de la place tout entier pointillé pendant quelques instants par un palpitant et neigeux rideau parcouru de remous, de courants multiples [. . .] et (du fait que le dessin du vol suivait une spirale montante puis descendante autour de l'esplanade) contraires, les centaines de taches claires et frémissantes s'entre-croisant en dents de peigne sur de plans différents [. . .], comme un rideau mouvant" (*Le palace*, 23); "l'épais plafond de fumée coagulée flottant comme un dais au-dessus des têtes de spectateurs, ondulant faiblement, parcouru par de lents remous sirupeux, se tordant et se dénouant avec une reptilienne paresse, ses écharpes traversées par le pinceau bleuâtre jailli de la cabine de projection et qui révélait ses lentes dérives, comme une sorte de laitance, de placenta, apparaissant et disparaissant dans l'oblique et pyramidale faisceau de lumière, rigide, multiple, changeant brusquement, passant de l'argent au gris, strié, se divisant, se brouillant, se scindant" (*Gé*, 211; cf. *G*, 144).

26. Several passages in *Les Géorgiques* are devoted to the same incident. See, for instance:

> The brief skirmish at the ambush into which the squadron has fallen seems over. Everything is now quiet. After a moment he sees a mosaic of irregular polygons of different sizes, pale grey, blue grey, chalky, ochre and pink. He is on all fours on the ground. In the middle of the track, in the strip protected from the vehicle wheels, small tufts of grass and tiny plants with star-shaped serrated leaves grow between the stones. He can no longer hear the machine-guns firing. (*G*, 34–35; *Gé*, 51)

A subsequent attack is described in the following way:

> It was then (then: whilst they were moving away) that the second bomb exploded—or the second cluster (still the impression of multiplicity because of the crackling, the secondary explosions which seemed to come from within the first), again behind and to the left, but this time very close to the road, so deafening that he thinks he has been hit, knocked by the blast no doubt, perceived as well (the blast) as a rapid succession of blows all over the body, like violent punches, at the same time as if blinded (unless he instinctively closed his eyes?): something obscure, brown, shattering into pieces, a rush of triangles, like infinite fragments of flying glass exploding (although it all takes place in the countryside with no house in the vicinity), the edges of the triangles luminous, dazzling, the noise (no longer that of the explosion but of what?) like the din of breaking glass whilst an odd smell of ether stings his nostrils. (*G*, 121–22; *Gé*, 177–78)

This kind of "jeux colorés" (*Gé*, 62; *G*, 42), the play of colored triangles and polygons, pervades the book (*Gé*, 37, 40, 42–44, 55–56, 177; *G*, 25, 27, 29, 37, 121–22); so does that of the sound of shattered glass (see in particular *Gé*, 177; *G*, 121–22). For an earlier treatment of the same episode see *FR*, 120–22; *RF*, 149–51.

27. Here is a description of the same phenomenon in *Histoire:* "quand le monde visible se sépare en quelque sorte de vous perdant ce visage familier et rassurant qu'il a (parce qu'en réalité on ne le regarde pas), prenant soudain un aspect inconnu vaguement effrayant, les objets cessant de s'identifier avec les symboles verbaux par quoi nous les possédons" (292). See also the Heidegger epigraph to the last part of *La Bataille de Pharsale* (*BP*, 129; *BPh*, 187); and Duffy, "Art as Defamiliarisation in the Theory and Practice of Claude Simon."

28. Cf. also *FR*, 97, 231; *RF*, 121, 296.

29. Both *La Bataille de Pharsale* and *La route des Flandres* emphasize the importance of geography in their very titles. The battlefield that the narrator of *La Bataille* is looking for in Thessaly turns out to have been the venue of several battles, none of which the inhabitants of the area can identify with any certainty. The road of Flanders is better known as the "Spanish Road." See Gould, *Claude Simon's Mythic Muse*, 42n. *Les Géorgiques* is equally concerned with the sites of what the novel presents, in analogy to the seasons, as a sort of cyclical destruction; cf. *G*, 74, 107; *Gé*, 136, 447; and *A*, 24; *Ac*, 39 (more on this below).

30. See *G*, 85; *Gé*, 124.

31. "They too wearing those cast-off rags the colour of bile, of mud, as if a kind of corruption were covering them, corroding them, attacking them even as they stood, first their clothes, then spreading insidiously like the very color of war, of earth, gradually taking possession, their faces ashen, their rags muddy, their eyes muddy too, with that filthy, vague tinge that already seemed to assimilate them to this clay, this mud, this dust from which they had sprung and to which, wandering, abject, dazed and sad, they returned a little more each day" (*FR*, 129; *RF*, 162). For Georges' later agony in the mud, in the "original matter (matrix)," see *FR*, 180–81; *RF*, 229–30; for the dead horse, in a state of decomposition, see *FR*, 23–26, 81, 179–80, 227; *RF*, 25–28, 99, 227–28, 290. Simon has spoken of the book as being the story of Georges' death in an interview with Hubert Juin, *Les lettres françaises*, Oct. 6–12, 1960 (quoted after Dällenbach's "Le tissu de la mémoire," afterword to *La route des Flandres* [*RF*, 310]).

32. See also *Gé*, 102, 352. A passage in *L'Acacia* describes the loss of "all logic and all coherence" and the parallel assertion of "forces habitually concealed by some artifice (or in sleep, by pure indolence on their part) and resuming their imprescriptible rights, animated by their formidable ferocity at once blind, neg-

ligent, and summary, obeying the irrefutable logic, that irrefutable coherence proper to the elements and to natural laws" (*A, 222; Ac, 294;* see also *A, 19; Ac, 33*).

33. Shortly after realizing the need to go underground so as to avoid persecution by the Stalinist branch of the Republican forces, "O." understands "that all problems, philosophical or other, were wiped out at a stroke, and even resolved, except one: running and hiding" (*G, 180; Gé, 266;* see also *G, 215, 231; Gé, 318–19, 343*). The mockery of bookish knowledge is also a major theme in *La route des Flandres* (see *FR, 29–32, 99; RF, 33–35, 123, 209–10*).

34. For the term *art brut* see Claude Simon's letter to Jean Dubuffet, Sept. 6, 1981, in Dubuffet and Simon, *Correspondance, 1970–1984,* 32.

35. Not surprisingly, Simon's "images" have been a major subject in the critical literature. It is impossible to do justice to the number of treatments—one could even say that, given their pervasiveness, all of Simon scholarship is, in one way or the other, about his images—but I would like to name the studies that have been crucial in shaping my own understanding of Simon's *univers imaginaire.* They are, in particular, Mougin, *L'effet d'image;* Nitsch, *Sprache und Gewalt bei Claude Simon;* and Duffy, *Reading between the Lines.* See also Ferrato-Combe, *Écrire en peintre;* and Britton, *Claude Simon.*

36. A gifted draftsman, Simon wanted to be a painter himself and went to art school when he was young. Although he abandoned the idea in favor of literature, he would occasionally try his hand in other media, producing, most notably, some collages and a very interesting volume of photography, *Photographies.* See also his *Album d'un amateur.* For Simon's relation to photography see Albers, *Photographische Momente bei Claude Simon;* and Ribaupierre, *Le roman généalogique,* esp. 47–125.

37. Simon, "Fiction Word by Word," 43–44. Another poetological image conjured against the idea of narrative progression, from beginning to end, is that of the Blind Orion's *errance* in the preface to *Orion Aveugle.*

38. Mitchell, *Iconology,* 10.

39. See Simon, "Roman et mémoire": "ma perception (et par conséquent ma mémoire) se trouvent encombrées d'une multitude de ces 'traductions codées' qui, depuis mon enfance, sont venues la gauchir: est-il besoin d'énumérer, en désordre, les souvenirs des écritures saintes, de tableaux représentant leurs épisodes, des textes latins ou autres, que l'on m'a fait apprendre par cœur au collège, la mythologie antique, des figures et des raisonnements mathématiques, des images cinématographiques, etc., etc." (191–92).

40. See, once more, the preface to *Orion Aveugle.*

41. Simon, *The World about Us,* 4. "La description (la composition) peut se continuer (ou être complétée) à peu près indéfiniment—merci beaucoup! selon la

minutie apportée à son exécution, l'entraînement des métaphores proposées, l'addition d'autres objets visibles dans leur entier ou fragmentés par l'usure, le temps, un choc (soit encore qu'ils n'apparaissent qu'en partie dans le cadre du tableau), sans compter les diverses hypothèses que peut susciter le spectacle" (*Leçon des choses,* 10–11). For a more systematic reflection on this dynamic see my "Métaphores et métamorphoses chez Claude Simon."

42. Mougin, *L'effet d'image,* passim. In addition Mougin, who is part of the research collective "Hubert de Phalèse," has furnished us with an invaluable research tool, namely an index of Simon's works that is accessible online (see www.cavi.univ-paris3.fr/phalese/csac.htm). Drawing on new information technologies, the same group of researchers has produced a comprehensive "code" of *La route de Flandres* (see Phalèse, *Le code de "La route de Flandres"*). Again, the combination of a statistical approach and microscopic readings on which the code is based is truly "eye-opening" with regard to the novel's images.

43. The German linguist and critic Harald Weinrich aptly speaks of "Bild-Spanne," elegantly spanning (!) both the tension and distance between the two terms; see the seminal article on the semantics of "audacious" metaphors, "Semantik kühner Metaphern."

44. See Mougin, *L'effet d'image,* 43–64. On the "nonaudacious" character of Simon's comparisons and their reliance on sensory resemblance see also Buuren, "L'essence des choses."

45. Deguy, "Claude Simon and Representation," 67. Rossum-Guyon, in "La mise en spectacle chez Claude Simon," states, "Le recours à la Mimésis II a chaque fois pour effet de renforcer Mimésis I suivant le principe que l'Art est plus vrai que la vie" (90). She defines "Mimésis I" as "représentation directe de la réalité: la formule 'Je croyais voir' fonctionnant . . . comme une hypotypose motivant, sur le plan de la vraisemblance, l'introduction d'une description élaborée de telle manière que le lecteur a l'impression de se trouver 'devant la chose même'" and "Mimésis II" as "imitation de l'art" (89).

46. Cf. *FR,* 104; *RF,* 129.

47. See Ferrato-Combe, *Écrire en peintre,* 117–29.

48. *Iliad* 6.394–496. Cf. *A,* 163–64; *Ac,* 217–18. See also Mougin, *Lecture de "L'Acacia" de Claude Simon,* 45.

49. See, e.g., the "Waterloo" episode in *Les Misérables:* "Il y a des moments dans les batailles où l'âme durcit l'homme jusqu'à changer le soldat en statue, et où toute cette chair se fait granit" (Hugo, *Les Misérables,* 438).

50. The episode reappears in both *Les Géorgiques* (*G,* 65–68; *Gé,* 93–98) and *L'Acacia* (*A,* 177–82; *Ac,* 237–43).

51. See *G,* 121–22; *Gé,* 177–78 (quoted at note 26 above).

52. See the special issue of *Critique,* no. 414, "La terre et la guerre dans l'œuvre

de Claude Simon" (Nov. 1981); Dällenbach, *Claude Simon*, esp. 135–39; and Schreckenberg, *Im Acker der Geschichten.*

53. On models of history as eternal recurrence (in Marx, Nietzsche, Blanqui, Benjamin, Klossowski, and Simon) see Hamel, "La poétique d'Orphée."

54. On the *comme si* see Apeldoorn, "Comme si . . . figure d'écriture." Apeldoorn sees in the *comme si* "une certaine fascination pour une causalité primitive, de l'ordre mécanique ou de l'ordre de puissances maléfiques" (21) and concludes: "C'est grâce à elle [la digression du 'comme si'], pourrait-on dire, que l'auteur est libéré du poids de raconter et se voue à l'exploitation de ce qui le préoccupe fondamentalement: il nous livre ses pulsions archétypales" (32). See also Gleize, "Comme si c'était une fiction"; and Mougin, *L'effet d'image*, 113–44.

55. See, e.g., Jongeneel, "Movement into Space"; Rousset, "La guerre en peinture"; and Duffy, *Reading between the Lines*, 82–98. The paintings described are Piero della Francesca, *Battle between Heraclius and Chosroes*, c. 1466; Paolo Uccello, *Battle of San Romano*, c. 1435–55; Pieter Brueghel the Elder, *Battle against the Philistines on the Gilboa*, 1562; and Nicolas Poussin, *Joshua's Victory over the Amorites*, 1625.

56. For an image of this strange amalgamation see above (p. 74).

57. See Kaempfer, *Poétique du récit de guerre*, 24–35. Kaempfer's book is a study of *La Bataille de Pharsale* in relation to other war narratives, ancient (Caesar, Lucan) and modern (Napoleon, Tolstoy, Céline, Cendrars, et al.). Kaempfer links the gruesome image of the spear (sword or arrow) hitting the soldier in the face with the *punctum* of the sniper's bullet striking Reixach, as he is drawing his saber, a gesture as heroic as it is absurd. The notion of *punctum* was introduced by Roland Barthes in his book on photography, *Camera Lucida.*

58. The first part of *La Bataille de Pharsale*, "Achilles Running Motionless," begins with the description of a bird's shadow passing over someone's face: "Yellow and then black in a wink of an eye then yellow again" (*BP*, 3; *BPh*, 9). As so often in Claude Simon, it sounds a number of motifs, all of which will resurface time and again in the novel. (Chief among them is the image of the arrow hitting the soldier straight in the face.) On the importance of Poussin see Duffy, *Reading between the Lines*, 197–247. One of the novelist's most sustained elaborations of his poetics of errance and quest, blindness and sacrifice is inspired by, or rather developed apropos of, Poussin's painting *Blind Orion Searching for the Rising Sun* (1658); see Simon, *Orion Aveugle*; see also Nitsch, *Sprache und Gewalt bei Claude Simon*, 1–33.

59. Apart from the authors of Roman antiquity already mentioned, Proust is a central reference throughout *La Bataille de Pharsale*, in particular his reflections on jealousy, which is at the center of the other type of "battle" the protago-

nist is engaged in. The Proust epigraph to the book's second part, "Lexicon," highlights the desire "to see": "Je fixais avec attention devant mon esprit quelque image qui m'avait forcé à la regarder, un nuage, un triangle, un clocher, une fleur, un caillou, en sentant qu'il y avait peut-être sous ces signes quelque chose de tout autre que je devais tâcher de découvrir"; "I considered closely some image which had compelled my attention, a cloud, a triangle, a steeple, a flower, a pebble, feeling that perhaps beneath these signs there was something else I must try to discover" (*BPh*, 99; *BP*, 67). On the relation to Proust in *La Bataille de Pharsale* see Rossum-Guyon, "De Claude Simon à Proust"; on intertextuality more generally see Orr, *Claude Simon*.

60. *BP*, 127; *BPh*, 186; see also note 21 above.

61. See the fine commentary on *La route des Flandres* in the recent Pléiade edition of Simon's works (Simon, *Œuvres*, 1274–1313, esp. 1293).

62. See Duffy, *Reading between the Lines*, 59–141.

63. "I was lying dead at the bottom of the ditch devoured by the ants my whole body slowly turning by a thousand tiny mutations into lifeless substance . . . nourishing the earth" (*FR*, 191; *RF*, 244); see also *FR*, 179–81; *RF*, 228–30, where Georges is comparing his own "slow transmutation" to that of the dead horse, which he sees again as he is cowering in the ditch, hiding from a German sentry.

64. See *FR*, 69, 120, 159, 212; *RF*, 83, 150–51, 202, 232.

65. On the last pages of *Le jardin des plantes*, Claude Simon's penultimate novel, the author has recapitulated the fateful episode once more, capturing the scene as a kind of still, but this time from the sniper's perspective: "Seen through the telescopic lens of the rifle (machine gun?), the four cavalrymen approaching along the road, at a walk. Two thin black lines meet perpendicularly at the center, their intersection moves slowly from left to right and right to left over the group of cavalrymen. A sudden glint of sunlight on the stripes of one of the riders' sleeves. . . . The group of cavalrymen is now very near. The intersection of the horizontal and vertical lines in the gun sight comes to rest on the chest of the leftmost officer. (Sound: the clattering of the hooves coming nearer, slight chirping of birds)" (Simon, *The jardin des plantes*, 285; cf. Simon, *Le jardin des plantes*, 374; see also 231).

Chapter Three: The Resistance to Pathos and the Pathos of Resistance

An earlier version of this chapter appeared as "The Resistance to Pathos and the Pathos of Resistance: Peter Weiss," in *Germanic Review* 83, no. 3 (summer 2008): 241–66. I would like to thank the publisher for permission to reprint it here.

1. Weiss, *Marat/Sade*, 109–10; *Die Verfolgung und Ermordung Jean Paul Marats dargestellt durch die Schauspielgruppe des Hospizes zu Charenton unter*

Anleitung des Herrn de Sade, 132. The play was translated into English by Geoffrey Skelton, Robert Cohen, and Daniel Theisen.

2. The critical literature on David's masterpiece from 1793 is abundant. The following observations are indebted to Träger, *Der Tod des Marat,* 63–70; Johnson, *Jacques-Louis David,* 95–120; Pankow, *Brieflichkeit,* 17–80; and Starobinski, *1789.*

3. "Die Zahl der Hinrichtungen, die er [Marat] von Zeit zu Zeit zur Rettung des Vaterlandes forderte schwankte. Bereits 1790 empfahl er die Errichtung von 860 Galgen. Am 27. Mai 1791 schrieb der 'Ami du peuple,' vor elf Monaten hätten noch 500 Köpfe genügt, heute seien 50.000 nötig und bis zum Jahresende würden vielleicht 500.000 rollen. Am 24. Oktober wurde er von Charles-Jean-Marie Barbaroux im Nationalkonvent beschuldigt, 200.000 Köpfe gefordert zu haben. Im Rathaus von Paris rief Marat aus, was er dann auch drucken ließ: 'Gebt mir 300.000 Köpfe, und ich antworte, daß das Vaterland gerettet sein wird. . . Laßt uns damit beginnen, die Bäcker, Kolonialwarenhändler, alle Kaufleute in ihren Ladentüren aufzuhängen.' In seinen letzten Lebenstagen sollen sich seine Forderungen auf 273.000 Köpfen eingependelt haben" (Träger, *Der Tod des Marat,* 144–45). The motif of the writing hand also brings to mind representations of the disembodied hand of God but also an engraving that depicts a hand without a body signing the death sentence of Louis XVI (see Johnson, *Jacques-Louis David,* 106–8).

4. Apparently, the smile Corday had on her face as she mounted the scaffold persisted even after her decapitation, a fact that left spectators indignant. If this is true, then the allusive smile on Marat's face would be his answer to his killer's unrepentant attitude even in death. For an illustration of Corday's smile see Pankow, *Brieflichkeit,* 70.

5. See Sontag, "Marat/Sade/Artaud."

6. Rector, "Die Verfolgung und Ermordung Jean-Paul Marats," 64.

7. Weiss, *Marat/Sade,* 58, 51.

8. Ibid., 57, 100–101.

9. See Weiss, *Vanishing Point,* 195; *Fluchtpunkt,* 211.

10. *Vanishing Point,* 196; *Fluchtpunkt,* 212 ("Dein Schmerz ist eitel; Du bist die Erschütterung, die Dich überkommt, nicht wert").

11. See Lessing, *Laocoön,* 16; *Laokoon,* 28.

12. See Rector, "Laokoon oder der vergebliche Kampf gegen die Bilder"; and Müller-Richter, "Bilderwelten und Wortwelten."

13. Weiss, "Laokoon oder Über die Grenzen der Sprache," 192.

14. "'Laokoon oder über die Grenzen der Sprache' argues for language against the image, yet at the same time it produces a set of images that will remain both defining and definitive" (Hell, "From Laokoon to Ge," 26).

15. Weiss, *The Investigation,* 118; *Die Ermittlung,* 9 ("Bei der Aufführung

dieses Dramas soll nicht der Versuch unternommen werden, den Gerichtshof, vor dem die Verhandlungen über das Lager geführt wurden, zu rekonstruieren. Eine solche Rekonstruktion erscheint dem Schreiber des Dramas ebenso unmöglich, wie es die Darstellung des Lagers auf der Bühne wäre"). In parenthetical citations in the text proper, I will distinguish between the English and German titles by using the following abbreviations: *I (The Investigation)*; *E (Die Ermittlung)*.

16. See, e.g., Kempen, *Die Rede vor Gericht,* 177–248.

17. See Young, *Writing and Rewriting the Holocaust,* 69–79.

18. See Krause, *Faschismus als Theorie und Erfahrung,* 356–439; and Weiß, *Auschwitz in der geteilten Welt.*

19. Weiss, "Meine Ortschaft," 114 ("Es ist eine Ortschaft, für die ich bestimmt war und der ich entkam").

20. "Ich hatte es gesehen, als ich davon hörte und davon las. Jetzt sehe ich es nicht mehr" ("Meine Ortschaft," 118).

21. Even some of the most skeptical critics of the novel singled out this episode as a remarkable achievement. Ferenc Fehér, for example, writes that it is "beyond any doubt one of the greatest chapters of modern German prose" (Fehér, "The Swan Song of German Khrushchevism," 160).

22. Weiss, *Die Ästhetik des Widerstands,* 3:217 ("im starken Licht [sah man] jede Falte, jeden Riß, jede blutunterlaufene Beule in den Gesichtern, und die Abschürfungen, die tiefen runden Verbrennungsmale, die verschorften oder eiternden Wunden an den Oberkörpern"). Quotes from the first volume of *Die Ästhetik des Widerstands* are from Joachim Neugroschel's translation, *The Aesthetics of Resistance;* subsequent citations of each will be given in the text using the abbreviations *AW* and *AR* for the translation of the first volume respectively; all other translations from volumes 2 and 3 of *AW* are my own.

23. For a more detailed account of these references see Müller, *Haltlose Reflexion,* 168–69; and Wiethölter, "'Mnemosyne' oder 'Die Höllenfahrt der Erinnerung,'" 240–41.

24. See 3:214, which invokes, if only in passing, three famous representatives of that tradition: Tilman Riemenschneider, Veit Stoß, and Jörg Ratgeb.

25. Weiss's account is, in fact, based on Poelchau, *Die letzten Stunden.* The pastor's memoirs consist largely of brief characterizations of the people he accompanied during their last hours and of excerpts from their farewell letters. Weiss has integrated some of this material. His depiction of Poelchau's own thoughts and feelings is fictional though.

26. The name is probably no coincidence. There is also a figure named Schwarz in *The Investigation,* accompanied by an assistant named *Weiß.* And like their counterparts in the novel they are involved in "administering" death. See Weiss, *Die Ermittlung,* 154.

27. See, e.g., Lindner, "Anästhesie."

28. For a complete catalogue of all the artworks invoked in the novel see Badenberg, "Kommentiertes Verzeichnis der in der 'Ästhetik des Widerstands' erwähnten Künstler und Kunstwerke."

29. Succinctly put, the chorus of voices replaces the omniscient narrator; the collective cast of the novel replaces individual characters; discussion replaces plot; development and progress are replaced by structures of repetition. In the words of one commentator: "Die Grundbewegung des Romans ist . . . nicht die des Sukzessiven, sondern des Iterativen" (Rector, "Örtlichkeit und Phantasie," 113).

30. For a discussion of the novel's apparent polyphony see Fehér, "The Swan Song of German Khrushchevism"; and Butzer, "Erinnerung als Diskurs der Vergegenwärtigung in Peter Weiss' *Die Ästhetik des Widerstands.*"

31. One example among many, summing up a discussion about the representation of working class figures from Mantegna to Vermeer and Chardin: "Once the historically determined hierarchies, the proportions of a specific era were exposed, we were confronted with a permanent image of reality, and we could discern to what extent the artist had prepared the future development and what stance he had taken on the suppression carried from century to century" (*AR*, 73, cf. also 300). ["Waren die historisch bedingten Ordnungen, die Größenverhältnisse einer bestimmten Zeit einmal bloßgelegt worden, so trat uns ein dauerhaftes Wirklichkeitsbild entgegen, und es ließ sich ausmachen, in welchem Grad der Künstler die zukünftige Entwicklung vorbereitet und welche Haltung er gegenüber der von Jahrhundert zu Jahrhundert getragnen Unterdrückung eingenommen hatte" (*AW*, 1:86, cf. also 341).]

32. For a critical discussion of this issue see Koch, "Das angestrengte Beharren auf Gesinnungs-Kompromissen und die heimliche Hoffnung des Peter Weiss."

33. See Eitner, *Géricault*, 190; and Heinrich, *Floß der Medusa*, 16.

34. See Heinrich, *Floß der Medusa*, 16.

35. The fascination with Géricault is, above all, a fascination with the artist's attempt to reimagine the despair and the horrors on the raft. But in this reconstruction he goes too far and comes close to losing his sanity. According to some visitors of his studio, Géricault surrounded himself with body parts from the morgue so as better to render the complexion of the corpses.

36. "We looked back at a prehistoric past, and for an instant the prospect of the future likewise filled up with a massacre impenetrable to the thought of liberation" (*AR*, 9); "Wir blickten in eine Vorzeit zurück, und einen Augenblick lang füllte sich auch die Perspektive des Kommenden mit einem Massaker, das sich vom Gedanken an Befreiung nicht durchdringen ließ" (*AW*, 1:14).

37. See, e.g., *AR*, 71; *AW*, 1:83.

38. The belief in the unity of their efforts, though perhaps illusory, cannot do

"without the contempt for individual death, without the belief in a path taken by many and that included collective death" ["ohne die Verachtung des individuellen Tods, ohne den Glauben an einen Weg, der von vielen beschritten wird und zu dem eben auch der gemeinsame Tod gehört" (*AW*, 3:228)].

39. "War nicht die Geschichte der Menschheit eine Geschichte des Mordens, waren Menschen nicht seit jeher . . . zu Hunderttausenden, zu Millionen versklavt, abgeschlachtet worden."

40. See, e.g., *AR*, 281–90 (esp. 289–90); *AW*, 1:320–30 (esp. 329–30), which recapitulates the invasions and struggles around the city of Denia, from its beginnings as a Greek settlement called Hemeroskopeion, to the present of the narrative. For another example see *AW*, 3:47–48. There is a remarkable similarity between these telescopic flashbacks, cutting through the centuries, and the ekphrastic descriptions. Both achieve their primary effect of compression and a sense of urgency by means of enumeration and accumulation.

41. See AR, 253–76; AW, 1:288–314. The voice of dissent is that of one Marcauer, who is later arrested and, presumably, executed. The section ends with Marcauer's memories of the terrified gaze of the people facing the firing squad on Goya's *El tres de mayo*. The narrator expresses his regret over her disappearance but very explicitly refrains from further pursuing the issue.

42. "Trauer würde mich überkommen, wenn ich ihrer gedächte, Tag und Nacht würden sie mich begleiten, und bei jedem Schritt . . . würde ich mich fragen, woher sie die Kraft genommen hatten zu ihrem Mut und zu ihrer Ausdauer, und die einzige Erklärung würde nur diese bebende, zähe, kühne Hoffnung sein, wie es sie auch weiterhin in allen Kerkern gibt."

Chapter Four: Medeamachine

A part of this chapter has been published previously as "'Death to the Enemies of the Revolution!' Heiner Müller's *Versuchsreihe*," *Telos* 144 (fall 2008): 52–65. I would like to thank the publisher for permission to reprint it here.

1. Müller, *Explosion of a Memory*, 137 (translation modified). See "Das Bild eine Versuchsanordnung," in *Bildbeschreibung*, 16.

2. See Berndt, "*oder alles ist anders.*"

3. Webb, "*Ekphrasis* Ancient and Modern"; see also Graf, "Ekphrasis." I adopt the term *presence-effects* from Gumbrecht, *The Production of Presence*.

4. See Müller, *Krieg ohne Schlacht*, 342–43.

5. "Der wesentliche Effekt, den Müller erzielt, besteht in der völligen Kontingenz des Textes" (Berndt, "*oder alles ist anders*," 301). The author himself has stressed the arbitrary character of the action in an endnote to his text: "Die Handlung ist beliebig" (see Müller, *Bildbeschreibung*, 14). In the words of Manfred

Schneider: the text is "infected" with contingency (Schneider, "Im Namen des Bildes").

6. Müller, *Explosion of a Memory*, 137–38.

7. Ibid., 138.

8. See Bonnaud, "The Invasion of the Body Snatchers." For more on the connection to *The Birds* see Vogl, "Gefieder, Gewölk."

9. See Benjamin, "On the Concept of History," 392; see also Hell, "Remnants of Totalitarianism," esp. 6–8.

10. Müller, "Luckless Angel"; see also Müller, "Der glücklose Engel."

11. See Primavesi, "Heiner Müllers Theater der Grausamkeit."

12. "Töten, mit Demut, das ist der theologische Glutkern des Terrorismus" (Müller, *Krieg ohne Schlacht*, 316). (To kill, with humility, that is the theological fervor at the core of terrorism.)

13. See Matt, *Verkommene Söhne, mißratene Töchter*, 96–100.

14. This view was first presented in one of the earliest articles on the play by the Brecht expert Werner Mittenzwei, "Eine alte Fabel, neu erzählt." See also the discussion published in *Sinn und Form* in 1966 between Mittenzwei, Müller, and Wilhelm Girnus, "Gespräch mit Heiner Müller," 143–46.

15. See Kraus, "Heiner Müller und die griechische Tragödie"; see also Huller, *Griechisches Theater in Deutschland*, 46–102, esp. 71–79.

16. *The Horatian*, 108. Cf. *Der Horatier:*

Und der Horatier, im Arm noch den Schwertschwung
Mit dem er getötet hatte den Kuriatier
Um den seine Schwester weinte jetzt
Stieß das Schwert, auf dem das Blut des Beweinten
Noch nicht getrocknet war
In die Brust der Weinenden
Daß das Blut auf die Erde fiel. Er sagte:
Geh zu ihm, den Du mehr liebst als Rom. (46)

17. The episode is in book 2, part 5, chapter 20; see Sholokhov, *And Quiet Flows the Don*, 567–71.

18. In a commemorative article the public persona Heiner Müller was remembered as "ein Panzer aus Pointen, Zynismus und Zitaten" (Peter Laudenbach, "Heiner Müller privat," *Der Tagesspiegel* [Berlin], July 10, 2005). See also the three volumes of interviews published as *Gesammelte Irrtümer*.

19. Lessing, *Laocoön*, 24; cf. Lessing, *Laokoon*, 36. For the remark on pity as the sole aim of the tragic stage see Lessing, *Laocoön*, 29; *Laokoon*, 45.

20. Lessing, *Laocoön*, 126 (Lessing is, in fact, quoting his friend Moses

Mendelssohn here). "Die Empfindungen des Ekels sind also allezeit Natur, niemals Nachahmung" (*Laokoon,* 169). See also Menninghaus, *Disgust,* esp. chaps. 1 and 2; and Wellbery, "Das Gesetz der Schönheit."

21. Lessing, *Laocoön,* 28–29; *Laokoon,* 44.

22. See Schneider, "Kunst in der Postnarkose."

23. "Spuck aus Dein Mitgefühl, es schmeckt nach Blut / kein Platz für die Tugend hier und keine Zeit jetzt"; cf. also, "Nur blind für seine Wunde heilst du die / Nur taub für seinen Jammer stillst du den" (Müller, *Philoktet,* 14).

24. "Weil er nicht lügen will, muß er töten" (Müller, *Geschichten aus der Produktion,* 145).

25. See Emmerich, "Der vernünftige, der schreckliche Mythos"; see also Horkheimer and Adorno, *Dialectic of Enlightenment,* 35–62.

26. Müller, "Brief an den Regisseur der bulgarischen Erstaufführung von Philoktet." For other prominent statements on the play see especially Müller, *Rotwelsch* and Müller, *Krieg ohne Schlacht.*

27. Müller, "Brief an den Regisseur der bulgarischen Erstaufführung von Philoktet," 107.

28. Christoph Menke has spelled out the implications of Müller's passing references to Hegel. He argues that Philoctetes and Odysseus represent two modes of reflexivity (as opposed to Neoptolemos's putative wholeness and "plasticity") that, instead of overcoming the tragic conflict, exacerbate the clash between the political claims of the city and the existential claims of the individual. See Menke, *Die Gegenwart der Tragödie,* 203–14; *Tragic Play,* 167–78.

29. "In diesem Handel bist du nicht der erste / Der was er nicht will tut" (Müller, *Philoktet,* 13).

30. Odysseus is, says Müller, "eine Figur der Grenzüberschreitung" ("Brief an den Regisseur der bulgarischen Erstaufführung von Philoktet," 104).

31. "Macher und Liquidator der Tragödie" (ibid.).

32. "Odysseus der Pragmatiker das Werkzeug" (ibid., 105).

33. "Das Stück ist natürlich nur spielbar, wenn dem Publikum verwehrt wird, sich in den Philoktet einzufühlen, spätestens von dem Punkt an, wo sein Griechenhaß in einen Haß auf die ganze Menschheit umschlägt, weil er keine Alternative sieht" (Müller, *Geschichten aus der Produktion,* 145).

34. *Der Horatier,* 47; *The Horatian,* 110 ("between laurel and ax").

35. For more on the relation to the play's "intertexts" see Klaus-Detlef Müller, "Nämlich die Worte müssen rein bleiben." On Corneille's *Horace* see Fumaroli, "La tragédie de la cité terrestre dans *Horace.*" On the relation between *The Horatian* and Brecht's learning play see Silberman, "Heiner Müllers Fortschreibung der Brechtschen Dialektik."

36. See, e.g.:

And the laurel bearer said:
His merit cancels his guilt
And the sword bearer said:
His guilt cancels his merit
And the laurel bearer asked:
Shall the conqueror be executed?
And the sword bearer asked:
Shall the murderer be honored? (Müller, *The Horatian*, 111)
[Und der Lorbeerträger sagte:
Sein Verdienst löscht seine Schuld
Und der Beilträger sagte:
Seine Schuld löscht sein Verdienst
Und der Lorbeerträger fragte:
Soll der Sieger gerichtet werden?
Und der Beilträger fragte:
Soll der Mörder geehrt werden? (*Der Horatier*, 49)]

37. *The Horatian*, 114; *Der Horatier*, 53.

38. *The Horatian*, 114 ("Tödlich dem Menschen ist das Unkenntliche" [*Der Horatier*, 53]).

39. *The Horatian*, 114 ("Nämlich die Worte müssen rein bleiben" [*Der Horatier*, 53]).

40. *The Horatian*, 114 ("nicht verbergend den Rest / Der nicht aufging im unaufhaltbaren Wandel" [*Der Horatier*, 53]).

41. Müller, *Mauser*, 57; ("We said: It's work like any other work" /... / "And it was work unlike any other work" [*Mauser*, in *The Battle*, passim]).

42. *Mauser*, in *The Battle*, 129, 130.

43. Müller, *The Battle*, 134 ("Die Stadt Witebsk steht für alle Orte, an denen eine Revolution gezwungen war ist sein wird, ihre Feinde zu töten" [*Mauser*, 69]).

44. *Mauser*, in *The Battle*, 134 ("Wer bist du andrer als wir" [*Mauser*, 62]).

45. *Mauser*, in *The Battle*, 125 ("Die Revolution selbst / Ist nicht eins mit sich selber" [*Mauser*, 59]).

46. *Mauser*, in *The Battle*, 128 ("Vor meinem Revolver ein Mensch" [*Mauser*, 62]).

47. *Mauser*, in *The Battle*, 133 ("DAMIT ETWAS KOMMT MUSS ETWAS GEHEN DIE ERSTE GESTALT DER HOFFNUNG IST DIE FURCHT DIE ERSTE GESTALT DES NEUEN IST DER SCHRECKEN" [*Mauser*, 68–69 (capitalized in the original)]).

48. *Mauser*, in *The Battle*, 121.

[Wissend, das tägliche Brot der Revolution
Ist der Tod ihrer Feinde, wissend, das Gras noch
Müssen wir ausreißen, damit es grün bleibt. (*Mauser*, 55)]

49. *Mauser*, in *The Battle*, 129; cf. *Mauser*, 64.

50. Domdey, *Produktivkraft Tod*, 298–302.

51. See Müller, "Brief an den Regisseur der bulgarischen Erstaufführung von Philoktet," 105. Müller uses the expression in a commentary on Odysseus, the least likely of the three protagonists (or rather antagonists) of *Philoktet* to elicit our sympathies, let alone our admiration, but the one who is supposed to announce a new kind of political subject.

52. "Die christliche Endzeit der *Maßnahme* ist abgelaufen" (*Mauser*, 85).

53. Müller, *Waterfront Wasteland Medea Material Landscape with Argonauts*, 50. Cf. *Verkommenes Ufer Medeamaterial Landschaft mit Argonauten*:

Mein Eigentum die Bilder der Erschlagnen
Die Schreie der Geschundnen mein Besitz
Seit ich aus Kolchis auszog meiner Heimat
Auf Deiner Blutspur Blut aus meinesgleichen. (94)

54. "Das Bild: der verwundete Mensch, der in der Zeitlupe seine Verbände sich abreißt, dem im Zeitraffer die Verbände wieder angelegt werden usw. ad infinitum" (Müller, *Wolokolamsker Chaussee*, 149).

55. Frank Hörnigk regards the image as "ein Bild des Krieges, ein Bild, das keine Begrenzung findet, solange die Wunde noch offen, noch nicht abgeheilt ist —oder immer wieder neu verbunden werden muß, um sie zu verstecken. Diese Wunde hat ihren Namen: er lautet Stalinismus. Gleichwohl geht der Text 'Wolokolamsker Chaussee' nicht in diesem Begriff auf. Er reicht weiter, wird aufgehoben in der Frage nach der Geschichte des Sozialismus generell in diesem Jahrhundert und den noch möglichen oder verlorenen Perspektiven" (Hörnigk, "Bilder des Krieges und der Gewalt," 67).

56. The titles themselves underscore the episodic and serial character of these works: *Hamletmachine* (1977), *Waterfront Wasteland Medea Material Landscape with Argonauts* (1982), *Life of Gundling Frederick of Prussia Lessing Sleep Dream Scream* (1976). On the notion of postdramatic theater see Lehmann, *Postdramatic Theater*.

57. See Müller, "Kopftheater," 108. Many critics have stressed the *imagistic* quality of the postdramatic works. Apropos of *Hamletmaschine* Uwe Wittstock speaks of cascades of images ["erdrückende Bild-Katarakte"] (see "Nachwort," in

Müller, *Der Auftrag und andere Revolutionsstücke*); Heinrich Vormweg has characterized the play as an orgy of images ["geradezu eine Bilderorgie"] (see Vormweg, "Sprache—die Heimat der Bilder," 21).

58. *Der Lohndrücker, Der Horatier,* and *Kentauren* in 1988; *Hamlet / Maschine* in 1990; *Mauser, Herakles 2, Quartett,* and *Der Findling* in 1991 (all at Deutsches Theater Berlin); *Duell Traktor Fatzer* in 1993 (at the Berliner Ensemble). For critical literature on some of the productions see especially Barnett, *Literature versus Theatre;* as well as Keim, *Theatralität in den späten Dramen Heiner Müllers;* for documentation of some of Müller's work as a director of his own plays see Linzer and Ullrich, *Regie Heiner Müller.*

59. See Schulz, "Waste Land / Verkommenes Ufer."

60. Müller, *Verkommenes Ufer Medeamaterial Landschaft mit Argonauten,* 92 (capitalized in the original); English translation quoted from Müller, *Theatremachine,* 48.

61. *Tractor,* in Müller, *The Battle,* 61; for the poem see *ABC* in Müller, *Explosion of a Memory,* 57.

62. *Verkommenes Ufer Medeamaterial Landschaft mit Argonauten,* 92; *Waterfront Wasteland Medea Material Landscape with Argonauts,* 48.

63. Brecht, *The Measures Taken,* 34 (translation modified).

64. Žižek, *The Fragile Absolute,* 173n99. See also Schulz, "Medea"; and Domdey, *Produktivkraft Tod,* 305–6.

65. Domdey, *Produktivkraft Tod,* 305–6.

66. One of the best accounts of *Hamletmaschine* remains the chapter by Lehmann and Schulz in the first monograph on the playwright; see Schulz, *Heiner Müller.*

67. Müller, *Hamletmachine,* 91; *Hamletmaschine,* 93. The imagery of petrification, stasis, and paralysis, so typical of the later work, usually carries negative connotations. In one instance, though, it is suggested that the utopian promise needs to be buried in order to be saved, like a message in a bottle for future generations. See Lehmann, "Leben der Steine."

68. *Hamletmachine,* 91; *Hamletmaschine,* 93–94.

69. *Hamletmaschine,* 91–92 (translation slightly altered). Cf.:

Ich stehe im Schweißgeruch der Menge und werfe Steine auf Polizisten Soldaten Panzer Panzerglas. Ich blicke durch die Flügeltür aus Panzerglas auf die andrängende Menge und rieche meinen Angstschweiß. Ich schüttle, von Brechreiz gewürgt, meine Faust gegen mich, der hinter dem Panzerglas steht. Ich sehe, geschüttelt von Furcht und Verachtung, in der andrängenden Menge mich, Schaum vor meinem Mund, meine Faust gegen mich schütteln. . . . Ich bin der Soldat im Panzerturm, mein Kopf ist leer unter dem Helm, der erstickte Schrei unter den Ketten. . . . Ich knüpfe die Schlinge, wenn die Rädelsführer aufgehängt werden, ziehe den Schemel weg, breche mein Genick. Ich bin mein Gefangener. . . . Meine Rollen sind Speichel und Spucknapf Messer und Wunde Zahn und Gurgel Hals und Strick. . . . Blutend in der Menge. Aufatmend hinter der Flügeltür." (*Hamletmaschine*, 94–95)

70. "Mein Ekel / Ist ein Privileg" (*Hamletmaschine*, 96). It is in his caricatures of Western consumer culture that the author's cultural conservatism is most evident.

71. *Hamletmachine*, 89; *Hamletmaschine*, 91.

72. *Hamletmachine*, 94; *Hamletmaschine*, 97 ("Es lebe der Haß, die Verachtung, der Aufstand, der Tod"). The slogan recalls that of the Falange—"¡Viva la muerte!" (Long live death!)—but also the more recent appropriations of the same idea by Islamic suicide terrorists: "You love life; we love death!" Heiner Müller's flirtation with terrorism doesn't exactly come as a surprise: "Töten, mit Demut, das ist der theologische Glutkern des Terrorismus" (*Krieg ohne Schlacht*, 316). See note 12 above.

73. "Die Instanz, auf die hin Handlung in Gang gesetzt, das Opfer gebracht, die Argumentation ausgerichtet wird, bleibt leer. Sie heißt 'Krieg' und ist der abwesende, als fraglose *condition* gesetzte Ausgangs- und Endpunkt der Fabel" (Schulz, "Gelächter aus toten Bäuchen," 765).

74. Hölderlin, *Poems and Fragments*, 586–87 (translation modified). Cf.:

Und vieles
Wie auf den Schultern eine
Last von Scheitern ist
Zu behalten. (Hölderlin, "Mnemosyne," 199)

See also Müller, *Rotwelsch*, 88.

75. In recent years Slavoj Žižek has advocated a similar form of violence, one that consists above all in undoing the ties that bind us to the symbolic order. The paradigmatic example of this is not so much Antigone as Medea (see Žižek, "Afterword," 223).

76. Müller, *Explosion of a Memory*, 132; *Bildbeschreibung*, 14.

Epilogue

1. The "idiocy" of the real is the dimension elaborated by Clément Rosset, whose many books on this issue seem to have had virtually no impact on the psychoanalytic accounts of the real. At the same time, Rosset himself does not seem particularly interested in the alternatives to his engagement with the subject. See Rosset, *Le réel*; and Rosset, *L'école de réel*.

2. In a conversation with Peter Hallward, Badiou characterized the real "as being, in a situation, in any given symbolic field, the point of impasse, or the point of impossibility, which precisely allows us to think the situation as a whole, according to its real" (Badiou, "Politics and Philosophy," 121). He adds that "emancipatory politics always consists in making seem possible precisely that which, from within the situation, is declared to be impossible."

3. Even though this is not spelled out in *The Century*, in many respects the real must be regarded as another name for one of the central categories of Badiou's thought, that of the event, and in this regard it is hardly surprising that it is such an emphatic notion. Associated as it is with the ideas of urgency, suddenness, and violence, the real is mobilized as a kind of *antidote* against the culture of spectacle and superficiality that, in Badiou's eyes, marks our social and political present.

4. Sontag, *Regarding the Pain of Others*, 26; Barthes, *Camera Lucida*, passim.

5. See, e.g., Hammer, *Bacon and Sutherland;* and Fischer, *Vis-à-vis.*

6. Seipel, Steffen, and Vitali, *Francis Bacon und die Bildtradition.* Bacon has further emphasized the continuity between his works and the tradition by insisting that his paintings be framed in gold.

7. This material has now been catalogued and documented. See Cappock, *Francis Bacon's Studio;* Harrison and Daniels, *Francis Bacon;* and Harrison, *In camera, Francis Bacon.*

8. Other examples include *Second Version of "Painting 1946"* (1974) or the 1988 version of *Three Studies for Figures at the Base of a Crucifixion,* from 1944. Many of the triptychs can be regarded as reworkings of earlier attempts at the same themes. I am thinking in particular of the triptychs commemorating George Dyer and his squalid death (see *Triptych,* August 1972, as well as *Triptych,* May–June 1973).

9. "It's a magnificent armature on which you can hang all types of feeling and sensation" (Sylvester, *The Brutality of Fact,* 44). In a later passage he added that the crucifixion does not only interest him as a technical device but in terms of its "poignancy" (ibid., 83).

10. *Le mal du siècle* is invoked in Leiris, *Francis Bacon, Full Face and in Profile,* 19. For a very forceful argument against generalities of this sort, rather common in the critical literature, see Werckmeister, *Citadel Culture,* 70–93, esp. 86–91. (This criticism is leveled specifically against Wieland Schmied's *Francis Bacon: Commitment and Conflict.*) Werckmeister is also skeptical of the artist's own prioritizing of form over content, which downplays what he sees as the central obsession of Bacon's work: the suicides of his two companions, Peter Lacey (d. 1962) and George Dyer (1934–71). For another critical and, indeed, polemical assessment of Bacon see Berger, "Bacon and Disney."

11. Bacon's appeal to sensation is the basis for Gilles Deleuze's important study of the painter, *Francis Bacon: The Logic of Sensation*.

12. "When talking about the violence of paint, it's nothing to do with the violence of war. It's to do with an attempt to remake the violence of reality itself" (Sylvester, *The Brutality of Fact*, 81).

13. Ibid., 46.

14. Quoted in Russell, *Francis Bacon*, 162.

15. Sylvester, *The Brutality of Fact*, 56. On the portraits see also Kundera, "Le geste brutal du peintre."

16. Sylvester, *The Brutality of Fact*, 22.

17. Ibid., 179.

18. Deleuze, *Francis Bacon*, 15–16.

19. Sylvester, *The Brutality of Fact*, 146.

20. The paintings seem to feature affects without a subject, as one might put it in view of Deleuze's later writings on aesthetics. See, e.g., Deleuze and Guattari, *What Is Philosophy?* 164.

21. Sylvester, *The Brutality of Fact*, 83. See also, Deleuze, *Francis Bacon*, 52. On the ostensible amorality of Bacon's paintings see Menke, "Der ästhetische Blick," 230–46.

22. See Agamben, *Homo Sacer*.

23. The character on the painting is itself a bit bull-like, a bulk of a man, who has reminded some critics of twentieth-century dictators, in particular of Mussolini.

24. Sylvester, *The Brutality of Fact*, 83.

25. The magisterial study by Deleuze, undoubtedly the most sustained effort to think about Bacon's work along the lines suggested by the artist himself, stressing questions of formal organization, materiality, and the appeal to sensation, is a case in point. By Deleuze's account, the disturbing mutations effected by these paintings do not at all pertain to the order of human drama and the tragic, or the order, as he puts it, of the spectacle. In some sense, wanting to look at Bacon in terms of agency, purpose, or intentionality is starting in the wrong place. Rather than being concerned with questions of meaning, psychology, or what he calls the "figurative," Deleuze views the paintings as being invested in capturing invisible processes, forces, and rhythms, elements of a vitalistic ontology, which forms the underlying premise of his study but is not elaborated in the book itself. See Deleuze, *Francis Bacon*, 31–38 (on sensation), 48–54 (on forces), 60–70 (on rhythms), and passim. On the ontological underpinnings of Deleuze's aesthetics see Deleuze and Guattari, *What Is Philosophy?* 163–99.

BIBLIOGRAPHY

Agamben, Giorgio. *Homo Sacer: Sovereign Power and Bare Life.* Translated by Daniel Heller-Roazen. Stanford, CA: Stanford University Press, 1998.

Albers, Irene. *Photographische Momente bei Claude Simon.* Würzburg: Königshausen und Neumann, 2002.

Anderson, Mark. *Kafka's Clothes: Ornament and Aestheticism in the Habsburg Fin de Siècle.* Oxford: Oxford University Press, 1992.

Apeldoorn, Jo van. "Comme si . . . figure de l'écriture." In *Pratiques de la description,* 17–37. Amsterdam: Rodopi, 1982.

Arasse, Daniel. *The Guillotine and the Terror.* Translated by Christopher Miller. London: Lane, 1989. Originally published as *La guillotine et l'imaginaire de la Terreur* (Paris: Flammarion, 1987).

Auerbach, Erich. "Gloria passionis." In *Literatursprache und Publikum in der lateinischen Spätantike und im Mittelalter.* Bern: Francke, 1958. English translation in *Literary Language and Its Public in Late Latin Antiquity and in the Middle Ages,* translated by Ralph Manheim, 67–81. Princeton, NJ: Princeton University Press, 1993.

———. "Passio als Leidenschaft." *PMLA* 56, no. 4 (Dec. 1941): 1179–96. Reprinted in *Gesammelte Aufsätze zur romanischen Philologie,* 161–75. Bern: Francke, 1967.

Auffret, Dominique. *Kojève.* Paris: Grasset, 1990.

Badenberg, Nana. "Kommentiertes Verzeichnis der in der 'Ästhetik des Widerstands' erwähnten Künstler und Kunstwerke." In *Die Bilderwelt des Peter Weiss,* edited by Alexander Honold and Ulrich Schreiber, 163–230. Berlin: Argument, 1995.

Badiou, Alain. "Beyond Formalization. An Interview with Peter Hallward." *Angelaki* 8, no. 2 (Aug. 2003): 111–36.

———. *The Century.* Translated by Alberto Toscano. Cambridge, UK: Polity, 2007.

———. *Conditions.* Translated by Steven Corcoran. London: Continuum, 2008.

———. *Ethics: An Essay in the Understanding of Evil.* Translated by Peter Hallward. London: Verso, 2001.

————. "Politics and Philosophy: An Interview with Alain Badiou." In Badiou, *Ethics*, 95–144.

Barck, Karlheinz, Martin Fontius, et al., eds. *Ästhetische Grundbegriffe: Historisches Wörterbuch in sieben Bänden.* Vol. 4, *Medien-populär.* Stuttgart: Metzler, 2002.

Barnett, David. *Literature versus Theatre: Textual Problems and Theatrical Realization in the Later Plays of Heiner Müller.* Bern: Peter Lang, 1998.

Barthes, Roland. *Camera Lucida.* Translated by Richard Howard. New York: Hill and Wang, 1981.

————. "The Reality Effect." In *The Rustle of Language,* translated by Richard Howard, 141–48. New York: Hill and Wang, 1986.

Bataille, Georges. *The Accursed Share: An Essay on General Economy.* Vol. 1, *Consumption.* Translated by Robert Hurley. New York: Zone Books, 1991.

————. "Attraction and Repulsion II." In Hollier, *The College of Sociology (1937–39),* 113–24.

————. *Erotism.* Translated by Mary Dalwood. San Francisco: City Lights, 1986.

————. *Expérience intérieure.* Vol. 1 of *La somme athéologique.* Paris: Gallimard, 1954.

————. *Guilty.* Translated by Bruce Boone. San Francisco: Lapis Press, 1988. Originally published as *Le coupable.* Vol. 2 of *La somme athéologique.* Paris: Gallimard, 1961.

————. *Œuvres complètes.* Vol. 5. Paris: Gallimard, 1973.

————. *The Tears of Eros.* Translated by Peter Connor. San Francisco: City Lights, 1989.

————. *Theory of Religion.* Translated by Robert Hurley. New York: Zone Books, 1989.

Benjamin, Walter. "On the Concept of History." Translated by Harry Zohn. In *Selected Writings,* Vol. 4, *1938–1940,* 389–411. Cambridge, MA: Belknap, 2003.

Berger, John. "Bacon and Disney" (1972). In *Selected Essays,* edited by Geoff Dyer, 315–19. New York: Pantheon, 2001.

Berndt, Frauke. "*oder alles ist anders*—Zur Gattungstradition der Ekphrasis in Heiner Müllers *Bildbeschreibung.*" In *Behext von Bildern?* edited by Heinz Drügh and Maria Moog-Grünewald, 287–312. Heidelberg: Carl Winter Universitätsverlag, 2001.

Bohrer, Karl Heinz. "Pathos im Zivilisationsprozeß." In *Großer Stil,* 34–57. Munich: Hanser, 2007.

Bois, Yve-Alain, and Rosalind Kraus. *Formless: A User's Guide.* New York: Zone Books, 1997. Originally published as *L'informe: Mode d'emploi* (Paris: Editions Centre Pompidou, 1996).

Bonnaud, Irène. "The Invasion of the Body Snatchers." In Haß, *Heiner Müller, Bildbeschreibung,* 135–43.

Bourgon, Jérôme. "Agony by Proxy: Voices, Views, and Values about lingchi Execution." Nov. 2005. http://turandot.ish-lyon.cnrs.fr/Essay.php?ID=40.

———. "Chinese Executions: Visualising Their Differences with European Supplices." *European Journal of East Asian Studies* 2, no. 1 (2003): 154–84.

Brecht, Bertolt. *The Measures Taken.* Translated by Carl R. Mueller. In *"The Measures Taken" and Other Lehrstücke,* edited by John Willet and Ralph Manheim, 7–34. New York: Arcade, 2001.

Britton, Celia. *Claude Simon: Writing the Visible.* Cambridge, UK: Cambridge University Press, 1987.

Brook, Timothy, Jérôme Bourgon, and Gregory Blue. *Death by a Thousand Cuts.* Cambridge, MA: Harvard University Press, 2008.

Buch, Robert. "Métaphores et métamorphoses chez Claude Simon." In *Transports: Les métaphores de Claude Simon,* edited by Wolfram Nitsch and Irene Albers, 165–86. Frankfurt: Peter Lang, 2006.

Butzer, Günter. "Erinnerung als Diskurs der Vergegenwärtigung in Peter Weiss' *Die Ästhetik des Widerstands.*" In *Peter Weiss Jahrbuch* 2 (1993): 51–86.

Buuren, Maarten van. "L'essence des choses: Etude de la description dans l'œuvre de Claude Simon." *Poétique,* no. 11 (1980): 324–33.

Caillois, Roger. "Festival." In Hollier, *The College of Sociology (1937–39),* 279–303.

———. *Man and the Sacred.* Translated by Meyer Barash. Urbana: University of Illinois Press, 2001.

Campe, Rüdiger. "Affizieren und Selbstaffizieren: Rhetorisch-anthropologische Näherung ausgehend von Quintilian Institutio oratoria VI, 1–2." In *Rhetorische Anthropologie: Studien zum Homo rhetoricus,* edited by Josef Kopperschmidt, 135–52. Munich: Fink, 2000.

Cappock, Margarita. *Francis Bacon's Studio.* London: Merrell, 2005.

Connor, Peter Tracey. *Georges Bataille and the Mysticism of Sin.* Baltimore: Johns Hopkins University Press, 2000.

Corngold, Stanley. *Lambent Traces: Franz Kafka.* Princeton, NJ: Princeton University Press, 2006.

Cortázar, Julio. *Rayuela.* Buenos Aires: Editorial Sudamericana, 1963.

Dachselt, Rainer. *Pathos: Tradition und Aktualität einer vergessenen Kategorie der Poetik.* Heidelberg: Carl Winter, 2003.

Dällenbach, Lucien. *Claude Simon.* Paris: Seuil, 1988.

———. "La Question primordiale." In *Sur Claude Simon,* 65–93. Paris: Minuit, 1987.

Da Vinci, Leonardo. *Leonardo on Painting.* Edited by Martin Kemp. Translated by Martin Kemp and Margaret Walker. New Haven, CT: Yale University Press, 1989.

Deguy, Michel. "Claude Simon and Representation." 1962. In *Claude Simon,* edited by Celia Britton, 59–81. London: Longman, 1993.

Deleuze, Gilles. *Francis Bacon: The Logic of Sensation.* Translated by Daniel W. Smith. Minneapolis: University of Minnesota Press, 2003.

Deleuze, Gilles, and Félix Guattari. *What Is Philosophy?* Translated by Hugh Tomlinson and Graham Burchell. New York: Columbia University Press, 1994.

Didi-Huberman, Georges. *La ressemblance informe ou le gai savoir visuel selon Georges Bataille.* Paris: Macula, 1995.

Domdey, Horst. *Produktivkraft Tod: Das Drama Heiner Müllers.* Cologne: Böhlau, 1998.

Dubuffet, Jean, and Claude Simon. *Correspondance, 1970–1984.* Paris: L'Echoppe, 1994.

Duffy, Jean H. "Art as Defamiliarisation in the Theory and Practice of Claude Simon." *Romance Studies,* no. 2 (summer 1983): 108–23.

———. "Claude Simon, Merleau-Ponty and Perception." *French Studies* 46 (spring 1992): 33–55.

———. *Reading between the Lines: Claude Simon and the Visual Arts.* Liverpool: Liverpool University Press, 1998.

Dülmen, Richard van. *Theatre of Horror: Crime and Punishment in Early Modern Germany.* Translated by Elisabeth Neu. Oxford: Polity, 1990. Originally published as *Theater des Schreckens: Gerichtspraxis und Strafrituale in der frühen Neuzeit* (Munich: C. H. Beck, 1985).

Duncan, Alastair. "Simon and Sartre." *Review of Contemporary Fiction* 5 (1985): 90–95.

Edgerton, Samuel. *Pictures and Punishment.* Ithaca, NY: Cornell University Press, 1985.

Eitner, Lorenz. *Géricault: His Life and Work.* London: Orbis, 1983.

Elizondo, Salvador. *Farabeuf o la crónica de un instante.* México, DF: Joaquín Mortiz, 1965.

Elkins, James. *The Object Stares Back.* New York: Simon and Schuster, 1996.

———. "The Very Theory of Transgression: Bataille, *Lingchi,* and Surrealism." *Australian and New Zealand Journal of Art* 5, no. 2 (2004): 5–19.

Emmerich, Wolfgang. "Der vernünftige, der schreckliche Mythos: Heiner Müllers Umgang mit der griechischen Mythologie." In *Heiner Müller Material,* edited by Frank Hörnigk, 138–56. Leipzig: Reclam, 1989.

Enders, Jody. *The Medieval Theater of Cruelty.* Ithaca, NY: Cornell University Press, 1999.

Evans, Dylan. *An Introductory Dictionary of Lacanian Psychoanalysis.* New York: Routledge, 1996.

Fehér, Ferenc. "The Swan Song of German Khrushchevism—with a Historic Lag: Peter Weiss's *Die Ästhetik des Widerstands.*" *New German Critique,* no. 30 (fall 1983): 157–69.

Ferrato-Combe, Brigitte. *Écrire en peintre: Claude Simon et la peinture.* Grenoble: ELLUG, 1998.

Fischer, Peter, ed. *Vis-à-vis: Bacon & Picasso.* Luzern: Kunstmuseum Luzern, 2007.

Foucault, Michel. *Discipline and Punish.* Translated by Alan Sheridan. New York: Pantheon, 1977. Originally published as *Surveiller et Punir* (Paris, Gallimard, 1975).

Fumaroli, Marc. "La tragédie de la cité terrestre dans *Horace.*" In *Diversité, c'est ma devise,* edited by Frank-Rutger Hausmann, Christoph Miething, und Margarete Zimmermann, 157–90. Paris: Papers on French Seventeenth Century Literature, 1994.

Gleize, Joëlle. "Comme si c'était une fiction: Sur un dispositif analogique dans *L'Acacia* de Claude Simon." *Michigan Romance Studies,* no. 13 (1993): 81–102.

Goebel, Rolf. *Constructing China: Kafka's Orientalist Discourse.* Columbia, SC: Camden House, 1997.

———. "Kafka and Postcolonial Critique: *Der Verschollene,* 'In der Strafkolonie,' 'Beim Bau der chinesischen Mauer.'" In Rolleston, *A Companion to the Works of Franz Kafka,* 187–212.

Gombrich, Ernst H. *Aby Warburg: An Intellectual Biography.* Chicago: University of Chicago Press, 1986.

Gould, Karen L. *Claude Simon's Mythic Muse.* Columbia, SC: French Literary Publications, 1979.

Gould, Thomas. *The Ancient Quarrel between Poetry and Philosophy.* Princeton, NJ: Princeton University Press, 1990.

Graf, Fritz. "Ekphrasis: Die Entstehung der Gattung in der Antike." In *Beschreibungskunst, Kunstbeschreibung: Ekphrasis von der Antike bis zur Gegenwart,* edited by Gottfried Boehm and Helmut Pfotenhauer, 143–55. Munich: Fink, 1995.

Gray, Richard T. "Disjunctive Signs: Semiotics, Aesthetics, and Failed Mediation in 'In der Strafkolonie.'" In Rolleston, *A Companion to the Works of Franz Kafka,* 213–45.

Gumbrecht, Hans Ulrich. *The Production of Presence.* Stanford, CA: Stanford University Press, 2004.

Hallward, Peter. *Badiou: A Subject to Truth.* Minneapolis: University of Minnesota Press, 2003.

Hamel, Jean-François. "La poétique d'Orphée: Les révolutions de la mémoire historique chez Claude Simon." In *Revenances de l'histoire: Répétition, narrativité, modernité,* 175–210. Paris: Minuit, 2006.

Hammer, Martin. *Bacon and Sutherland.* New Haven, CT: Yale University Press, 2005.

Harrison, Martin. *In camera, Francis Bacon: Photography, Film, and the Practice of Painting.* New York: Thames and Hudson, 2005.

Harrison, Martin, and Rebecca Daniels. *Francis Bacon: Incunabula.* London: Thames and Hudson, 2008.

Haß, Ulrike, ed. *Heiner Müller, Bildbeschreibung: Ende der Vorstellung.* Berlin: Theater der Zeit, 2005.

Heindl, Robert. *Der Berufsverbrecher.* Berlin: Pan-Verlag R. Heise, 1927.

———. *Meine Reise nach den Strafkolonien.* Berlin: Ullstein, 1913.

———. "Strafrechtstheorie und Praxis." In *Jahrbuch für Charakterologie,* Vol. 1, 89–152. Berlin: Pan-Verlag R. Heise, 1924.

Heinrich, Klaus. *Floß der Medusa.* Basel: Stroemfeld, 1995.

Hell, Julia. "From Laokoon to Ge: Resistance to Jewish Authorship in Peter Weiss's *Die Ästhetik des Widerstands.*" In *Rethinking Peter Weiss,* edited by Jost Hermand and Marc Silberman, 21–44. New York: Peter Lang, 2000.

———. "Remnants of Totalitarianism: Hannah Arendt, Heiner Müller, Slavoj Žižek, and the Re-Invention of Politics." *Telos* 136 (fall 2006): 1–28.

Hobsbawm, Eric. *The Age of Extremes.* New York: Pantheon, 1994.

Hölderlin, Friedrich. "Mnemosyne: Dritte Fassung." In *Werke,* edited by Pierre Bertaux, 199–200. Munich: Winkler, 1963.

———. *Poems and Fragments.* Translated by Michael Hamburger. London: Anvil Poetry Press, 2004.

Hollier, Denis, ed. *The College of Sociology (1937–39).* Minneapolis: University of Minnesota Press, 1988.

Hollywood, Amy. *Sensible Ecstasy: Mysticism, Sexual Difference, and the Demands of History.* Chicago: University of Chicago Press, 2002.

Honold, Alexander. "In der Strafkolonie." In *Kafka-Handbuch,* edited by Bettina von Jagow and Oliver Jahraus, 493–95. Göttingen: Vandenhoeck und Ruprecht, 2008.

Horkheimer, Max, and Theodor W. Adorno. *Dialectic of Enlightenment: Philosophical Fragments.* Edited by Gunzelin Schmid Noerr. Translated by Edmund Jephcott. Stanford, CA: Stanford University Press, 2002.

Hörnigk, Frank. "Bilder des Krieges und der Gewalt: Heiner Müller, 'Wolokolamsker Chaussee.'" In *DDR-Literatur '89 im Gespräch,* edited by Siegfried Rönisch, 67–75. Berlin: Aufbau-Verlag, 1990.

Howard, Richard. "Divination by Ashes: An Introduction to Claude Simon, 1995." In *Paper Trail*, 148–55. New York: Farrar, Strauss and Giroux, 2004.

Hsia, Adrian, ed. *Kafka and China*. New York: Peter Lang, 1996.

Hugo, Victor. *Les Misérables*. Paris: Gallimard/Folio, 1995.

Huller, Eva C. *Griechisches Theater in Deutschland: Mythos und Tragödie bei Heiner Müller und Botho Strauß*. Köln: Böhlau, 2007.

Johnson, Dorothy. *Jacques-Louis David: Art in Metamorphosis*. Princeton, NJ: Princeton University Press, 1993.

Jongeneel, Els. "Movement into Space: La belligérance de l'image dans *La Bataille de Pharsale* de Claude Simon." *Revue Romane* 26, no. 1 (1991): 78–99.

Kaempfer, Jean. *Poétique du récit de guerre*. Paris: José Corti, 1998.

Kafka, Franz. *Briefe an Milena*. Edited by Jürgen Born and Michael Müller. Frankfurt: Fischer, 1986.

———. *In der Strafkolonie*. In *Drucke zu Lebzeiten*. Edited by Wolf Kittler, Hans-Gerd Koch, und Gerhard Neumann, 201–48. Frankfurt: Fischer, 1994.

———. *In the Penal Colony*. Translated by Stanley Corngold. In *Selected Stories*. Edited by Stanley Corngold, 66–87. New York: Norton, 2007.

———. *The Penal Colony*. Translated by Willa and Edwin Muir. New York: Schocken, 1961.

Keim, Katharina. *Theatralität in den späten Dramen Heiner Müllers*. Tübingen: Niemeyer, 1998.

Kempen, Anke van. *Die Rede vor Gericht: Prozeß, Tribunal, Ermittlung: Forensische Rede und Sprachreflexion bei Heinrich von Kleist, Georg Büchner, Peter Weiss*. Freiburg: Rombach, 2005.

Kittler, Wolf. "In dubio pro reo: Kafkas 'Strafkolonie.'" In *Kafkas Institutionen*, edited by Arne Höcker and Oliver Simons, 35–72. Bielefeld: Transcript, 2007.

———. "Schreibmaschinen, Sprechmaschinen: Effekte technischer Medien im Werk Franz Kafkas." In *Franz Kafka, Schriftverkehr*, edited by Gerhard Neumann and Wolf Kittler, 75–163. Freiburg: Rombach, 1990.

Koch, Rainer. "Das angestrengte Beharren auf Gesinnungs-Kompromissen und die heimliche Hoffnung des Peter Weiss." *Peter Weiss Jahrbuch* 2 (1993): 87–117.

Kraus, Manfred. "Heiner Müller und die griechische Tragödie." *Poetica* 3/4 (1985): 299–339.

Krause, Rolf D. *Faschismus als Theorie und Erfahrung: "Die Ermittlung" und ihr Autor Peter Weiss*. Frankfurt: Lang, 1982.

Kremer, Detlef. *Kafka: Die Erotik des Schreibens*. Mainz: Philo, 1998.

Kundera, Milan. "Le geste brutal du peintre." In *Bacon: Portraits et autoportraits*, 7–18. Paris: Belles Lettres, 1996.

Lacan, Jacques. *Écrits*. Translated by Alan Sheridan. New York: Norton, 1977.

———. *The Ego in Freud's Theory and in the Technique of Psychoanalysis, 1954–1955*. Edited by Jacques-Alain Miller. Translated by Sylvana Tomaselli. New York: Norton, 1991.

———. *The Ethics of Psychoanalysis, 1959–1960*. Translated by Dennis Porter. New York: Norton, 1997. Originally published as *Le séminaire, livre VII: L'éthique de la psychanalyse, 1959–1960*. Paris: Seuil, 1986.

———. *The Four Fundamental Concepts of Psycho-Analysis*. Edited by Jacques-Alain Miller. Translated by Alan Sheridan. New York: Norton, 1988.

———. *On Feminine Sexuality: The Limits of Love and Knowledge, 1972–1973*. Translated by Bruce Fink. New York: Norton, 1998.

Largier, Niklaus. *In Praise of the Whip: A Cultural History of Arousal*. Translated by Graham Harman. New York: Zone Books, 2007.

Lehmann, Hans-Thies. "Leben der Steine: Kurze Phantasmagorie über Heiner Müllers Stein-Schriften." In Schulte and Mayer, *Der Text ist der Coyote*, 299–304.

———. *Postdramatic Theater*. Translated by Karen Jürs-Munby. London: Routledge, 2006.

Leiris, Michel. *Francis Bacon, Full Face and in Profile*. Translated by John Weightman. New York: Rizzoli, 1983.

Lessing, Gotthold Ephraim. *Laocoön: An Essay on the Limits of Poetry and Painting*. Translated by Edward Allen McCormick. Baltimore: Johns Hopkins University Press, 1984.

———. *Laokoon*. Edited by Wilfried Barner. Frankfurt: Deutscher Klassiker Verlag, 2007.

Lindner, Burkhardt. "Anästhesie: Die dantesche 'Ästhetik des Widerstands' und die 'Ermittlung.'" In *Ästhetik, Revolte, Widerstand: Zum literarischen Werk von Peter Weiss,* edited by Jürgen Garbers et al., 114–28. Jena: Universitätsverlag Jena, 1990.

Linzer, Martin, and Peter Ullrich, eds. *Regie Heiner Müller*. Berlin: Zentrum für Theaterdokumentation, 1993.

Livy. *History of Rome*. Vol. 1, Books 1–2. Translated by B. O. Foster. Loeb Classical Library 114. Cambridge, MA: Harvard University Press, 1961.

Lubrich, Oliver, ed. *Berichte aus der Abwurfzone: Ausländer erleben den Bombenkrieg in Deutschland, 1939 bis 1945*. Frankfurt: Eichborn, 2007.

Matt, Peter von. *Verkommene Söhne, mißratene Töchter*. Munich: Hanser, 1995.

Menke, Christoph. "Der ästhetische Blick: Affekt und Gewalt, Lust und Katharsis." In *Auge und Affekt,* edited by Gertrud Koch, 230–46. Frankfurt: Fischer, 1995.

———. *Die Gegenwart der Tragödie: Versuch über Urteil und Spiel*. Frankfurt: Suhrkamp, 2005. Translated by James Phillips as *Tragic Play: Irony and The-*

ater from Sophocles to Beckett (New York: Columbia University Press, 2009).

Menninghaus, Winfried. Disgust: Theory and History of a Strong Sensation. Translated by Howard Eiland and Joel Golb. Albany: State University of New York Press, 2003.

Merleau-Ponty, Maurice. "Five Notes on Claude Simon." 1961. In Claude Simon, edited by Celia Britton, 35–40. London: Longman, 1993.

Mitchell, W. J. T. Iconology: Image, Text, Ideology. Chicago: University of Chicago Press, 1986.

Mittenzwei, Werner. "Eine alte Fabel, neu erzählt." Sinn und Form 17, no. 6 (1965): 948–56.

Mittenzwei, Werner, Heiner Müller, and Wilhelm Girnus. "Gespräch mit Heiner Müller." 1966. In Geschichten aus der Produktion, vol. 1, 137–46. Berlin: Rotbuch, 1974.

Mladek, Klaus. "'Ein eigentümlicher Apparat': Kafkas 'In der Strafkolonie.'" In Franz Kafka, edited by H. L. Arnold, 115–42. Munich: Text + Kritik, 1994.

Mougin, Pascal. Lecture de "L'Acacia" de Claude Simon: L'imaginaire biographique. Paris: Lettres modernes, 1996.

———. L'effet d'image: Essai sur Claude Simon. Paris: L'Harmattan, 1997.

Müller, Heiner. "Brief an den Regisseur der bulgarischen Erstaufführung von Philoktet." In Herzstück, 102–10.

———. Der Auftrag und andere Revolutionsstücke. Edited by Uwe Wittstock. Stuttgart: Reclam, 1988.

———. "Der glücklose Engel." In Die Gedichte: Werke 1, 53. Frankfurt: Suhrkamp, 1998.

———. Explosion of a Memory. In Theatremachine, 137–38. Originally published as Bildbeschreibung. In Shakespeare Factory, Vol. 1, 7–14. Berlin: Rotbuch-Verlag, 1985.

———. Gesammelte Irrtümer. Frankfurt: Verlag der Autoren, 1986, 1990, 1994.

———. Geschichten aus der Produktion. Vol. 1. Berlin: Rotbuch-Verlag, 1974.

———. Hamletmachine. In Theatremachine, 85–94. Originally published as Hamletmaschine. In Mauser, 89–97 (Berlin: Rotbuch-Verlag, 1978).

———. Herzstück. Berlin: Rotbuch-Verlag, 1983.

———. The Horatian. In The Battle: Plays, Prose, Poems. Translated by Carl Weber, 103–16. New York: PAJ Publications, 1989. Originally published as Der Horatier. In Mauser, 45–54 (Berlin: Rotbuch-Verlag, 1978).

———. "Kopftheater." In Linzer and Ullrich, Regie Heiner Müller, 108.

———. Krieg ohne Schlacht. Cologne: Kiepenheuer and Witsch, 1992.

———. "Luckless Angel." Translated by Bernard and Caroline Schütze. In Germania, 99. New York: Semiotext/e, 1990.

———. *Mauser.* In *The Battle.* Translated by Carl Weber, 117–34. New York: PAJ Publications, 1989. Originally published as *Mauser,* 55–69 (Berlin: Rotbuch-Verlag, 1978).

———. *Philoktet.* In *Mauser,* 7–42. Berlin: Rotbuch-Verlag, 1978.

———. *Rotwelsch.* Berlin: Merve, 1982.

———. *Theatremachine.* Edited and translated by Marc von Henning. London: Faber and Faber, 1995.

———. *Verkommenes Ufer Medeamaterial Landschaft mit Argonauten.* In *Herzstück,* 91–101.

———. *Waterfront Wasteland Medea Material Landscape with Argonauts.* In *Theatremachine,* 45–57.

———. *Wolokolamsker Chaussee.* Frankfurt: Verlag der Autoren, 1988.

Müller, Karl-Josef. *Haltlose Reflexion: Über die Grenzen der Kunst in Peter Weiss' "Ästhetik des Widerstands."* Würzburg: Königshausen und Neumann, 1992.

Müller, Klaus-Detlef. "Nämlich die Worte müssen rein bleiben: 'Arbeit an der Differenz' in Heiner Müllers *Der Horatier.*" In *Auf klassischem Boden begeistert: Antike-Rezeption in der deutschen Literatur,* edited by Olaf Hildebrand and Thomas Pittroff, 467–82. Freiburg: Rombach, 2004.

Müller-Richter, Klaus. "Bilderwelten und Wortwelten: Gegensatz oder Komplement." In *Peter Weiss Jahrbuch* 6 (1997): 116–37.

Müller-Seidel, Walter. *Die Deportation des Menschen: Kafkas Erzählung "In der Strafkolonie" im europäischen Kontext.* Stuttgart: Metzler, 1986.

Neumeyer, Harald. "'Das Land der Paradoxa' (Robert Heindl): Franz Kafkas *In der Strafkolonie* und die Deportationsdebatte um 1900." In *Textverkehr: Franz Kafka und die Tradition,* edited by Claude Liebrand and Franziska Schlößler, 291–334. Würzburg: Königshausen und Neumann, 2004.

Nietzsche, Friedrich. *On the Genealogy of Morals.* Translated by Walter Kaufmann. New York: Vintage, 1989.

Nitsch, Wolfram. *Sprache und Gewalt bei Claude Simon.* Tübingen: Gunter Narr, 1992.

Öhlschläger, Claudia. *Beschädigtes Leben, erzählte Risse: W. G. Sebalds poetische Ordnung des Unglücks.* Freiburg: Rombach, 2006.

Orr, Mary. *Claude Simon: The Intertextual Dimension.* Glasgow: University of Glasgow French and German Publications, 1993.

Pan, David. "Kafka as a Populist: Re-reading 'In the Penal Colony.'" *Telos* 101 (fall 1994): 3–40.

Pankow, Edgar. *Brieflichkeit: Revolution eines Sprachbildes: Jacques-Louis David, Friedrich Hölderlin, Jean Paul, Edgar Allan Poe.* Munich: Fink, 2002.

Phalèse, Hubert de. *Le code de La Route de Flandres.* Paris: Nizet, 1997.

Poelchau, Harald. *Die letzten Stunden: Erinnerungen eines Gefängnispfarrers.* Berlin: Volk und Welt, 1949.

Port, Ulrich. "'Katharsis des Leidens': Aby Warburgs 'Pathosformeln' und ihre konzeptuellen Hintergründe in Rhetorik, Poetik, und Tragödientheorie." *Deutsche Vierteljahrsschrift für Literaturwissenschaft und Geistesgeschichte* 73 (1999): 5–42.

Prendergast, Christopher. *Napoleon and History Painting.* Oxford: Clarendon Press, 1997.

Presner, Todd. "'What a Synoptic and Artificial View Reveals': Extreme History and the Modernism of W. G. Sebald's Realism." *Criticism* 46, no. 3 (summer 2004): 341–60.

Primavesi, Patrick. "Heiner Müllers Theater der Grausamkeit." In Schulte and Mayer, *Der Text ist der Coyote,* 143–66.

Puppi, Lionello. *Torment in Art: Pain, Violence, and Martyrdom.* New York: Rizzoli, 1991. Originally published as *Le splendore dei supplizi* (Milan: Berenice, 1990).

Raulff, Ulrich. *Der unsichtbare Augenblick: Zeitkonzepte in der Geschichte.* Göttingen: Wallstein, 1999.

Rector, Martin. "Die Verfolgung und Ermordung Jean-Paul Marats." In *Peter Weiss' Dramen,* edited by Martin Rector and Christoph Weiß, 57–88. Opladen: Westdeutscher Verlag, 1999.

———. "Laokoon oder der vergebliche Kampf gegen die Bilder." In *Peter Weiss Jahrbuch* 1 (1992): 24–41.

———. "Örtlichkeit und Phantasie: Zur inneren Konstruktion der 'Ästhetik des Widerstands.'" In *Die Ästhetik des Widerstands,* edited by Alexander Stephan, 104–33. Frankfurt: Suhrkamp, 1983.

Ribaupierre, Claire de. *Le roman généalogique: Claude Simon et Georges Perec.* Brussels: La Part de l'Œil, 2002.

Rohde, Bertram. *Und blätterte ein wenig in der Bibel: Studien zu Kafkas Bibellektüren und ihren Auswirkungen auf sein Werk.* Würzburg: Könighausen und Neumann, 2002.

Rolleston, James, ed. *A Companion to the Works of Franz Kafka.* Rochester, NY: Camden House, 2002.

Rosset, Clément. *L'école de réel.* Paris: Minuit, 2008.

———. *Le réel: Traité de l'idiotie.* Paris: Minuit, 1977.

Rossum-Guyon, Françoise van. "De Claude Simon à Proust: Un exemple d'intertextualité." *Les lettres nouvelles* (Sept.–Oct. 1972): 107–37.

———. "La mise en spectacle chez Claude Simon." In *Claude Simon: Analyse, théorie,* edited by Jean Ricardou, 88–118. Paris: UGE, 1975.

Rousset, Jean. "La guerre en peinture." In *Passages, échanges et transpositions,* 165–75. Paris: José Corti, 1990.

Russell, John. *Francis Bacon.* Greenwich, CT: New York Graphic Society, 1971.

Santner, Eric. "Miracles Happen: Benjamin, Rosenzweig, Freud, and the Matter of the Neighbor." In Žižek, Santner, and Reinhard, *The Neighbor,* 76–133.

———. *On Creaturely Life: Rilke, Benjamin, Sebald.* Chicago: University of Chicago Press, 2006.

Schiller, Friedrich. *On the Pathetic.* Translated by Daniel O. Dahlstrom. In *Essays,* edited by Walter Hinderer and D. O. Dahlstrom, 45–69. New York: Continuum, 1993.

———. "Über das Pathetische." 1793. In *Theoretische Schriften,* edited by Rolf-Peter Janz, 423–51. Frankfurt: Deutscher Klassiker Verlag, 1992.

Schmied, Wieland. *Francis Bacon: Commitment and Conflict.* Translated by John Ormrod. Munich: Prestel, 1996.

Schneider, Manfred. "Im Namen des Bildes: Über den Grund des Sprechens." In Haß, *Heiner Müller, Bildbeschreibung,* 112–20.

———. "Kunst in der Postnarkose: Laokoon Philoktet Prometheus Marsyas Schrei." In Schulte and Mayer, *Der Text ist der Coyote,* 120–42.

Schreckenberg, Stefan. *Im Acker der Geschichten: Formen historischer Sinnstiftung in Claude Simons "Les Géorgiques."* Heidelberg: Carl Winter, 2003.

Schulte, Christoph, and Brigitte Maria Mayer, eds. *Der Text ist der Coyote: Heiner Müller Bestandsaufnahme.* Frankfurt: Suhrkamp, 2004.

Schulz, Genia. "Gelächter aus toten Bäuchen: Dekonstruktion und Rekonstruktion des Erhabenen bei Heiner Müller." *Merkur* 487–88, nos. 9/10 (Sept.–Oct. 1989): 764–77.

———. *Heiner Müller.* Stuttgart: Metzler, 1980.

———. "Medea: Zu einem Motiv im Werk Heiner Müllers." In *Weiblichkeit und Tod in der Literatur,* edited by Renate Berger and Inge Stephan, 241–64. Köln: Böhlau, 1987.

———. "Waste Land / Verkommenes Ufer." In *Explosion of a Memory, Heiner Müller DDR: Ein Arbeitsbuch,* edited by Wolfgang Storch, 103–4. Berlin: Edition Hentrich, 1988.

Sebald, W. G. *Austerlitz.* Translated by Anthea Bell. New York: Random House, 2001. Originally published as *Austerlitz* (Munich: Hanser, 2001).

———. *On the Natural History of Destruction.* Translated by Anthea Bell. New York: Random House, 2003. Originally published as *Literatur und Luftkrieg* (Munich: Hanser, 1999).

———. *The Rings of Saturn.* Translated by Michael Hulse. New York: New Directions, 1998. Originally published as *Die Ringe des Saturn* (Frankfurt: Eichborn, 1995).

————. *Vertigo*. Translated by Michael Hulse. London: Harvill Press, 2000.

Seipel, Wilfried, Barbara Steffen, Christoph Vitali, eds. *Francis Bacon und die Bildtradition*. Wien: Kunsthistorisches Museum, 2003.

Settis, Salvatore. "Pathos und Ethos: Morphologie und Funktion." In *Vorträge aus dem Warburg-Haus*. Vol. 1, 31–74. Berlin: Akademie Verlag, 1997.

Sholokhov, Mikhail. *And Quiet Flows the Don*. Translated by Robert Daglish. Revised and edited by Brian Murphy. New York: Carroll and Graf, 1996.

Silberman, Marc. "Heiner Müllers Fortschreibung der Brechtschen Dialektik." In Schulte and Mayer, *Der Text ist der Coyote*, 197–210.

Simon, Claude. *The Acacia*. Translated by Richard Howard. New York: Pantheon, 1991. Originally published as *L'Acacia* (Paris: Minuit, 1989).

————. *Album d'un amateur*. Remagen-Rolandseck: Rommerskirchen, 1988.

————. *The Battle of Pharsalus*. Translated by Richard Howard. New York: Braziller, 1971. Originally published as *La Bataille de Pharsale* (Paris: Minuit, 1969).

————. "The Crossing of the Image." Interview with Claud Duverlie. *Diacritics* (Dec. 1977): 47–58.

————. "Fiction Word by Word." Translated by Barbara Wright. *Review of Contemporary Fiction* 5, no. 1 (spring 1985): 24–46. Originally published as "La fiction mot à mot." *Nouveau Roman: Hier, aujourd'hui*. Vol. 2, edited by Jean Ricardou, 73–97 (Paris: Collection 10/18, 1972).

————. *The Flanders Road*. Translated by Richard Howard. London: John Calder, 1985. Originally published as *La route des Flandres* (1960; Paris: Minuit, 1985).

————. "Für wen schreibt denn Sartre?" *Kursbuch* 1 (1965): 126–33.

————. *The Georgics*. Translated by Beryl Fletcher and John Fletcher. London: John Calder, 1989. Originally published as *Les Géorgiques* (Paris: Minuit, 1981).

————. *Histoire*. Translated by Richard Howard. New York: G. Braziller 1968. Originally published as *Histoire* (Paris: Minuit, 1962).

————. *The Jardin des Plantes*. Translated by Jordan Stump. Evanston, IL: Northwestern University Press, 2001. Originally published as *Le Jardin des Plantes* (Paris: Minuit, 1997).

————. *Le palace*. Paris: Minuit, 1962.

————. "Nobel Lecture, December 9, 1985." In *Nobel Lectures: Literature, 1981–1990*, edited by Sture Allén and Tore Frängsmyr, 63–74. Singapore: World Scientific, n.d.

————. *Œuvres*. Edited by Alastair B. Duncan, with Jean H. Duffy. Paris: Gallimard, 2006.

————. *Orion Aveugle*. Geneva: Skira, 1970.

———. *Photographies.* Paris: Maeght, 1992.

———. "Réponses à quelque questions écrites de Ludovic Janvier." *Entretiens* 31 (1971): 15–29.

———. "Roman, Description et Action." *Studi di letteratura francese.* Vol. 8, *Il romanzo in discussioni,* 12–27. Firenze: L. S. Olschki, 1982.

———. "Roman et mémoire." *Revue des Sciences Humaines,* no. 220 (Oct.–Dec. 1990): 191–92.

———. *The World about Us.* Translated by Daniel Weissbort. Princeton, NJ: Ontario Review Press, 1983. Originally published as *Leçon des choses* (Paris: Minuit, 1975).

Sontag, Susan. "Marat/Sade/Artaud." In *Against Interpretation,* 163–76. New York: Picador, 2001.

———. *Regarding the Pain of Others.* New York: Farrar, Straus and Giroux, 2003.

Spierenberg, Pieter. *The Spectacle of Suffering.* Cambridge, UK: Cambridge University Press, 1984.

Starobinski, Jean. *1789: The Emblems of Reason.* Cambridge, MA: MIT Press, 1988.

Sylvester, David. *The Brutality of Fact: Interviews with Francis Bacon.* New York: Thames and Hudson, 1987.

Träger, Jörg. *Der Tod des Marat: Revolution eines Menschenbildes.* Köln: Dumont, 1986.

Treichel, Hans-Ulrich. "Fleischwerdung der Schrift und Schriftwerdung des Leibes: Franz Kafkas 'In der Strafkolonie.'" In *Auslöschungsverfahren,* 37–51. Munich: Fink, 1995.

Ubilluz, Juan Carlos. *Sacred Eroticism: Georges Bataille and Pierre Klossowski in the Latin American Erotic Novel.* Lewisburg, PA: Bucknell University Press, 2006.

Ueding, Gert, ed. *Historisches Wörterbuch der Rhetorik.* Vol. 6. Tübingen: Niemeyer, 2003.

Vogl, Joseph. "Gefieder, Gewölk: Anläßlich einer Fußnote Heiner Müllers." In Haß, *Heiner Müller, Bildbeschreibung,* 187–98.

Vormweg, Heinrich. "Sprache—die Heimat der Bilder." In *Heiner Müller,* edited by Heinz Ludwig Arnold, 20–31. Munich: Text + Kritik, 1982.

Warburg, Aby. *Der Bilderatlas Mnemosyne.* In *Gesammelte Schriften,* Vol. 2.1, edited by Martin Warnke. Berlin: Akademie Verlag, 2000.

———. "Dürer und die italienische Antike." 1906. In *Ausgewählte Schriften und Würdigungen,* edited by Dieter Wuttke, 125–30. Baden-Baden: Verlag Valentin Koerner, 1980.

Webb, Ruth. "*Ekphrasis* Ancient and Modern: The Invention of a Genre." *Word & Image* 15, no. 1 (Jan.–March 1999): 7–18.

Weinrich, Harald. "Semantik kühner Metaphern." In *Sprache in Texten*, 295–316. Stuttgart: Klett, 1976.

Weiß, Christoph. *Auschwitz in der geteilten Welt: Peter Weiss und die "Ermittlung" im Kalten Krieg*. St. Ingbert: Röhrig Universitätsverlag, 2000.

Weiss, Peter. *The Aesthetics of Resistance*. Vol. 1. Translated by Joachim Neugroschel. Durham, NC: Duke University Press, 2005.

———. *Die Ästhetik des Widerstands*. Vols. 1, 2, and 3. Frankfurt: Suhrkamp, 1975, 1978, 1981.

———. *Die Ermittlung*. In *Dramen* 2:7–199. Frankfurt: Suhrkamp, 1968.

———. *Die Verfolgung und Ermordung Jean Paul Marats dargestellt durch die Schauspielgruppe des Hospizes zu Charenton unter Anleitung des Herrn de Sade*. Frankfurt: Suhrkamp, 1964.

———. *The Investigation*. Translated by Job Swan, Ulu Grosbard, and Robert Cohen. In Weiss, *Marat/Sade; The Investigation; and The Shadow of the Body of the Coachman*, 117–296.

———. "Laokoon oder Über die Grenzen der Sprache." In *Rapporte*, 170–87. Frankfurt: Suhrkamp, 1968.

———. *Marat/Sade*. Translated by Geoffrey Skelton, Robert Cohen, and Daniel Theisen. In Weiss, *Marat/Sade; The Investigation; and The Shadow of the Body of the Coachman*, 41–116.

———. *Marat/Sade; The Investigation; and The Shadow of the Body of the Coachman*. Edited by Robert Cohen. New York: Continuum, 1998.

———. "Meine Ortschaft." In *Rapporte*, 113–24. Frankfurt: Suhrkamp, 1968.

———. *Vanishing Point*. In *Exile*. Translated by E. B. Garside, Alastair Hamilton, and Christopher Levenson. New York: Delacorte, 1968. Originally published as *Fluchtpunkt* (Frankfurt: Suhrkamp, 1962).

Wellbery, David E. "Das Gesetz der Schönheit: Lessings Ästhetik der Repräsentation." In *Was heißt "Darstellen"?* edited by Christiaan L. Hart Nibbrig, 175–204. Frankfurt: Suhrkamp, 1994.

Werckmeister, O. K. *Citadel Culture*. Chicago: University of Chicago Press, 1991.

Wiethölter, Waltraud. "'Mnemosyne' oder 'Die Höllenfahrt der Erinnerung': Zur Ikono-Graphie von Peter Weiss' *Die Ästhetik des Widerstands*." In *Zur Ästhetik der Moderne*, 217–82. Tübingen: Niemeyer, 1992.

Young, James E. *Writing and Rewriting the Holocaust: Narrative and the Consequences of Interpretation*. Bloomington: Indiana University Press, 1988.

Zierl, Andreas. *Affekte in der Tragödie: Orestie, Oidipus Tyrannos, und die Poetik des Aristoteles*. Berlin: Akademie Verlag, 1991.

Zilcosky, John. *Kafka's Travels: Exoticism, Colonialism, and the Traffic of Writing*. New York: Palgrave Macmillan, 2003.

Žižek, Slavoj. *The Abyss of Freedom*. In *The Abyss of Freedom / Ages of the World*, by Slavoj Žižek and F. W. J. von Schelling. Ann Arbor: University of Michigan Press, 1997.

———. "Afterword: Lenin's Choice." In V. I. Lenin, *Revolution at the Gates: A Selection of Writings from February to October 1917,* edited by Slavoj Žižek, 165–336. London: Verso, 2002.

———. *Le plus sublime des hystériques: Hegel passe.* Paris: Point Hors Ligne, 1988.

———. *Tarrying with the Negative.* Durham, NC: Duke University Press, 1993.

———. *The Ticklish Subject.* New York: Verso, 1999.

Žižek, Slavoj, Eric L. Santner, and Kenneth Reinhard. *The Neighbor: Three Inquiries in Political Theology.* Chicago: University of Chicago Press, 2005.

Zumbusch, Cornelia. *Wissenschaft in Bildern: Symbol und dialektisches Bild in Aby Warburgs Mnemosyne-Atlas und Walter Benjamins Passagen-Werk.* Berlin: Akademie Verlag, 2004.

Zupančič, Alenka. *Esthétique du désir, éthique de la jouissance.* Lecques: Théétète éditions, 2002.

———. *The Shortest Shadow: Nietzsche's Philosophy of the Two.* Cambridge, MA: MIT Press, 2003.

dom, 35; mythoheroic, 62; of pathos, 25; war, 24, 76
illusion, 29, 59, 78, 81, 149
Imaginary, the: affect and, 158; collective, 34, 72; cultural, 96; and Symbolic, 9–10, 25, 146, 165
immanence, 15, 18, 22, 162
immateriality, 17, 159
Inferno (Dante), 108, 115
intensity: affective, 95, 98; in Bacon, 155, 157, 163; presence, 17; and tension, 114
In the Penal Colony (Kafka), 24–25, 31–32, 39–41, 43, 48–53
Investigation, The (Die Ermittlung) (Weiss), 26, 95, 98–99, 102–5, 108, 112, 114
Iphigenia, 97

Jakobson, Roman, 72

Kafka, Franz, works: *Country Doctor*, 30; *In the Penal Colony*, 24–25, 31–32, 39–41, 43, 48–53; "The Metamorphosis," 174n54; *Report for an Academy*, 174n54; *The Trial*, 40
kairos, 146
Kant, Immanuel, 9, 12
katabasis, 120
Klee, Paul, 121
Kleist, Heinrich von, 124

Lacan, Jacques, 2, 4–15, 18–19, 72, 146, 151–52
"Laokoon oder Über die Grenzen der Sprache" (Weiss), 95–98, 103, 108, 112, 114, 128
Last Judgement (Michelangelo), 114
Lenin, Vladimir, 1
Lessing, Gotthold Ephraim, 71, 97, 128–29
Livy, 124, 132
Lotar, Eli, 30
Lucan, 83
Lukács, Georg, 155
Lynch, David, 120

Mallarmé, Stéphane, 1, 15
Mandelstam, Osip, 1, 15

Mao Zedong, 1
Marat, Jean-Paul, 90–95, 98, 151
Marat/Sade (Weiss), 90, 92–95, 98
martyr, 33, 48, 92
Marx, Karl, 54
Massacre of the Innocents (Poussin), 158
materiality, 17, 69, 119, 156
Mauser (Müller), 26, 123–24, 127, 131, 133–34, 136–39, 144
Mauss, Marcel, 28, 36
Measures Taken, The (Brecht), 127–28, 137, 141
Medea, 15, 118, 123, 138–41, 143–44
Medusa, 11, 14–16
Merleau-Ponty, Maurice, 177n22
metamorphosis, 41–42, 66, 79, 105, 112, 150
"Metamorphosis, The" (Kafka), 174n54
metaphor, 61–62, 70–73, 75–76, 80
Michelangelo, 91, 114, 153
Miró, Joan, 66
mise en image, 49, 61–62, 98
mise en scène, 22, 98, 163–64
models, iconic, 77, 157
Moscow trials, 109
Müller, Heiner, works: *Germania Tod in Berlin*, 138; *Hamletmaschine*, 138–39, 141–43; *The Horatian*, 26, 123–24, 126–27, 131–33, 140, 144; *Mauser*, 26, 123–24, 127, 131, 133–34, 136–39, 144; *Philoctetes*, 26, 123–26, 128–33, 138, 144; *Verkommenes Ufer Medeamaterial Landschaft mit Argonauten*, 123, 128–29, 133; *Zement*, 138
Munch, Edvard, 158
Muybridge, Eadweard, 153, 160
mysticism, 147

Napoleon, 57
Nazism, 148
Nietzsche, Friedrich, 1, 51
Novelli, Gastone, 66

objet a, 12–13
October Revolution, 148
Oedipus, 153
Ophelia, 142–43

128–29; of pathos, 98; of public execution, 25, 33, 43; of punishment, 39,
47; religious subtext of, 33; of suffering, 8, 16–19, 25, 43, 104–5, 108,
115, 148–49; of violence, 34, 98, 104,
148, 164; war as, 76
spectral, 15, 17, 21, 78, 158
Sphinx, 153
Stalin, Joseph, 130, 141
Stalinism, 148
state portrait, 160
Stendhal, 56–57, 59
sublation, 38, 149
sublimation, 12
subtraction, 5, 14
Surrealist, 29–30, 153
Sutherland, Graham, 153
Sweeney Agonistes (Eliot), 155
Sylvester, David, 152, 154–55, 160–61
Symbolic, the, 9; the Imaginary and, 9–
10, 165; matrix, 11; vs. the real, 13;
the somatic and, 31; space of, 25; this
side of, 151–52
symbolic order, 3, 17; Antigone, 11; beyond, 32; constraints of, 51; and the
imaginary, 25; initiation into, 53; inscription in, 51; outside of, 53; power
of, 15; protective shield of, 52, 151;
shattering, 31; sublimation, 12; undoing the, 25, 32

tableau/tableaux, 90, 92, 95, 116, 120,
122, 140, 142, 143, 150
Tears of Eros (Bataille), 28, 34, 36, 38,
52, 68, 106
Thanatos, 155
theatricality, 8, 40, 54, 80, 153
Three Studies for a Crucifixion 1962
(Bacon), 161
*Three Studies for Figures at the Base of
a Crucifixion 1944* (Bacon), 155

totalitarianism, 130
tragedy, 19–20, 32, 121, 123, 131, 138–
39
transcendence, 36, 39, 49, 108
transfiguration, 23, 147, 164–65; in
Kafka, 32, 34, 40–43, 47, 49, 52,
150; in Weiss, 107
transgression, 55, 165; in Bataille, 25,
28–32, 35–39, 51–52, 150; in
Mauser, 127
Trial, The (Kafka), 40
triptych, 123, 139–40, 151, 163–64
trompe l'œile, 55, 88–89

Uccello, Paolo, 82
Ugolino, 113

Velázquez, Diego, 153–54
verisimilitude, 150
*Verkommenes Ufer Medeamaterial
Landschaft mit Argonauten* (Müller),
123, 128–29, 133

Warburg, Aby, 21
Warhol, Andy, 153
Waterloo, 24–25, 54–55, 57, 151
Weimar Republic, 109
Weiss, Peter, works: *Fluchtpunkt (Van-
ishing Point)*, 106; *The Investigation
(Die Ermittlung)*, 26, 95, 98–99, 102–
5, 108, 112, 114; "Laokoon oder
Über die Grenzen der Sprache," 95–
98, 103, 108, 112, 114, 128; *Marat/
Sade*, 90, 92–95, 98
World War I, 76
World War II, 24, 58–59, 62, 65, 140

Zement (Müller), 138
Žižek, Slavoj, 6, 9, 11–13, 15, 141